The Science Of Self-Hypnosis

The Evidence Based Way To Hypnotise Yourself

Adam Eason

Awake Media Productions Ltd

28 Winston Avenue

Poole

Dorset

BH12 1PE

Published by Awake Media Productions Ltd

First Published — December 2013

ISBN 978-0-9575667-1-2

© Adam Eason, 2013

I dedicate this book to my children.

While I was writing this book, my son was in the background laughing, shouting, wrestling with dinosaurs and driving his car into walls. He often runs into my garden office, jumps on the chairs, screams excitedly to himself with great satisfaction, then runs out again. We often watch the moon together and cheer when the clouds pass so it appears brighter

My daughter is responsible for the variety of damp patches my clothes have had while I wrote this book. She is a brilliant dribbler. She laughs when I blow my nose. She has red hair like mine. I love how she looks when I rock her to sleep.

They turn all my frowns into smiles. I love you Ollie. I love you Bella. Being your Dad is my favourite thing.

CONTENTS

Foreword, by Dr Steve Murray

I am extremely honoured to be asked to write the foreword of this excellent book on self-hypnosis.

I met Adam in June 2013 at a hypnosis conference, where he was speaking on the topic of **"Evidence-Based Practice"**. I was giving a talk on my anecdotal experiences of hypnosis in cardiology patients - the irony of this may be lost on you at the moment, but after reading this book, I hope you'll understand!

But what wisdom can I offer? I'm certainly not one of those clever NLP types with those ingenious linguistics - one who can twist words effortlessly and use artful ambiguity whilst magically transforming the lives and experiences of clients. In fact I'm a rather old fashioned, authoritarian type of hypnotist. Neither am I as well read on the subject as Mr Eason - *(the first part of this book is one of the best reviews of the literature to date that I've read)*.

So I will fall back on the advice oft given to writers - *"write about what you know"*: my day job is working as a consultant cardiologist, sub-specialising in heart rhythm problems. Please, bear with me as I write on a topic something I do know about: by the end I think you will appreciate the relevance.

It was a long known fact that after a heart attack, those patients who had a lot of extra, out of place, heart beats (known as "premature ventricular contractions" of PVCs) had a higher risk of dying suddenly as compared to those without PVCs.

For many years US physicians would routinely prescribe drugs to suppress these PVCs after a heart attack (for some reason us Europeans just never took to it) . The drugs were very effective at suppressing these extra beats, as it turned out, and it became standard practice for years.

It was only in the mid 1980s that this strategy was subjected to a double-blind, randomised controlled trial - meaning patients were randomly assigned to either placebo or active drug; the double blind element meant that neither patient nor doctor knew what the tablets were. In this way any bias is minimised from both doctor and study patient.

The proposed research was very controversial, with some physicians branding the study unethical, as it would surely expose patients to the unnecessary risk of placebo treatment. In other words, the practice was so well established it seemed negligent to test it.

From 1986 to 1998 over 1700 patients were enrolled across 27 centres in the US into the *"Cardiac Arrhythmia Suppression Trial"* or CAST, as it became known.

The findings resulted in a paradigm shift in the management of these patients. It transpired that the drugs caused significantly more deaths than the placebo. Almost 8% of the active treatment patients were dead within 10 months, as compared to only 3% in the placebo arm; now these numbers may not sound that impressive, but the scale of the practice meant that very large numbers were being harmed in day to day medical practice. In fact it was estimated that the number of heart attack patients killed from these drugs over the years exceeded the numbers of combatants killed in WWII, the Korean War and Vietnam war put together.

Ignore evidence based practice at your peril - literally.

Since the publication of CAST, cardiology has been blessed by many large scale trials, and furthermore most new treatments are routinely backed by clinical evidence. Even within my own career we have had unexpected results which have fundamentally changed practice overnight, with findings that are genuinely counter-intuitive (those interested could search for the AFFIRM study to learn how the effort spent in keeping patients in normal rhythm as opposed to just leaving them in an abnormal rhythm which is well known to effect life expectancy is actually a wasted effort!)

Intuitive thinking can be very powerful, and is often regarded as the product of our subconscious minds - quietly working away in the background, dreaming up new and creative solutions.

However, all is not so straightforward and this powerful tool can also produce bias, superstitious thinking, stereotypes and even dangerous assumptions! In order to better understand this, you need to read this book.

You may even be surprised to learn that you **don't** have a 'subconscious' anymore!

A lack of evidence does not necessarily equate to a lack of effectiveness however. In some cases the trial is just waiting to be done, or the research may not be robust enough. Also, being selective with the evidence can be just as bad a practice as ignoring it; for instance if there are 5 studies in the literature, choosing the one with the best results to make your argument is obviously disingenuous. Ignoring the negative studies verges on deception. *"Publication-bias"* is the phenomenon describing the tendency of both researchers and editors to favour "positive" findings for publication, whilst "negative" trials may languish in the bottom drawer of the researcher's desk.

Nevertheless, there is a strong argument for drawing on the evidence we have, and ideally, adding to it through well designed, peer-reviewed studies.

Adam has clearly set out his approaches in the book from an evidence based perspective. His clear and balanced treatment of the literature will make uncomfortable reading for some I suspect; there are a lot of hypnosis gurus out there, each with their own system or style. Indeed, I have paid for and read many of their books, filled with inspiring anecdotes, and miraculous accounts of change. They may well be reproducible in the expert hands of the authors, but in my own experience I find my results to be sub-optimal. The beauty of evidence based strategies is that if you apply the techniques in a standardised way, then you can expect comparable results to those of the original researchers. The methods will also be clear and transparent to the reader, and will not rely on one special person or centre *(in medicine this is controlled for using "multi-centre" trials, where the effect of particularly talented practitioners is controlled for by trialling the treatment in a variety of centres, or even countries/cultures).*

So thanks to Adam's evidence-based approach you can expect the techniques contained within this book to work.

To finish, I feel I must defend the "controlled trial", as many people feel that the medical profession use this methodology because they don't like the placebo effect. To be clear, doctors love the placebo effect! We use it all the time within the bounds of ethical practice and rely on it in much of our practice. However, if you are testing a drug or procedure, you want to measure the effect of it, and it alone - you don't want the placebo effect muddying the water. In other words, the randomised controlled trial is a major acknowledgment of the placebo effect - what we are saying is that it's so powerful an effect that it can lead us to erroneously ascribed powerful healing effects to treatments that are, in fact, not efficacious.

And the placebo effect leads us neatly back to hypnosis, which Adam quotes Kirsch as saying the "non-deceptive mega-placebo".

Sounds too good to be true to me - show me the evidence and Adam does.

Foreward written by Dr Steve Murray

Consultant Cardiologist & Electrophysiologist Regional
Cardiothoracic Centre
Freeman Hospital,
Newcastle upon Tyne

Introduction:
My Evidence-Based Rationale

Before we get on to actually doing self-hypnosis, it is going to benefit you to understand the subject. If you know the underpinning rationale, and have the correct expectations, it'll help you to adopt the right attitude and know how to derive maximum benefit from self-hypnosis.

I am going to do my best to help you with that understanding in what may initially seem like a convoluted way. In this introduction, I am going to informally explain the stance and values that underpin this book. In chapter one, I'll explain and explore the model of hypnosis that this book adheres to. Then you can begin to learn how to develop your hypnotic skills, learn the main protocol that I use in this book and learn how to apply self-hypnosis to help with certain areas of your life.

Although I'll examine this more closely later, let me pose the question: what is hypnosis?

That really is the $64,000,000.00 question. Any book that is intending to explain how to use hypnosis in a self-directed fashion, needs to explain what hypnosis is. As you'll see, this is not the simplest of tasks, and I wish it were simpler.

Before I attempt to give any kind of explanation about the working model of hypnosis in this book, I need to explain something. This book attempts to be as evidence based as it possibly can, and while

I have a personal experience of self-hypnosis that I do not consider insubstantial, this is not a book based upon anecdotal evidence or conjecture.

In my therapy rooms and within my own teaching, I adhere to a very particular model of hypnosis that will be explained in chapter one. In order to do that, I want to show you how I arrived at this model and explain the reasons it is relevant to this book.

In this book I will use evidence-based practice, which has a scientific approach that works towards new discovery. This practice does not claim to have all the answers, but it uses evidence to arrive at certain results. The more evidence we gather, the more our forecasts tend to improve.

The world relies on scientific evidence for almost everything. Almost all safety mechanisms – from car brakes to food hygiene, from gas appliance maintenance to front door locks – rely on scientific evidence. Given that you follow the generally accepted scientific advice, you don't tend to rely on anyone's gut feeling or anecdotal evidence when it comes to the important aspects of everyday life.

You would not permit your doctor to tell your loved ones or children, ah no, my gut feeling is that you do not have cancer. Gargle some aspirin and that lump on your neck will soon get better, that's what another fellow I know did and he's fine today.

If we accept science and evidence-based approaches in other facets of our lives, it makes sense that it is incorporated into our work as self-hypnotists, rather than responding to myth, pseudoscience or anecdotal evidence.

I trained as a hypnotherapist originally in 1997. I was taught a very particular method that the vast majority of hypnotherapists are trained. I believed in that model and did not question it, accepting it as the truth and blissfully not knowing any better. Central to that model was the notion that we all have a distinct conscious and subconscious mind.

My career in this field was propelled as a result of my first book, which I wrote in 2004. It is entitled "The Secrets of Self-Hypnosis: Harnessing the Power of Your Unconscious Mind". It was a best-seller. Among the many things that I read in the years after writing that book, I came upon a wonderful quote by the philosopher and psychologist, William James, which is over 100 years old. James had this to say about the existence of the unconscious mind:

"The sovereign means for believing what one likes in psychology and of turning what might become a science into a tumbling ground for whimsies"
- William James, 1884,

I felt hurt.

Today, I am embarrassed by my first book. Right here, I am re-writing my own bestselling book, as it is centered on a model that I no longer believe in or adhere to.

Today, the majority of cognitive psychologists and neuroscientists dispute the concept of dualism: that of the mind being distinct to the brain. There is no centre of consciousness, no centre of decision-making. It made for some initial discomfort as reality hit me. My book was showing people how to communicate with their unconscious mind that I had just found out did not exist. Pah!

Dualism of mind is probably only useful as a metaphor, and even then, only if you are comfortable with mistruths. Why not simply explain it as it is?

Still today, I get emails from people all around the world, desperately spoiling for a rumble with me: You wrote a book with the unconscious mind in the title and yet you blog saying it does not exist… Heck, we change and develop over the years.

We all ought to be developing and changing as our careers progress. All hypnotherapy associations that I have had anything to do with have expected continued professional development, and I think we all need to develop, progress and move on.

The irony for me, another bitter pill to swallow, is that most of the evidence supporting the model I adhere to in this book, existed before I was even born; it is not new.

The Unconscious Mind?

I recall an early experience with a hypnotherapist. He was an utterly lovely man. He hypnotised me (what I considered to be hypnosis in those days) and I was unaware of most of the session thereafter, as I slumped into a very relaxing nap of some kind. He had a gentle tone, used very fancy, confusing language that sounded like he knew what he was doing, and he brought me up and out of hypnosis. I felt a bit spaced out and felt like I had truly been in the 'trance' he had told me I would go into prior to the session. I said to him at the end of the session "so what happens, now? I can't recall anything from the session, has the change happened?" He smiled and said that my unconscious mind had taken it all in and was going to make the changes for me. I later found out that this therapist referred to his approach as Ericksonian, based upon the work of a prominent hypnotherapist called Milton Erickson, and he claimed it was the best method of hypnosis.

Therapeutically, this was an impotent experience for me. No change happened. I kept on thinking, **when is my unconscious mind going to do something amazing?** When is it going to tell me about the changes? This is a typical occurrence in therapy rooms and strikes me as a bit of an 'Emperor's New Clothes' approach to hypnosis.

In Stephen Lankton's chapter in the *Oxford handbook of Hypnosis (2008)* which refers to the Ericksonian approach, he states that the approach required preparation and consideration, and that it was not just about trusting the unconscious mind to do the right thing. In fact, he states it is a **"dangerous false assumption"** *(2008, p. 469)*. Yet the approach did characterise the unconscious mind as a separate entity that was a force for good:

> *"Your unconscious knows how to protect you ....*
> *Your unconscious mind knows what is right and*
> *what is good. When you need protection, it will*
> *protect you"*
>
> *(Milton Erickson, cited in Erickson & Rossi, 1979, p 296)*

5

Despite Stephen Lankton's efforts to educate us on the Ericksonian approach, to the contrary, since I first qualified as a hypnotherapist in 1997, I have encountered many hypnosis professionals who believe it is fine to think in terms of 'magical thinking' and that the all-seeing, ultra wise, benevolent, demi-God that lives within us will serve us perfectly – the unconscious mind knows what we want, why not let it sort things out?

No. Don't.

This book is going to be a sobering antidote to that type of approach. My advice is that you do not rely on any such notion of trusting your unconscious mind. Rather, I highly recommend that you prepare thoroughly, that you approach self-hypnosis in a systematic way that encourages you to know what is going on, that equips you with skills and the wonderful notion of self-efficacy. That is, you feel capable and confident in making change in your life, not relying on something beyond your conscious awareness.

- Should there be a distinction made between the unconscious and conscious minds?

- Is it actually just nonsense?

- Do these two minds actually exist separately from each other?

- Or is it, as some tend to favour as a theory, a simple metaphor that helps us illustrate hypnosis in action?

Many still believe and work to this model of the mind in relation to hypnosis:

"The conscious mind is the part of the mind which thinks, feels and acts in the present . The unconscious mind is a much greater part of the mind, and normally we are quite unaware of its existence. It is the seat of all our memories, our past experiences, and indeed of all that we have ever learned. In this respect it resembles a large filing cabinet to which we can refer in order to refresh memory whenever we need to do so."
(Hartland, 1971, p 13).

For many hypnosis professionals the existence of an unconscious mind is essential. Yet, why is it then, that virtually the entire academic fraternity and researcher community do not adhere to this notion?

Many frontline hypnotherapy professionals characterise the unconscious mind as being a vast storehouse of memories, that it has great knowledge and wisdom, that it is literal, that it processes information in a way that is different to the conscious mind and makes various other distinctions. Then when we come to the field of hypnosis, it takes on another dimension. It is then believed that hypnosis enables us to communicate with the unconscious mind and ask or direct the unconscious mind to do certain useful things. This is how I was originally taught, and how many are still taught today, but it is not necessarily a valid explanation of what is actually going on.

When people are told this by someone who totally believes in it, they treat it as empirical truth and accept that we all have two totally separate minds, doing totally separate things. Many people are not shown how to adopt responsibility and the appropriate skills to make change for themselves, to learn to be in control, because they wait for something magical to occur.

> *That the mind is divided into these two parts, the conscious and the unconscious, is an over-simplistic and potentially a very misleading idea and one that unnecessarily limits our progress in understanding human psychology and hypnosis in particular*
> (Heap and Aravind, 2002, p. 203).

We all tend to commonly say that we have thoughts, ideas, memories, images, perceptions, and so on. Like they are things we can carry around in a wheelbarrow. We say such things as 'I have just had an excellent idea'; 'I had a great thought today'; 'I have a vivid image of this person'; and 'I have happy memories of last Christmas'.

In reality, what we are describing here are activities that we have engaged in. Processes that we have just done. It is more appropriate to say that we think rather than that there are things called thoughts that we have. Likewise, we imagine rather than have images. We remember rather than have things called memories. When we stop remembering, the memories do not go anywhere. They are not stored away as files are stored in a filing cabinet; though it may seem that way when we do the process of remembering.

With regard to activities of thinking, remembering, imagining, and so on, all of these are represented by neural activities that are, as of yet unknown (and maybe ultimately unknowable), and are associated with the conscious experiences that we call 'having memories, thoughts, images,' and so on.

Suppose that, having decided you have done enough reading for the moment, you put this book down, and go and do something else. However, later on, you start to think about some of the ideas that I have written about here. Surely you can only do this if there is something, some representation of this material, 'a memory', that exists in your mind that you retrieve, when you decide to, as you would draw a file from a filing cabinet?

We can say that this is so only in a manner of speaking, but a more accurate and potentially less misleading description is to say that, as you are reading this, neuro-biochemical changes are occurring in your brain that enable you, in the future, to engage in the activity of recalling this material.

Don't these observable neuronal properties constitute your memory of this information? If I use the example of shaking hands, having experienced a handshake with another person earlier in the day, a physiotherapist or biologist may perform a careful examination of a person's arm and hand later on that day, and as a result of that examination, conclude that indeed the arm is capable of moving and doing the handshake process. However much they examine the arm though, they will not locate 'a handshake.' It is not a thing that exists, is it?

What relevance does this have to the concept of the unconscious mind? In an attempt to put it as concisely as possible (this is a subject matter that could have entire books dedicated to it alone, but is not wholly relevant to the central theme of this book) it is simply that the unconscious mind does not exist. In the context of the model that this book adheres to, it does not exist. There, I said it. We can talk about doing things unconsciously, but as a separate entity, distinct from the brain, distinct from another separate entity known as the conscious mind, it does not exist.

If you examine the depths of research in the field of hypnosis over the last century, from major contributors such as Hull and White in the 1930s and 1940s, Hilgard in the 1950s, Barber and Orne in the 1960s, those engaged in the theory wars of the 1970s, such as Barber and Spanos, and other authors up to the 1990s, such as Kirsch, Lynn, McConkey and Sheehan – none of them discussed the unconscious mind. It has not forged a part of academics understanding of hypnosis, and therefore if this is going to be an evidence-based approach to self-hypnosis, the unconscious mind is not going to feature beyond this introductory chapter.

Were it not for the fact that my previous book on the subject had the unconscious mind in the title, I would not have even mentioned it here in the introduction. I felt obliged to address it, as it was so central to what was written before.

Trusting Gut Feelings?

Throughout this book, as well as making use an evidence-based rationale, I want to champion critical thinking as opposed to trusting your gut feelings.

Let's take the example of a smoker who has just quit using will power alone. He goes to buy a packet of chewing gum with his morning paper and the cigarette packets on the back shelf beckon and attempt to lure our smoker back in: *Come on and smoke me, I'm all delicious and smoky, you know you want to, come and get me, you'll feel so great if you just give in and smoke me.*

Our smoker has will power though and fights back to the calls of the cigarettes: *Not on your nelly, be gone vile cigarettes, I am no slave to you…Absolutely not…You are a big no no… Well, maybe just this time, I'll buy a pack and just have one final smoke and then that's it… Definitely no more…*
And the victor is the cigarette packet.

Many people in personal development circles believe that will power is no way near as impressive as our intuition, instincts and gut feelings. We are often told to just trust our gut and it will lead us in the right direction, it knows best. In that case, what about our smoker? That was a gut feeling he had to fight off. The gut feeling was making him want to smoke and it is common knowledge that smoking is not in our best or healthiest interests, is it?

I think sometimes we need to strike a balance and know when to fight or override intuition and gut feelings, and apply some intelligence too. Our intuition can also be a bit wild from time to time. My bookshelf has a whopper of a dictionary on it, and that dictionary defines intuition as this:

NOUN

1. *Knowledge or belief obtained neither by reason nor perception.*

2. *Instinctive knowledge or belief.*

3. *A hunch or unjustified belief*

(Collins English Dictionary, 2003).

If that is the case, why do so many people hold so much faith in the absolute accuracy and correctness of intuition?

Is our intuition really a vast source of perfection?

Do we have an ultra-genius residing within us all that never gets things wrong?

I am not attempting to dismiss out of hand the intuition we have, but suggest that we don't treat it like some deity that needs prayer or the sacrifice of our souls. We all have some modest wisdom gleaned through a lifetime of experience, evolution, culture, development, awareness, education and so on. Yet, if I were to give my own intuition a school report, it would have a similar theme to my real-life school reports: "Could do better."

Rather than having to fight and battle with our intuition as our smoker did (and often losing) we can retrain our intuitive selves with evidence. As a hypnotherapist of many years, I think that is partly what therapy is about: rather than telling people to "sort themselves out", therapy has evolved to retrain our minds, retrain our intuition and natural way of doing things, instead of the problematic behaviours and thought patterns that require therapeutic intervention.

Maybe will power does come off worse when compared with the power of intuition, maybe it does not. Surely we all benefit from educating our intuition to be even more accurate and effective; which is not too dissimilar from learning to use self-hypnosis to make beneficial changes in your life.

Why Self-Hypnotists Need Critical Thinking Skills

In a nutshell, critical thinking is the ability to think clearly and rationally. Importantly for self-hypnotists, it includes the ability to engage in reflective and independent thinking. Critical thinkers identify, construct and evaluate arguments, and they use due diligence and consideration when presenting information. Critical thinkers detect inconsistencies and common mistakes in reasoning, such as noticing if someone offers up solely subjective anecdotal evidence to support their theory. Critical thinkers solve problems systematically. Importantly for us as self-hypnotists, critical thinkers reflect on the justification of one's own beliefs and values. (i.e. they don't carry on bloody-mindedly believing in something because that is how they were taught it several years ago).

Being a critical thinker is not just about being able to regurgitate and accumulate information. A person with a good memory and who knows a lot of facts is not necessarily good at critical thinking. For an extreme example, look at autistic savants (as seen in the film *The Rain Man*) who have phenomenal memories but poor critical evaluation skills. A critical thinker is able to deduce consequences from what he knows, and knows how to utilise information to solve problems and to seek relevant sources of information to inform himself, locating valid evidence.

As students of self-hypnosis, critical thinking can help us acquire knowledge, improve our skills, and strengthen our understanding. We want to promote critical thinking and not stifle it.

Having an attitude that prefers to be given the correct answers, rather than figuring them out for yourself, stifles critical thinking. Having an attitude that insists on not reflecting or thinking a great deal about decisions, instead just relying on gut feelings, stifles critical thinking. Having an attitude that refuses to acknowledge or review the mistakes you have made, stifles critical thinking. Having an attitude that does not like to be criticised or challenged in any way, also stifles critical thinking.

Psychologists and philosophers learn critical thinking as an inherent part of their learning and education. In order to be an effective self-hypnotist, then surely critical thinking needs to be a part of who and how you are and not just blind following, assumption-making and believing in anything and everything based on anecdotal evidence or pseudoscience.

Back to Evidence-Based Practice

Being an evidence-based practitioner as I am, means offering up some congruency of evidence. After some lengthy conversations with academics and professional peers in recent years, I now openly state on my website that my audios have not all been individually tested. We removed a lot of them, offered some for free, and vouched for those that had evidence supporting them or the principles that underpinned them.

As I incorporated evidence-based approaches into my work, the benefits to my clients, my success rates and entire business has been transformed for the better as a result. Now that excites me. Having an evidence-based approach excites me, where the field constantly develops and is therefore dynamic. In actual fact, many people are blissfully working in the field of hypnosis without any idea of the true depth of the scientific studies we have to support our field.

In July 2013, I visited PubMed website and searched for papers on hypnotherapy. There were 12,907 studies! However, they don't make comfortable reading for some corners of the professional hypnosis community, as many professionals perpetuate myth and misconception that the evidence refutes.

Also on PubMed there are 50,445 studies on cognitive behavioural therapy (CBT), and this wealth of evidence tends to be why it is offered most predominantly by the NHS (national health service) here in England. Us hypnotherapy professionals have nearly 13,000 studies to look at (and counting). Many good ones too. This is exciting, but it would be more exciting if there were more randomised, controlled trials. Nevertheless we can still be excited.

Evidence-based practice is engaging; it is easier to explain how and why something is likely to work if the justification for believing in it is sound and consistent. Importantly, it is downright responsible and ethical to offer up an evidence-based approach rather than one built purely upon gut feeling, anecdotal evidence, egos and armchair philosophy.

I wanted to write a self-hypnosis book based upon reliable studies and scientific evidence, as opposed to anecdotal, philosophising, gut feeling, divine insight or guesswork; or where one is encouraged to "trust your unconscious mind," which cannot be truly quantified.

The American Psychological Association defined evidence-based practice in Psychology as *"the integration of the best available research with clinical expertise in the context of patient characteristics, culture, and preferences"*.

One of my goals with this book is to ensure that any reader studying this subject does not merely play lip service to the concept of evidence-based self-hypnosis, nor are they completely limited by an overly scientific approach that lacks usability.

I am often confronted with discussion on the (seemingly) forever-debated notion of *Art versus Science* in the field of hypnosis. As far back as 1965, Ernest Hilgard provided us with evidence that still today stands up to rigour, and suggests that *"hypnosis depends more on the efforts of the subject than any 'artistry' of hypnotist"* (Hilgard, 1965).

There is general consensus among academics of this: most pioneers of the subject, from James Braid who coined the term hypnosis and created the field of hypnotherapy, to Irving Kirsch who has conducted more research on this subject than anyone, tend to support the notion that the subject is the one who imagines, engages in cognitive processes, etc. Hypnosis depends on the individual's efforts more than the artistic skills of the hypnotist.

If you are now saying, *yes but Adam, I'm an artist! I use hypnosis and express myself... Much like those people who engage in interpretive dance and flow with all creation...* Well, you'll still get to be creative and artistic with my approach to self-hypnosis, but hypnosis is not dependent upon someone else's artistry in order for you to benefit from it.

If you believe that hypnosis is reliant on the artistry or character of the individual, then the training needs to offer intangible skills; and how do you teach that, how do you measure that progress? How do you write a book that shows you how to do that?

I do not want to encourage pooh-poohing of much in this life, but anecdotal evidence and teaching anecdotally, as if subjective experience is credible evidence, is something I think we should pooh-pooh and stick our tongue out at. It is the scourge of modern hypnotherapy and the field of self-hypnosis.

There is a proliferation and use of subjective/anecdotal 'evidence' in this field. Therapists and trainers often say that they *"know what works"* – relying on anecdote or their own experience of success in treating clients. This often flies in the face of what the evidence tells us. Often therapists get results for a wide variety of other reasons. For example, the congruence of the therapist enhances belief in the process. Many therapists get results not because of the techniques they are using, many of which lack evidence, but because the therapist believes in it so much, which is in turn transmitted to the client.

The search for the one true universal definition that explains hypnosis continues. There are many rumbles that are ongoing in the forums of the front lines of hypnotherapy and academia. However, the evidence base that I use when learning self-hypnosis is here for us to benefit from. I really do not and cannot understand why so many self-hypnosis books, manuals or trainings do not include any science? In my personal library, I own 17 books with the words 'self-hypnosis' in the title, and just five of those have credible scientific references punctuating them.

Notes on This Book

There is a lot of repetition in this book. Mainly because some of the material is theoretical and academic, therefore if it is repeated in a variety of ways, I hope that you manage to understand it with ease. Also, there are a lot of step-by-step techniques that you'll have to read and learn rather than use directly from the book; because you'll be hypnotised with your eyes closed when doing the techniques. Therefore, if you have learned the processes by having the notions repeated from time to time, it'll make it easier to practically apply.

Please use the content of this book in a systematic way. It is not designed to be read straight through from front to back. You need to practice certain parts of what you are learning, before you move on to develop your skills. Those skipping through will not derive the benefit that is to be had through the diligent application of the content of this book.

I refer to 'him' throughout this book when giving examples or when talking about someone being hypnotised or using self-hypnosis. I often think of myself as the example I am giving and therefore use the male term.

Enjoy this book.

PART ONE

Chapter One:
What Is The Cognitive Behavioural Approach To Self-Hypnosis

We begin at the beginning then. I hesitated about starting the book in the way that I have. Essentially I want this book to be a manual on how to learn and develop the skill of self-hypnosis and this chapter is very theoretical.

A lot of hypnotherapists, psychotherapists, psychologists and mental health professionals that use hypnosis within their work, sometimes offer a disinterested and unconcerned response to being confronted with such theory and rationale that I offer in this opening chapter.

Some might incorrectly state that some of the debates, discussions and points raised within this chapter are nothing more than *"academic debate"*, and as a result, do not have any practical significance. The points I shall be making about the nonstate theories of hypnosis and the cognitive-behavioural conceptualisation of hypnosis, do in fact have incredibly important practical benefits and implications. Having an understanding of these things has been shown to lead to the development of hypnotic skills and enhanced responsiveness to hypnosis, which is very important as we learn how to use self-hypnosis. I will later explain this in more depth.

This chapter then provides the rationale for and explanation of this book's approach to self-hypnosis. Therapeutic hypnosis is seen and considered by some (hypnotherapists in particular) to be an independent modality of therapy that is comparable to psychodynamic, behavioural, or cognitive approaches to therapy.

In recent times though, hypnosis has been used as an adjunct to other forms of psychotherapy and this is documented greatly in the work of Kirsch et al.*(1995)* in *"Hypnosis as an adjunct to cognitive-behavioural psychotherapy: A meta-analysis"*. Similar works have also discussed hypnosis as an adjunct rather than as a stand alone therapy *(Rhue, Lynn and Kirsch, 1993)*.

Hypnotherapy in the modern world is quite different in theory and real life from the traditional approaches. Today, instead of just relying on delivering suggestions to someone who is hypnotised as a means of creating change (which you will also learn how to do in this book), we hypnotherapists also incorporate hypnosis into other well-established psychotherapeutic interventions. The same can be said about how we apply self-hypnosis.

We can subsequently employ a wide range of impressive therapeutic strategies, techniques and processes within our self-hypnosis sessions, as will be demonstrated within this book. The added beauty of this (in particular for the evidence-based approach offered in this book), is that we get to employ empirically supported interventions in conjunction with our self-hypnosis skills.

When you consider that currently, clinical hetero-hypnosis is not really recognised as an empirically supported treatment for any psychiatric disorder (though getting very close with some applications), does it not make sense for us to be using hypnosis as an adjunct to a therapeutic modality that does?

For example, hypnosis goes well with cognitive behavioural therapy (CBT) , because many of the processes and techniques used in the field of cognitive behavioural therapy (the mental imagery techniques) have real parallels to those used in hypnosis and self-hypnosis. There are some dissenting viewpoints about the level of enhancement that hypnosis offers CBT, often based upon expectancy and belief, as well as the hypnotisability factors that affect results. However, hypnosis has been used as a successful adjunct to CBT for a wide variety of issues and ailments.

The results of the previously mentioned Kirsch et al. *(1995)* meta-analyses, does indeed suggest that hypnosis may even enhance cognitive behavioural therapy. Other similar studies suggest the same, but the Kirsch et al. meta-analysis of 18 studies that compared CBT with and without hypnosis as an adjunct, found fairly significant improvements when hypnosis was used an adjunct to the treatment. It seems to make sense that we can therefore employ a number of strategies from the field of CBT within our self-hypnosis sessions.

It is an aim of this book that any student of self-hypnosis therefore learn how to use hypnosis in a more sophisticated manner than simply delivering suggestions; though we'll look at how to do that too. Instead, this book aims to incorporate strategies from the field of cognitive-behavioural therapy and use self-hypnosis as an adjunct with them.

That is one of the reasons that this book adheres to a cognitive-behavioural approach. However, in order to start using that approach, we need to explain what it actually is. That is, we need to understand how self-hypnosis is conceptualised within this approach, before we then learn how to use it to make changes in our lives.

Instead of now asking "what is hypnosis?" We need to ask "what do we mean by the cognitive-behavioural approach to hypnosis?"

As this is the model we shall be using throughout this book. The cognitive-behavioural re-conceptualisation of hypnosis replaces the often used notion of "hypnotic trance" with its explanation based upon more ordinary psychological processes.

The founder of hypnotism, James Braid, adopted an approach based on the Victorian philosophical psychology known as Scottish "common sense" realism. Hypnotism was discovered by Braid in 1841, and entailed a more common sense psychological explanation of the apparent effects of Mesmerism (a historical precursor of hypnotism). We'll revisit Braid often in this book.

Braid defined hypnotism as *"focused attention upon an expectant dominant idea or image" (Braid, cited in Robertson, 2008)*. Later, Hippolyte Bernheim, a very important figure in the history of hypnotism, said that there was no such thing as *"hypnosis"* other than heightened suggestibility, and named his approach *"suggestive therapeutics" (Bernheim, 1887)*.

Before we take any further steps forward, I need to explain that hypnotism is essentially the art and science of suggestion, and not that of inducing "trances" or altered states of consciousness. If you were hoping for an instructional manual on how to alter your state of consciousness and/or how to create a special trance state, then you will be disappointed; this book rejects that way of explaining hypnosis.

Much of what we now know about the subject was first expressed in the original writings of Braid, who coined the term *"hypnotism"*. He developed his theory and practice of hypnotism through constant experimentation and by carrying out public demonstrations in front of some of the leading scientists and academics of his day, one of whom, Prof. William B. Carpenter, became his ally and provided the original *"ideo-motor reflex"* conceptualisation of hypnotism.

Today, this phrase is most commonly used in reference to the process whereby a thought or mental image brings about a seemingly "reflexive" or automatic muscular reaction. When you imagine a movement occurring in the body, even if you attempt to hold that part of the body still, there is a movement generated, even if it is miniscule. This is best demonstrated in some of the hypnotic skills training we'll be doing later in this book.

Psychologists up to the present day have continued to carry out important research on hypnosis and its clinical applications. Some of the main researchers in the history of hypnotism were also key figures in the field of behavioural psychology, most notably Ivan Pavlov, Clark Hull and Hans Eysenck, and so again, it seems to be a natural and logical marriage. Well, not even a marriage, the two are historically and conceptually intertwined.

It should be noted though, that the model of hypnosis adhered to in this book predates cognitive behavioural therapy, and not just the contributions referred to already. Joseph Wolpe, the developer of systematic desensitisation and arguably the founder of behaviour therapy, originally described his technique as *"hypnotic desensitisation" (Wolpe, 1958, p. 203; Wolpe, 1954).*

Wolpe based his own hypnotic induction technique on the earlier writings of Lewis Wolberg, whose well known and influential textbook, Medical Hypnosis, described a similar hypno-therapeutic technique that was explained in terms of the same conditioning principles derived from behavioural psychology *(Wolberg, 1948a).*

Andrew Salter is a great contributor to the field of self-hypnosis and we will champion him later regarding that. Moreover, he was one of the co-founders of behaviour therapy too and was a hypnotist and one of the first authors to describe hypnotic skills training, which I will later focus on *(Salter, 1949).*

In the 1970s, Andre Weitzenhoffer, one of the leading researchers in the field of hypnosis, published a literature review illustrating the extent to which, for many decades, hypnotherapists had employed behavioural psychology concepts, derived from Hull and Pavlov, and used techniques overlapping behaviour therapy, forming an approach sometimes called *"behavioural hypnotherapy" (Weitzenhoffer, 1972).* More recently, the hypnosis researcher Irving Kirsch has emphasised that, in particular, many imagery-based techniques found in behaviour therapy and CBT, such as systematic desensitisation, covert sensitisation and covert modelling, basically resemble typical hypnotic interventions, *"minus the hypnosis label" (Kirsch, 1999).*

In my opinion, this is evidence enough for us to have a cognitive-behavioural approach to self-hypnosis, though there is still plenty more to discuss. Of course, self-hypnosis is in and of itself a cognitive process: hypnotic suggestions, mental imagery techniques and cognitive strategies have the intention of evoking ideas (cognitions) that lead to certain desired hypnotic responses.

As the field of cognitive behavioural therapy (CBT) developed in the 1960s and 1970s, pioneered by the work of Albert Ellis and Aaron T. Beck, it highlighted the role of cognition as being vitally important to well-being, particularly specific thoughts and underlying beliefs that people had. Ellis had also, as a much younger man, studied and been influenced by the auto-suggestion techniques of Emile Coué *(Ellis, 2004).* Coué has contributed greatly to the field of self-hypnosis as it is today, and will also be referred to often in this book.

A 1941 paper written by the personality theorist, Robert White, entitled "A preface to the theory of hypnotism" is considered by many to be the beginning of the cognitive-behavioural approach to hypnosis. Research cited by White in this seminal article suggests that responses to hypnosis are primarily a result of the conscious attitudes and voluntary efforts of the individual. As a result, he redefined hypnosis as follows: *"Hypnotic behaviour is meaningful, goal-directed striving, its most general goal being to behave like a hypnotised person as this is continuously defined by the operator and understood by the client" (White, 1941).*

White took the perspective that *"hypnosis"* is actually a verb rather than a noun. That is, it is a skill that the individual does and it is not a passive state that seems to automatically 'happen' in a mechanical fashion in response to something a hypnotist does. White supported the notion (though it was not the first time this notion was supported, as we shall see) that all hypnosis is, to some extent, self-hypnosis. Or a process of hypnotising oneself.

This started a range of studies and research papers to subsequently develop what is known as a non-state theory of hypnosis. Nonstate proponents base their understanding of hypnosis on ordinary psychological processes, rather than the hypothetical, shrouded in mystique notion of a special *"hypnotic trance."* This also enabled hypnosis study to be integrated into the wider field of general psychology.

The State Versus Nonstate Debate

In a nutshell, state proponents tend to emphasise the differences between hypnosis and everything else, whereas nonstate proponents emphasise the similarities between hypnosis and everything else.

State theorists believe hypnosis is a special state, that hypnosis is all about altered consciousness and gives the impression of it being magical in some way.

Nonstate theorists apply healthy scepticism when explaining hypnosis, they look at it in rational terms and with Braid's original approach of Scottish common sense. Braid did meet with some opposition though, mainly in the form of John Elliotson (a medical mesmerist and author of *The Zoist*) who aggressively and publicly denounced Braid's views.

The cognitive-behavioural approach to hypnosis (and of course, self-hypnosis) adopted by this book, rejects the concept of a "hypnotic trance", by which is meant some sort of a special or abnormal state, which is how hypnosis is often (and quite popularly) explained.

In contrast to that way of explaining hypnosis, based on extensive scientific research, we explain hypnosis in terms of a hypnotic "mind set" comprising of ordinary processes, such as our beliefs, our imagination, our expectations, our attitude toward hypnosis, our level of motivation, the depth of our engagement with the role of being hypnotised and some other factors that we'll also examine.

Throughout this book then, "hypnosis" simply refers to a set of attitudes and behaviours that facilitate hypnotic responses, and not an *"altered state of consciousness"* or *"hypnotic trance"* of some kind *(Barber, Spanos and Chaves, 1974).*

To add some meat to the bones to support this nonstate approach, decades of research that employed brain-imaging methodologies of hypnotised individuals have provided some fascinating findings. The main finding is that no single, consistent, uniform response in brain functioning (i.e. an altered state) has been identified in hypnotised individuals.

> *Technology allows researchers to see the brains of hypnotised individuals, but no-one has to date*

found the 'hypnotic state' or any kind of 'unitary
state' to indicate hypnosis
(Lynn, Kirsch and Hallquist, 2008, p. 130).

In fact, different neurological responses occur with
different types of hypnotic suggestions
(Horton and Crawford, 2004).

Based on these premises, how are we going to explain all those people who report a varied and wide array of subjective feelings during hypnosis? I have people from all over the world advise me of all manner of unusual responses that they attribute to my hypnosis audio recordings bought from my website. Firstly I explain to them that in studies, control group subjects who are simply asked to sit with their eyes shut for a similar period of time without being hypnotised, also tend to report unusual feelings.

Despite the rejection of the theory that hypnosis is a 'trance state', nonstate proponents still accept that many people report that they felt that they were "in a trance". Upon further examination, and despite people reporting similarities, these sensations are not uniform and neither are they at all necessary to effective hypnosis.

It would be better to understand these responses as side effects of suggestion rather than evidence of experiencing a "hypnotic trance." More often than not, these reported responses are simply the effect of sitting still with the eyes closed for a prolonged period, or they are just the ordinary effects of relaxation or mental imagery.

My experience has been that many people expect to be "spaced out", and they consider that to be evidence of hypnotic trance. This is misleading. That kind of experience is typically a result of responding to suggestion rather than evidence of a special altered state of consciousness.

Self-Hypnosis as a Hypnotic Mindset

According to the cognitive-behavioural approach that we are using here, the hypnotised individual does not respond mechanically to suggestions given, but rather in an active and goal-directed manner *(Lynn and Sivec, 1992)*. Similarly, cognitive-behavioural therapists have defined hypnosis as a coping strategy that individuals can learn to apply across a variety of problematic situations *(Golden, Dowd and Freidberg, 1987, p. xi)*. For budding or existing self-hypnotists, this is excellent news; the very premise of hypnosis being self-directed makes self-hypnosis something anyone can realistically learn and develop as a valuable skill.

As a self-hypnotist, you simply need to engage in the hypnotic mindset as an inherent part of the skills you are also about to learn in this book. A 'hypnotic mindset' simply means that you will be motivated to hypnotise yourself, you will be confident in your ability to respond, optimistic about the self-hypnosis process, and that you will expect to automatically experience the responses being self-suggested or imagined. If you adopt this mindset, you will respond better to all of the skills you develop in the later chapters of this book.

To explain this more explicitly, the hypnotic cognitive-set originally described by Barber *(1974)* and then formulated more recently by Robertson *(2012)* is explained in terms of five attitudes that you adopt throughout your self-hypnosis practice:

Firstly, is the attitude of **recognition**.

When you learn the variety of hypnotic induction methods later in this book, you'll simply recognise it as your trigger to initiate this progressive, favourable hypnotic mind-set. You do so by actively engaging your imagination to the best of your ability and in a way that you find convincing. You also respond to your own hypnotic suggestions with a depth of focus and absorption, so as to avoid distraction during your self-hypnosis sessions.

Secondly is the attitude of **attribution**.

This is whereby you accurately attribute your responses within and throughout self-hypnosis sessions to your own imagination, self-suggestions and expectations. That is, you do not permit yourself to think of your responses as just compliance or the "unconscious mind" doing it for you. You are actively responsible for the hypnotic response you get.

Thirdly, you adopt the attitude of **appraisal**.

Here you appraise the demands of your desired outcome in a favourable way. You view your hypnotic suggestions, cognitive strategies and mental imagery processes (that are shown throughout the remainder of this book) as serving you well, being consistent with your own personal values. You realise and appraise self-hypnosis to be a safe, ordinary process that requires a progressive mindset to develop as a valuable skill.

Fourth then, we have the attitude of **control.**

It is important that you realise that you are in control of your own self-hypnosis experience. It is a skill to develop, and therefore, you assure yourself of your ability to do self-hypnosis and engage in it in the ways laid out in this book. Continue to encourage yourself and take control of your attitude towards self-hypnosis. Consider yourself capable.

Additionally here, be in control of your own level of expectation. Expect the responses that you wish to occur, to actually occur. Expect them to happen automatically. Expect yourself to respond in the ways that you suggest or imagine in your self-hypnosis sessions.

The final attitude to adopt within the hypnotic mindset is that of **commitment.**

It is important that you allow yourself enough time to respond hypnotically to your suggestions. You do not want to rush yourself and likewise, you do not want to procrastinate or linger on things for too long. Additionally though, being committed means you invest the right amount of time and enthusiasm into using your self-hypnosis skills.

This hypnotic mindset may seem sobering and a far cry from the magical way hypnosis is often presented. Some people do not like having the magic whipped away from them. However, one important consequence of this is that the role of the hypnotic subject, the role of the self-hypnotist has now been demystified and made more easily learnable. In order for you to be a successful self-hypnotist, you learn the evidence-based hypnotic skills that are coming up and adopt this hypnotic mindset throughout.

This hypnotic mindset includes a number of themes that are duplicated in varying guises within this book, and for good reason. If you truly engage in these attitudes and adopt them inherently within your self-hypnosis sessions, the outcomes are going to be enhanced and advanced, and self-hypnosis is going to have much benefit for you.

We now conclude, **that hypnotism is basically about inducing a set of attitudes or mind-set.** The self-hypnotist learns to adopt a favourable attitude, to "get into the right mind-set", prior to engaging in the structured process that follows. Part of the reason for explaining all of this, is so that you can now apply these principles and learn to adopt the right anticipatory attitude.

Dispelling Popular Misconceptions

The third attitude explained within our hypnotic mindset pertains to you appraising hypnosis in a way that assures you of its safety, and in a way that is free from popular misconceptions. I thought I'd explain and dispel some popular misconceptions, so that you feel equipped in that regard and fully educated before this chapter is finished.

The following is based upon a handout I was given by Donald Robertson (his brilliant books are in the bibliography at the end of this book) on a course I took with his school back in 2006.

Go into any large bookshop nowadays and you will most likely find that their shelves are liberally stocked with books about hypnosis, and its numerous applications. Pick out any such book at random, open it anywhere and look anywhere on the page. The chances are that what you are reading is plainly wrong, is misleading, is questionable, has little support, or requires significant qualification for it to be accepted as a valid statement
(Heap, 2006).

Lynn, Kirsch et al. emphasise that *"clinicians can now rely on the following empirically derived information to educate their clients and inform their practice"*. Each point is substantiated by reference to a major piece of scientific research, most of which are well over a decade old now.

Some of these findings clash with popular misconception, popular psychology, New Age therapy, stage hypnosis hype and certain principles of hypnotic regression therapy and NLP/Ericksonian hypnosis. All are consistent, however, with the theory and practice of cognitive behavioural hypnotherapy, which is intended to be evidence-based. Not all of these points are totally relevant to self-hypnosis, but help to advance your understanding of this subject matter in an evidence-based manner.

The ability to experience hypnotic phenomena
does not indicate gullibility or weakness
(Barber, 1969).

This is a common misconception.

Hypnosis is not a sleep-like state
(Banyai, 1991).

Many people think hypnosis is similar to being asleep, when it is nothing of the sort. As you have read already, hypnosis requires you to be engaged and focused. Hypnosis is also not the same as relaxation. Banyai *(1991)* writes about and builds upon his earlier work from the 1970s with Ernest Hilgard, whereby he showed that by having a client exercise vigorously for a period of time prior to a hypnosis session, the client could still be hypnotised, but would not be at all relaxed. In fact, they would be alert and focused and have a heart rate and pulse that was very active.

A client undergoing relaxation training in any form of psychotherapy would not gain the benefits of the relaxation in the same way, making the two quite different.

Hypnosis depends more on the efforts and abilities
of the subject than on the skill of the hypnotist
(Hilgard, 1965).

I will mention this again in the next chapter, but it is incredibly good news for us as self-hypnotists. We are in control of our own hypnotic experiences with or without a hypnotist present.

Subjects retain the ability to control their behaviour during hypnosis, to refuse to respond to suggestions, and even to oppose suggestions (Lynn, Rhue and Weekes, 1990).

This is really more to do with hetero-hypnosis, however, it has implications for us self-hypnotists. We are ultimately in control of how suggestions affect and influence us. We'll be learning a great deal of how to enhance our responsiveness to suggestions later on.

Spontaneous amnesia is relatively rare (Simon & Salzburg, 1985).

Regardless of the impression Paul McKenna's TV show in the early 1990s gave, it is a common misconception that people forget what happened in hypnosis sessions.

The unwanted occurrence of amnesia can be easily prevented by telling yourself that you will be able to remember everything that is relevant from the session.

It is worth bearing in mind that you don't remember every single second of every single day – if I asked you to repeat back everything you have read in this book so far, you may struggle to repeat it exactly as you have read it, but you have not had amnesia. Hypnosis sessions are no different.

*Suggestions can be responded to with or without
hypnosis, and the function of a formal induction is
primarily to increase suggestibility to a minor
degree*
(Barber, 1969; Hilgard, 1965).

We shall be learning a number of inductions that are going to act as a cue for us to fully engage in our hypnotic mindset (detailed immediately prior to this section of the chapter).

*Hypnosis is not a dangerous procedure when
practiced by qualified clinicians and researchers*
(Lynn, Martin and Frauman, 1996).

Likewise, with the correct understanding and tuition offered here, self-hypnosis is not a dangerous procedure.

*Most hypnotised subjects are neither faking nor
merely complying with suggestions*
(Kirsch, Silva, Carone, Johnston and Simon, 1989).

*Hypnosis does not increase the accuracy of
memory*
(Sheehan and McConkey, 1993)

*or foster literal re-experiencing of childhood
events*
(Nash, 1987).

Today, hypnosis is no longer used as a means of eye-witness testimony, because it has been proven that hypnosis does not guarantee veracity of memory.

In fact, science has proven that memory is reconstructive, meaning that you view your memories through the person you are today and colour them accordingly.

> *Direct, traditionally-worded hypnotic techniques*
> *appear to be just as effective as permissive, open-*
> *ended, indirect suggestions*
> *(Lynn, Neufeld and Mare, 1993).*

Within our self-hypnosis sessions, we'll be learning to communicate in a simple, direct manner with no ambiguity or confusion.

> *A wide variety of hypnotic inductions can be*
> *effective (e.g. inductions that emphasise alertness*
> *can be just as effective as inductions that promote*
> *physical relaxation;*
> *(Banyai, 1991).*

Again, you'll learn a wide array of different induction techniques for starting your self-hypnosis sessions off.

> *Most hypnotised subjects do not describe their*
> *experience as "trance" but as focused attention on*
> *suggested events*
> *(McConkey, 1986).*

I think I have covered this in detail already in this chapter.

Hypnosis is not a reliable means of recovering repressed memories, but it might increase the danger of creating false memories
(Lynn and Nash, 1994).

There is a much broader discussion to be had on this subject (evidence shows hypnosis helps bring more memories/material up and enhances belief in those memories, potentially increasing the chances of false memory syndrome – responsible for some of the biggest litigation cases in psychiatric history in the 1990s) but for now, simply know that hypnosis is not a reliable means of recovering repressed memories.

Hypnotisability can be substantially modified
(Gorassini and Spanos, 1986; Spanos, 1991).

Many people initially measured as being low on a scale of hypnotic responsiveness can have that responsiveness increased. We focus on hypnotic skills designed to show you how to do this in a later chapter. The key point here is to explain that hypnotisability and responsiveness to hypnosis are not set in stone for everyone – they can be developed as with any skill.

Hypnotism then, as Braid explains marks a move away from the fantastical:

I beg farther to my remark, if my theory and pretensions, as to the nature, cause, and extent of the phenomena of nervous sleep (hypnotism) have none of the fascinations of the transcendental to

captivate the lovers of the marvellous, the
credulous and enthusiastic, which the pretensions
and alleged occult agency of the mesmerists have,
still I hope my views will be the less acceptable to
honest and sober-minded men, because they are
all level to our comprehension, and reconcilable
with well-known physiological and psychological
principles
(Braid, 1853, p. 36).

This chapter has explained the model of hypnosis that this book adheres to. That model and evidence supporting it rejects that hypnosis is an altered state, or a trance state, or that it is a magical, special state of any kind. Instead it supports the notion that hypnosis is actually a specific set of attitudes that you actively engage in, and you are responsible for the responses you get, not your unconscious mind. With this way of explaining and conceptualising hypnosis and self-hypnosis, lets look more specifically at self-hypnosis.

With our general approach explained, we'll now start being more specific about self-hypnosis.

In the foreword written by Martin Orne for the book *Self-Hypnosis: The Chicago Paradigm by* (Fromm and Kahn -1990) he states:

Perhaps the greatest single advancement made in the scientific study of hypnosis has been the realization that the ability to enter hypnosis is largely a skill of the patient, combining elements of focused attention, fantasy, and suspended belief. The role of the therapist working with the patient to use his or her hypnotic ability is to provide a context in which the patient can willingly express aspects of this cognitive skill......

Not only can the patient benefit from hypnosis during therapy, but self-hypnosis, once learned, can be used effectively outside the therapist's presence.

Before we learn how to do just that, I will first place self-hypnosis in context, focusing on the theory and background.

Chapter Two: Framing Self-Hypnosis

Having conceptualised hypnosis according to the cognitive behavioural, nonstate, evidence-based model, I now need to focus specifically on the theory and background of self-hypnosis for a variety of reasons:

I want to inform you about self-hypnosis in such a way that you'll find it easier to adopt the required positive mindset towards it.

To further aid your understanding of the subject, I want to contextualise self-hypnosis and show how it has developed historically.

I want you to have some correct and positive expectancy regarding what you can realistically achieve using hypnosis.

Therefore this chapter is going to offer up some historical context to self-hypnosis, address a couple of key notions that have plagued and persisted within the field of self-hypnosis, and offer up a portion of the evidence base that supports the efficacy of self-hypnosis.

What is Self-Hypnosis?

Following on from the first real definition of hypnosis that they put together, an executive committee of the American Psychological Association altered the APA definition of hypnosis to include the much used clinical technique of self-hypnosis, which they describe as *"the act of administering hypnotic procedures on one's own."* *(Green et al., 2005).*

Some people refute this and stand firm with the notion that any hypnosis must involve two people: a hypnotist and a subject. Therefore, they offer little credence or acceptance of the existence of the phenomenon of self-hypnosis. As far as they see it, self-hypnosis has no hypnotist present, therefore it cannot be considered actual hypnosis. My own subjective perspective (i.e. non-evidence based) is that the subject becomes the hypnotist. However, as we have already seen, the model of hypnosis we adhere to in this book is one whereby hypnosis is not reliant on someone else wielding it upon us; it is a hypnotic mindset we engage in ourselves.

Therefore, at one level, we can say that this refutation makes no sense, because as many academics, hypnotherapists, researchers and hypnosis professionals believe:
all hypnosis is self-hypnosis. They believe and suggest that although a hypnotist can conduct a hypnotic induction and give suggestions for a variety of experiences, it is actually the subject who has to engage in the process; without that engagement and participation by the subject, without their imagination, absorption, thought and feeling, no hypnosis occurs. We know that already, it was explained in our previous chapter.

Having said that, comparisons of self-hypnosis with more widely known 'hetero-hypnosis' show that they absolutely do have an important relationship that we self-hypnosis proponents cannot ignore, and a number of studies have gone in to exploring that relationship which I'll examine here *(Shor and Easton, 1973; Orne and McConkey, 1981; Johnson et al 1983).*

Some refute self-hypnosis on the grounds of it not being identical to hetero-hypnosis when it comes to the responsiveness to suggestions. It is indeed very likely to prove challenging to give yourself a suggestion for amnesia when you are the one reminding yourself what it is that you are forgetting. Likewise, it is likely to be more challenging to bring forth an hallucination before you in real-life terms (using self-hypnosis) when you are the one suggesting that you hallucinate it ('hallucination' infers it is not really there and you know that when suggesting it to yourself) rather than an external source helping you to believe it is the case. These circumstances are not impossible with self-hypnosis, but more challenging.

This is certainly not grounds for dismissing self-hypnosis and there is a great deal of cross-over between the two (hetero and self), despite them being different in so many other ways.

Is all Hypnosis Self-Hypnosis?

Most cognitive-behavioural theorists have adopted the view, as did James Braid (the founder of hypnotism), that "hetero-hypnosis", being hypnotised by another person, is essentially guided self-hypnosis. *(Golden, Dowd and Freidberg, 1987, p. 119).*

A number of researchers, and many clinicians, have found that simply asking subjects to "put yourself into hypnosis" is generally about as effective as performing the standard eye-fixation induction, or probably any other induction technique used by hypnotists (Barber, Spanos and Chaves, 1974).

Despite this evidence, there are still numerous hypnosis professionals, hypnotists and hypnotherapists out there who seem a bit 'ego-maniacal' and believe that they wield hypnosis upon their clients and subjects. They believe hypnosis is something that their hypnotic subjects must surrender to. These professionals do not tend to like the argument that evidence and studies available to us today suggest that the hypnotist does not actually have as much impact about what goes on in hypnosis, because virtually all the action is in the mind of the subject. That is, as I wrote earlier, **it is actually the subject who has to engage in the process; without that engagement and participation by the subject, without their imagination, absorption, thought and feeling, no hypnosis occurs.**

In fact, in 2006, the National Guild of Hypnotists (NGH) even stated in print that the hypnotist will "induct a client into a self-hypnotic state" *(2006)*. Several other hypnosis associations have followed in a similar vein.

As mentioned already, Theodore Barber *(1985)* stated that the vast majority of hypnotic procedures can be accurately defined as self-hypnosis. Additionally, work by Orne and McConkey *(1981)* and Sanders *(1991)* state the same. Parts therapy and regression proponent Roy Hunter and his mentor Charles Tebbetts state the same: that hypnosis is self-hypnosis. In fact, in Roy Hunter's book The Art Of Hypnotherapy, he states that Tebbetts, while still alive, began every hypnosis session with the statement "all hypnosis is self-hypnosis."

The founder of the American Board of Hypnotherapy held that

same opinion, as stated in The Wizard Within by Krasner *(1990)*. Michael Yapko *(1995)* suggested that whatever power the hypnotherapist has, is acquired from the client and of course, can be terminated by the client.

As far back as 1965, in Hypnosis Induction Technics, Tietelbaum stated that if a hypnotist attempts to be too powerful, then the client may lose rapport and reject the suggestions delivered in a session. Further suggesting that a sense of self-efficacy aids hypnosis.

It is the guys in the 19th century, born out of Mesmerism and the dark ages, that created the notions of hypnosis 'being done to' another individual. Imagine if that were the case? How comfortable would you be about hypnotists being set loose on the world? Surely they'd take over, wouldn't they? Well, the less scrupulous ones at any rate.

Ultimately, most researchers, academics and proponents of the nonstate, cognitive-behavioural model believe the person being hypnotised is responsible for generating the suggestion inside their own mind, the relevant imagery to go with it, and they combine their own experience and behaviour in response.

(I think I have made the point enough times, and will now move on to other areas. I hope it has registered with you, since it is fundamental to your development as a self-hypnotist).

The data available regarding the use of self-hypnosis in the therapeutic and clinical setting suggests that of the psychologists and medical practitioners who use hypnosis within their work, the majority teach their patients and clients self-hypnosis *(Sheehan and McConkey, 1979)*, and one study also shows that self-hypnosis is used in the majority of smoking cessation programmes *(Holroyd, 1980)*.

Self-hypnosis experienced a widespread acceptance as an integral part of therapeutic intervention as far back as the 1970s *(Sheehan and McConkey, 1979)*. The growing trend since then may well be related to the fact that the use of self-hypnosis gives individuals the chance of contributing to their own development within therapy, and to enjoy a feeling of being more in control of themselves. For those of us not in therapy, it becomes a learnable, enjoyable skill that can enrich many facets of our lives.

For example, in my hypnotherapy consulting rooms, if I am working with a client for overcoming or lowering chronic pain, by using self-hypnosis they get to discover that they can take control of a problem that may well have seemed out of control before; many individuals initially believe they are passive recipients of their ailments. The belief that they are capable of affecting change themselves, often leads to other impressive benefits within therapy too: an advanced self-image, belief in their own ability to cope, and an increase in positive expectation, which is deemed vital by many prominent psychotherapists *(Bandura, 1977)*.

Many authors and trainers I have encountered believe that this does more than advance the progress a client makes, but that it is beneficially therapeutic in its own right. More great news for us self-hypnotists.

One of the benefits of the self-hypnosis approach is that it means we can use hypnosis techniques at home and can be taught a number of techniques to create a repertoire of skills to use in a wide variety of areas in our lives. This is made difficult if the person being hypnotised believes that they can only enter hypnosis if the hypnotist needs to be around to induce it.

This way of explaining hypnosis to my hypnotherapy clients is also very useful because it helps to alleviate and overcome resistance and fear associated with the notion of being under the control of another person. Practicing self-hypnosis, the client can enhance the collaborative nature of successful therapy. They become an active (i.e. non-passive) component of the therapeutic process.

The hypnotherapist can be a facilitator rather than a dictator too. Of course, there are as many theories on this as there are hypnotists and hypnotherapists. I think for therapists in particular, it is important to at least consider the notion that all hypnosis is self-hypnosis because it empowers the hypnotherapy client, allays fears, puts them in control, creates a collaborative approach and seems to be more client-centred.

I think that as a student of self-hypnosis, someone learning how to use this for yourself, it helps to understand that you are in control. On one hand, we see that the role of the hypnotist is actually relatively minor, as compared with an individual's hypnotic aptitude, and all hypnosis can be conceived as self-hypnosis. On the other hand, a lot of self-hypnosis is actually taught in the context of a two-way relationship with the hypnotist or therapist, and so it can also rightly be argued that self-hypnosis is actually a variant of hetero-hypnosis *(e.g. Weitzenhoffer, 1957)* or the re-accessing of previous hetero-hypnosis experiences. For this reason, I think we can benefit from both perspectives and on my website *(www.adam-eason.com)* I offer a free, instantly downloadable hypnosis session guiding you through hypnosis so that you can practice it with my guidance, prior to or while you are doing it entirely for yourself.

There are a number of other really good arguments, theoretical inferences and notions of contrasting nature that arise from exploring the field of self-hypnosis.

For example, some do not fully support the above notions, instead opting for a separation of self-hypnosis and hetero-hypnosis; suggesting that they are both entirely separate entities to be treated as such, and though they correlate, the existence of one is not dependent on the other. I have used this notion to diffuse many a heated forum debate in the past.

In order to make any hard and fast claims to understanding self-hypnosis, we definitely require more exploration and further studies.

Let us now delve a little deeper.

Historical Context of Self-Hypnosis

The English term "hypnotism" was introduced in 1841 by the Scottish physician and surgeon James Braid.

Braid *(1846, 1855, cited in Robertson, 2008)* was the first investigator to systematically explore the phenomenon of self-hypnosis. used self-hypnosis to aid in his own health issues and was absolutely convinced that:

> *In as much as patients can throw themselves into*
> *the nervous sleep, and manifest all the usual*
> *phenomena of mesmerism, through their own*
> *unaided efforts ...*
> *it is obvious that there is no need for an exotic*
> *influence to produce the phenomena of*
> *mesmerism*
> *(Braid,1846, cited in Robertson, 2008).*

As I'll discuss later, Emile Coué *(1922)* later also demonstrated Braid's stance and both supported that stance by conducting a number of demonstrations of individuals experiencing hypnosis and displaying hypnotic phenomena without any direct involvement or intervention of another person

Within Braid's writings, he states that he started using "self-hypnotism" a couple of years after discovering hypnotism. He initially taught it to his clients, then began using it himself:

> *My first experiments on this point [i.e. self-*
> *hypnosis] were instituted in the presence of some*
> *friends on the 1st May, 1843, and following days. I*
> *believe they were the first experiments of the kind*
> *which had ever been tried, and they have*
> *succeeded in every case in which I have so*
> *operated.*
> *(Braid, 1855, cited in Robertson, 2008).*

In a later work, *Observations on Trance or Human Hybernation* *(1850)*, Braid provides what is seen by most as the earliest account of self-hypnosis use. He gave an account of how he used self-hypnosis to deal with the pain of a rheumatism attack. He followed all the protocols and instructions he gave his hypnosis patients and experienced much success.

He went on to be free of his rheumatism for six years. I continue to find it really difficult to deny the benefits of self-hypnosis when the very man who coined the term, essentially creating the field of hypnosis, used it in this way and wrote about it.

The next major historical proponent of self-hypnosis is Émile Coué. Coué is seen by many as one of the most influential figures in the development of self-hypnosis. Coué's system became a globally recognised self-help methodology at the beginning of the 20th century. His method of "conscious autosuggestion" was prevalent half a century before millions of people started doing transcendental meditation, for example.

As I mentioned earlier, Coué used so-called 'hypnotic phenomena' (arm levitation, cataplepsy etc. as you'll be taught later in this book) by simply teaching his clients and students to engage the imagination and affirm suggestions to themselves with a depth of meaning and real volition.

As well as using his system to get individuals engaged in phenomena, such as the hand clasp, hand stick and being stuck in a chair, Coué documented the pen-drop technique back in 1922 (by

Autosuggestion), and in 1923 by (*'my method'*). Using self-suggestion and imagination within self-hypnosis sessions, people achieved this type of hypnotic phenomena.

(Please note, Barber showed there is no phenomena exclusive to the field of hypnosis that cannot be achieved with suggestion alone, but I refer to the kind of hypnotic phenomena that is used by many hypnosis professionals to indicate hypnosis, and which is used as a 'convincer').

Coué would tell people to repeat self-suggestions, such as the famous *"day by day, in every way, I am getting better and better."* In coming chapters, I'll be writing about how to use Couéism in more detail.

Throughout this chapter, I make reference to a number of important contributions to the field of self-hypnosis and a selection of evidence. In particular, the body of work produced by Erika Fromm and Stephen Kahn in the 1980s is something I refer to later on in this book. However, for now, the only other isolated contribution to the history of self-hypnosis I want to refer to, is the contribution of Andrew Salter.

Many believe that Salter's 1941 academic journal article on self-hypnosis, "Three techniques of autohypnosis", was the first of its kind. Salter's story is an impressive one as he persisted to get his paper published despite running up against some opposition. Salter's article basically described the processes of self-hypnosis.

Thankfully, Professor Clark Leonard Hull, of Yale's Psychology Department at the time, chose to publish the article in the Journal of General Psychology, of which he was an editor. Hull is the author of an important work entitled, *Hypnosis & Suggestibility*, (of which I have a tattered old copy) and has been considered by many to be the world's greatest authority in the field of hypnosis. Therefore, it is encouraging (to me) that he supported the publication of this journal article on self-hypnosis.

Salter's technique was applied to over 200 subjects while being developed over a period of a couple of years. Within the aforementioned paper, Salter offered up his methods of teaching self-hypnosis to individuals by:

- Autohypnosis by post-hypnotic suggestion.

- Autohypnosis by memorised trance instructions. (Scripted suggestions.)

- Fractional autohypnosis. (Part learning.)
  (Salter, 1941)

This may not make much sense right now, but by the end of this book, if you revisit this chapter, it'll make more sense then.

It is believed that Salter's behavioural approach went on to influence the Carleton Skills Training Programme developed by Nicholas Spanos in the 1980s, as well as influencing other similar skills models designed at enhancing the responsiveness to hypnosis.

One of the four parts of the Carleton Skills Training Programme was designed to primarily enhance hypnotisability and to regularly practice the hypnotic strategies. The inherent thought is that self-hypnosis is possible and practicing helps enhance hypnotisability and responsiveness. We are going to revisit the Carelton Skills Training Programme in depth in the next chapter.

In a similar vein to the Carleton Skills Training Programme, other studies have also indicated that as well as the actual responsiveness and skill developing from the practice of self-hypnosis, an individual's confidence in their ability to use self-hypnosis is increased with practice *(Fromm et al., 1981)*.

Research Into Self-Hypnosis

Over the years, there has been a lot of empirical exploration and study of hetero-hypnosis. However, the same kind of exploration has not been paralleled in the field of self-hypnosis, although there have been some key studies that I will refer to shortly.

Firstly, I'll say this… I have bias. This is demonstrated in the very fact that I have written this book and dedicated so much of my professional career to the subject. I like to think that I am presenting information with some consideration of opposing sides of debate and argument, and offering information in a balanced manner, but my goal is to show self-hypnosis in a progressive light, and most of my writing on the subject offers my personal idea of what self-hypnosis is and how it should be done as influenced by evidence.

This is commonplace. Most researchers and authors tend to approach the subject in terms of their personal understanding and theory of what self-hypnosis is and how it is best done, and this is often reflected in their research. The approaches of modern authors on the topic tend to reveal a wide range of definitions that have been applied during the exploration of self-hypnosis.

In relation to the wide range of approaches to self-hypnosis, I want to state that no one approach can be considered to be the correct method, and none of the major authors tend to suggest or stress that a single method prevails. There is some contrast in the research approaches, for example, such as the amount of time or level of instruction that an individual should receive when practicing self-hypnosis.

Due to the nature of hypnosis studies, much of the research conducted by Fromm et al. *(1981)* used subjects who had previous experience of hetero-hypnosis, and this set the way for how they experienced the use of self-hypnosis within the research. It is often stated that having learned self-hypnosis (after having had a clinical hetero-hypnosis experience) is highly likely to influence the way an individual relates to and uses self-hypnosis *(Gardner, 1981; Sacerdote, 1981)*.

In contrast to this, some researchers have only worked with people who have had no previous clinical experience of hypnosis, and some have given their subjects minimal instructions on what to do or engage in *(Ruch, 1975)*. In other studies, subjects have been asked to read and follow a full induction procedure to themselves *(Shor and Easton, 1973)* which some have said is nearly the same as listening to an audio recording.

There have been key studies that have looked at comparing self-hypnosis and hetero-hypnosis. There have been indications from such studies that in both self-hypnosis and hetero-hypnosis, individuals experience a high level of absorption, as well as a lessening in their connection to reality *(Fromm et al., 1981)*.

However, there are ways in which these two methods appear to be different too. Individuals seem to experience more vivid imagery when using self-hypnosis *(Fromm et al., 1981)* though individuals state that they are more cognitively active and self-controlling when in self-hypnosis *(Johnson, 1981)*. So although the overall behavioural responses and experiences of subjects using self- hypnosis and hetero-hypnosis are indeed correlated, some individuals do respond in different ways to self-hypnosis than they do to hetero-hypnosis *(Fromm et al., 1981; Johnson, 1979, 1981)*.

The Benefits of Self-Hypnosis

I have seen and heard self-hypnosis described in a wide variety of ways. Overall though, it seems to be described by most who use and teach it, as something which results in beneficial outcomes for the self-hypnotist. I realise that some are going to read that as a no evidence-based bias statement,, but I think it is the truth. Although not all strictly empirically evidence based, let me attempt to illustrate my reasons.

There are studies that suggest that when an individual receives instruction from a therapist, self-hypnosis is an effective way to successfully treat anxiety *(Benson et al., 1978)*. We'll look at overcoming anxiety using self-hypnosis in a later chapter.

Anbar *(2003)* describes a means of successfully teaching a client self-hypnosis to help overcome anxiety and deal with her asthma.

Many authors suggest self-hypnosis used within smoking cessation treatments, dealing with weight reduction and other kinds of presenting issues as a means of enhancing efficacy of the overall therapeutic treatment.

Many books have been written on the subject, many poor, some excellent, but those authors and many of the readers go on to successfully employ self-hypnosis methods and techniques.

For those wishing to explore further, read

- *Self-Hypnosis The Chicago Paradigm* by Fromm and Kahn,

- *Teaching Self-Hypnosis* by David Soskis,

- *Strategic Self-Hypnosis* by Roger Straus, and

- *Clinical Self-Hypnosis* by Shirley Sanders.

Writing in the foreword to *Strategic Self-Hypnosis* the Straus book on self-hypnosis, Theodore Barber described four major insights that developed out of the "hypnosis renaissance" of the 1970s *(Straus, 1982, pp. ix-xi).*

Self-hypnosis was realised to be a much broader and more important concept than had previously been assumed, because hypnosis in general was increasingly understood to depend upon the active goal-directed imagination of the kind employed during self-hypnosis.

Self-hypnosis was shown to be, to a large extent, a learnable skill, which can be taught using familiar behavioural training methods, such as psycho-education, coaching, modelling, shaping and reinforcement etc.

Self-hypnosis gradually lost its "aura of mystery" as researchers explored the cognitive and behavioural strategies involved, and their similarity to other processes.

The value of self-hypnosis was understood to reach beyond psychotherapy and into other domains of life, such as education and the everyday self-management of emotion and behaviour for positive psychological functioning.

In 1981, an entire special edition of the *International Journal of Experimental and Clinical Hypnosis* was dedicated to the subject of self-hypnosis, and I hope another such edition is published in the future. I highly recommend anyone with a scholarly interest in self-hypnosis to read the 1981 edition.

In 2008, a man named Alex Lenkei used self-hypnosis and refused anaesthesia, to have a walnut sized lump of bone and gristle removed from his hand; his account included him hearing cracking and crunching of bones. He has had a total of 6 surgical procedures, his most recent (at the time of this book being written) came in 2013, where he had an ankle replacement surgery.

In 1986 Victor Rausch, a Canadian dental surgeon, used self-hypnosis to have his gall bladder removed. He charted it and made notes at the same time. He did not feel a thing.

Then there is my own friend and graduate of my school, Gareth Lee Morgan, who had his teeth removed using only self-hypnosis.

Google his name and mine, and read my full blog entry on my website describing it in detail.

Hundreds of women each year use self-hypnosis skills, giving birth within and outside of specific hypnobirthing protocols. This is the tip of the iceberg with regards to what I have seen and experienced.

Self-hypnosis exists and it's here to stay. Its benefits are well documented. It has evidence to support it and a history that key academics and researchers have contributed to.

I hope you have expectancy, I hope you have that set of attitudes to develop your hypnotic mindset, and I hope you get a feel for how the field of self-hypnosis has developed, because we are now going to start engaging in it.

Chapter Three: Hypnotic Skills Training

Before we move on to our structured protocol for self-hypnosis sessions, there is substantial evidence to suggest that people can learn to be more responsive and better hypnotic subjects *(Gorassini and Spanos, 1986; Spanos, 1991).* That is, we can learn to develop our self-hypnosis skills and abilities before we start with our structured sessions.

Up to now, the aim has been to educate you correctly about what hypnosis is and correct any previous misconceptions you may have had. The aim has also been to make sure that you realise the importance of adopting the progressive self-hypnosis mindset and favourable attitudes. The final preparation prior to starting to engage in the self-hypnosis protocol (coming up in the next chapter) is to engage in some hypnotic skills training and practice some self-suggestion experiments. This helps to develop your understanding of hypnosis in your own terms (rather than hearing about it from a theoretical perspective) and gives you some hypnotic experience to build on.

In chapter one, I explained that this model of hypnosis finds the similarities between hypnosis and other aspects of life, and it makes hypnosis an ordinary process–not an abnormal altered state of consciousness. It is for that reason that I have no hesitation in telling you that hypnosis is much easier than you realize, and you have done many similar things on numerous occasions without calling it 'self-hypnosis'.

Think about ordinary relaxation. Some people are better at relaxing than others. I remember when I first moved to Bournemouth and owned a health centre; at the end of the weekly yoga class, the instructor would ask everyone to relax and wind down with some guided relaxation. I was busy fidgeting and trying to get comfortable while others were properly zonked out. Some people find that relaxation is easier to induce when they focus attention on certain ideas, or use mental imagery, which is often used in yoga classes. People develop the ability to relax with practice, and after a while, can relax at will, despite not having much previous ability. When relaxation is done confidently and expectantly, and for a good period of time, the relaxation is often better.

Self-hypnosis is quite distinct from relaxation *(Banyai and Hilgard, 1976)*, though the two can go together wonderfully well (as we shall see later). However the way in which people develop the skill to relax and attain the right mental approach is similar to getting better at self-hypnosis.

If you wanted to relax deeply, you could take some time and gradually, progressively and systematically imagine each part of the body relaxing in turn, moving your attention all the way from your foot (the muscles within it softening) and then up to the lower leg, the knee, the upper leg and through the rest of the body. In this way, your entire body can be relaxed more deeply than it usually is. We are going to develop this skill later on in the book. Anyone can get better at relaxation with some repetition and practice.

These underlying skills involved in developing your ability to relax are virtually identical to the hypnotic skills you will learn in this chapter. You may not have drawn parallels between the ability to relax and self-hypnosis, but there is a clear correlation. In Chapter One I referred to this relationship as, the ideo-motor reflex: the use of the imagination to evoke bodily responses. When you engage your thoughts and ideas, there is often a physiological response.

James Braid often made direct comparisons of hypnotism to many everyday examples of suggestion, where thoughts and ideas influence our physiology. His examples included blushing or the change in skin pallor when listening to a story; actors able to shed tears by being so immersed in their roles; or mothers lactating at the mere thought of their baby crying. These are all examples of the ideo-motor reflex, where our thoughts and imagination create a physiological response. In this chapter, you are going to start engaging in this type of activity by purposefully applying your imagination to create particular responses and to start to develop your hypnotic skills.

The most empirically-supported programme to train subjects in hypnotic skills and improve responsiveness to hypnosis was led by Nicholas Spanos at Carleton University in Canada in the 1980s. The Carleton Skills Training Programme (CSTP) has been supported by numerous studies as an effective means of increasing hypnotic responsiveness among initially low-responding subjects.

Participants in the programme are trained to respond to a range of suggestions of varying kinds. In order to generate a kind of willing self-deception, the CSTP basically asks clients to role-play their responses to suggestions while interpreting them as automatic, which seems to generalise to future experiences of being hypnotised *(Gorassini and Spanos, 1999).* This is something we can all learn to do to develop our hypnotic skills and prepare us for using self-hypnosis protocols to make changes in our life.

You are sure to have become deeply absorbed or engrossed in a film or the content of a story to the extent that it evokes a physical and emotional reaction of some kind. It is the same sort of response we want to have to suggestions and mental imagery processes that we practice here.

In the brief version of the CSTP the instructions to clients are summed up in two sentences:

> *"Make the responses that are suggested, but pay*
> *no attention to the fact that you are making them.*
> *Instead, devote your full, undivided, and*
> *continuous attention to the suggestions"*
> *(Gorassini and Spanos, 1999, p. 171).*

With the coming exercises, simply assure and convince yourself of the responses that are required. Make yourself believe that the responses are happening automatically. Also remember to truly adopt the set of attitudes outlined in Chapter One with regards to having the progressive hypnotic mindset.

Role-modelling

It does not really occur in hypnotherapy consulting rooms today, but back in the 1840s, James Braid often hypnotised his patients in the presence of others, who subsequently became good hypnotic subjects as a result of seeing it happen to other people. Likewise, with the CSTP, participants are initially shown video clips of model hypnotic subjects demonstrating each suggestion test and commenting on what their experience was like.

It is difficult to offer this element of help in a book. However, you can visit my YouTube channel and watch a number of clips that demonstrate several of the kinds of hypnotic 'phenomena' that you are going to be engaging in shortly:
(www.youtube.com/adameasonhypnosis)

One of the simplest ways to start with the development of your hypnotic skills is to engage in the **bucket and balloon** imagination experiment.

You can be seated or stood for this. Whichever you are, have both arms stretched out in front of you with your fists clenched and your eyes closed.

Turn the right fist so that it is pointing palm upwards and now imagine that your right hand is holding the handle of a heavy bucket, making it feel tired and sink down.

At the same time, imagine your left arm is resting on a large inflatable balloon that is gradually expanding, making it feel light and rise.

To make the left arm rise up even more, here is an additional suggestion used in the CSTP:

> In response to this suggestion, you must do everything that is required of someone making believe such a thing. You must lift your arm up, and you must imagine that the arm is really a hollow balloon that is being pumped up full of helium, rising by itself, and anything else you wish to

imagine that is consistent with such a make-believe situation. Of course, your arm will not really go up by itself, you must raise it.

However, you can make it feel like it's going up by itself by focusing on the make-believe situation, that your arm is hollow and being filled with helium
(Gorassini and Spanos, 1999, p. 152).

By engaging your imagination and making yourself believe in the imagery, with each breath, imagine the right arm is getting heavier and the left arm is getting lighter. Do this for a couple of minutes with focus and absorption, expect the arms to respond, gently convince yourself using your imagination.

Once those 2-3 minutes have passed, open your eyes and have a look at the different positions your arms are in. It is usual for the heavy right arm to have moved more than the left one (gravity helped it feel heavy as well as your imagination). This brief and simple process is one initial way for us to illustrate how your imagination, thoughts and beliefs influence and affect your physiology.

Using Emile Coué's Convincers as Hypnotic Skills Training

Today, one of the most common things I am asked by people who have read my books or listened to my audio tracks (especially those teaching themselves self-hypnosis) is how can they tell if they were actually hypnotically engaged, if they were doing things right and responding to the suggestions? Therefore, the rest of this chapter will supply that evidence by conducting a series of experiments to fine tune your skills, enhance your belief and develop self-efficacy.

Within the therapy room, hypnotherapists can feedback or ratify an individual's on-going experience and give clear indications that they are in hypnosis.

At a lecture in 2011, I watched Professor Irving Kirsch discuss how the positive expectancy and belief of the client enhanced their hypnotisability and responsiveness to suggestions. Therefore, to enhance the beneficial responses we are looking for, it makes sense that we work out ways of enhancing our belief in our self-hypnosis skills. These skills help you build positive expectancy and give you evidence of your progress. Furthermore, if you have a positive expectancy to make life changes (to be examined) those changes are more likely to be actualized.

One of the greatest contributors to the field of self-hypnosis is Emile Coué, whose method of autosuggestion was enhanced and developed for individuals by teaching them a set of experiments to practice with. This enhanced their own degree of self-efficacy and made them more responsive to autosuggestions, as well as developing skill with the method (we'll be looking at how to use his method of autosuggestion later in the book).

Though Coué's method was not strictly known as self-hypnosis, it is considered a major contribution to the field of self-hypnosis and the parallels are great. In order to develop our hypnotic skills, I thought I'd share with you Coué's series of "waking suggestion" experiments. They are very similar to suggestibility tests that are employed by street and stage hypnotists, as well as those used in the consulting rooms of hypnotherapists.

These experiments require an engagement of the imagination and often result in what is referred to as ideo-motor or ideo-reflex responses (as explained previously). That is, when you truly engage the imagination, there is a physiological or sensory response to that which dominates the imagination; it creates a response of some kind.

With the experiments, it is important to avoid the 'effort error' that Coué often referred to. One of the biggest obstructions to successful outcomes with these experiments, is trying so hard that it induces anxiety. Convince yourself of the outcome with a gentle assuredness. Use your belief: believe in the successful outcome occurring and assume success. This is going to advance the responses you get and not impede your progress.

Prior to starting any of these experiments, make sure you are in a place where you are going to be undisturbed, can focus and concentrate, and are able to engage without distraction. Sit in a receptive, progressive, attentive posture, with your feet flat on the floor and your arms not touching each other.

Coué stated, as was central to his work, that if you engage the imagination strongly enough, where will and imagination conflict, imagination prevails. He would give examples of people using their will to unsuccessfully get themselves back to sleep when having insomnia, or to overcome problems by using too much forceful will that exasperated the issue at hand, instead of helping it.

Therefore, Coué extolled the virtues of the imagination and suggestion over the will.

The extensive work of Bandura in the 1970s, 1980s and 1990s demonstrates the need for self-efficacy; that is, the belief in our own ability to successfully achieve something, making it far easier to effectively fulfil. With this in mind, again I reiterate the importance of gentle convincing and reassuring yourself, believing in what you are doing as much as you can.

Before we move on to the next chapter, firstly, in order to fine tune your own self-hypnosis skills, to become more responsive and develop your belief in your own self-hypnosis, have a go at these particular experiments:

1. Salivating

I once watched a demonstration by a stage hypnotist whereby he held up a lemon, cut it into quarters, and then put it to his mouth and sucked the juice, while suggesting to the audience that they could taste it in their own mouths and were starting to salivate. He had not actually sucked on the lemon, it looked very real but he had pretended, though it got the desired effect from the audience. There were all kinds of contorted faces and giggles among us.

The smell and sight of various substances, or of other people eating them, functions like a conditioned stimulus for salivation. This is a process that I have been using for years in my self-hypnosis training seminars to demonstrate the power of the imagination against the will and determination alone, which is referred to by Coué in *My Method* (1922). If you simply told yourself, and tried to will yourself to dribble, you may not get the desired result. However, with this experiment, you **imagine** the scenario and let your imagination trigger the response.

Right now, close your eyes, truly imagine that you are taking a chilled lemon out of the fridge, it gets sliced in half and then quarters. You pick up one of the quarters, bring it to the mouth and sink your teeth right into it. Imagine the texture, the juices running in and around the mouth, under the tongue, make it all as vivid as possible and notice how your mouth responds. Even if it is a very subtle response, it is a response, illustrating the process discussed in previous chapters.

This demonstrates an ideo-dynamic response, which is the effect of that suggestion and your imagination influencing the autonomic processes of the body. You salivate and develop a sensation within your mouth as you engage your imagination.

2. Chevreul's Pendulum

Michel-Eugene Chevreul was a well-known French chemist who in the early 1800s investigated what was initially seen as an "occult" phenomenon of the pendulum, and he wanted to give it a plausible scientific explanation. In 1812, Chevreul discovered the psycho-physiological basis of dowsing, though it was not publicly realised until 1833 when his work was shared.

Chevreul's explorations and investigations showed that the pendulum effect is due to a simple, regular and very usual human reaction, which was seen as some sort of mystical phenomenon for years previously. Chevreul found that if you imagine something intensely, then the human body behaves in a way as if the imagined action, event or circumstance is actually happening. Today, Chevreul's pendulum is used to demonstrate the astonishing and remarkably strong effects of self-hypnosis by tutors, such as myself, on hypnosis training and self-hypnosis seminars.

First up then, grab yourself a piece of paper or card and draw a big circle with a cross inside it. You'll have a drawn circle with a cross in the middle of it dividing it into quarters. If you have not got your own pendulum, then you can easily make one. Get some cotton, some string, or any other similar material, and cut it to a length of 30-35 cm. Attach a small weight to the end; you can use a ring, or anything at the end that'll serve as the weight for the pendulum.

Now you need to take a seat at a table with your piece of paper/card on the table in front of you. Rest your elbow on the tabletop. Hold the string between your thumb and forefinger so that the pendulum weight can hang straight down; ideally 1-2 cm above the centre of the cross in the circle. Try to hold the pendulum as still and immovable as possible. Let your arm be as loose as possible while holding the string in this position.

Next, you are going to engage your imagination. While holding the pendulum as still with your arm as loose as possible, just imagine how it would feel if the pendulum started to swing vertically. In your mind, imagine it swinging, imagine watching it swing vertically along the line of your diagram. Don't do anything consciously to make it swing, simply imagine as vividly as you can that the pendulum is starting to swing all on its own. Make yourself believe that it is swinging.

After a couple of minutes of engaging your imagination, you may well be finding that the pendulum actually starts swinging. It is likely that at first, it'll be small swings and then these may grow to wide, bold swings in the vertical direction. When you have succeeded with the vertical swings, then you can do the same to imagine what it would feel like if the pendulum instead, started rotating clockwise.

The pendulum takes tiny movements one end (where you are holding it), magnifies them and they are expressed much more largely at the other end. When you are imagining the pendulum swinging, then the ideo-motor reflex occurring in your body makes very small, almost imperceptible movements in the right direction.

The pendulum is an energy accumulating system, so the minute imperceptible swings add up, and after a while the pendulum swings with easy-to-watch movements.

3. Hands Locked Together

With this experiment, you clasp your hands tightly together and hold your arms out straight. You now convince yourself that you cannot pull your hands apart, that they are stuck together. You imagine that they are stuck together and convince yourself of it.

Coué would recommend that individuals tell themselves "I will open my hands, but I CANNOT, I CANNOT!" while simultaneously imagining the hands to be stuck tightly together. The words are then repeated over and over in the mind in a convincing manner, using a tone that makes the words believable.

Note the linguistic pattern here too: you start off by telling yourself "I will open my hands" before you say "I cannot!" When you say "will" it presupposes that this thing will happen in the future but is not happening right now, and so it lends itself well to the notion of your hands being stuck together.

Engage your imagination and continue to tell yourself your hands are clenching tighter and cannot be separated. As long as the imagination is fixed on the idea, it will convince you that they are stuck. When you have convinced yourself that they are stuck, then tell yourself "I can open them" and imagine them coming apart to free them accordingly.

The use of "I cannot!" and "I can" is to be used with the other experiments here that follow.

4. Arm or Leg Catalepsy

When I say catalepsy, I am referring to either your leg or arm remaining solid, stuck and remaining in position, regardless of external stimulus. For example, you imagine that your arm is a steel bar, or made of a solid material that means it cannot bend and again you use a similar type of linguistic pattern with yourself: "I will be able to bend my arm, but I cannot, I cannot!" while simultaneously imagining the arm to be solid and incapable of bending.

The same process can be applied to the leg. You imagine that one or both legs are totally solid and because they are rigid, you are unable to walk. Convince yourself with imagination and strong belief.

Not totally dissimilar to this, you can also create a tightly clenched fist and suggest to yourself that it is locked tighter and tighter, using similar language and convincing imagery as used in the previous experiments.

Once you have tested this and convinced yourself of each of the experiments, give yourself permission for the limb and arm to bend, loosen, relax, tell yourself "I can bend it and loosen it", and then feel a sense of development and happiness with your progress.

5. *Sticking* Hands *and Fingers*

You may have seen video clips of me doing this type of thing with clients and students on YouTube. Coué uses similar experiments,getting something stuck to the hand or getting the hand stuck to something.

You can do a pen stick, or a card stick, whereby you take a firm grip of a pen or a playing card between the finger and thumb, and imagine the fingers to be locked in place, and the card or pen to be stuck in the hand. Again, you state the same kind of linguistic pattern to yourself, convincing yourself of the card or pen being stuck there: "I will drop the pen, but I cannot, I cannot now!"

When I do this with clients or students, the client/student is told that the more they try to drop the card/pen, the more rigidly locked the fingers become and the more stuck the card is. The fingers squeeze tighter and you imagine them being stuck firm and fast with as much purpose as you can imagine.

A similar process is to press your palm onto one of your legs or a tabletop and imagine that it is stuck tight and cannot be moved.

Imagine it stuck with glue, convince yourself with your imagination and communicate with yourself in your mind with total belief.

Engage in these five imagination experiments and convince yourself of the right outcomes; assume they are happening and when the imagination is vivid, and with the right level of belief and expectation invested, you'll start to get some evidence and proof that you are hypnotising yourself, and will become convinced of the effects of your self-suggestion, imagination and self-hypnosis skills.

Enjoy these exercises and train up your skills and belief. In the next chapter you'll learn some more of these convincers and hypnotic skills within the actual step-by-step protocol for self-hypnosis (especially with some of the inductions). The aim of this chapter has been to get you to realise that self-hypnosis responses are something you can train yourself to get better at, providing you with a set of processes to practice that will build a foundation of hypnotic skills using imagination, expectation, positive belief and the set of attitudes described in chapter one. We'll now move on to a structured method of self-hypnosis

Chapter Four: Doing Self-Hypnosis

To begin with, the self-hypnosis sessions you engage in will require you to loosely follow a five step structure, with a model that takes you through steps A to E:

STEP A – You Access hypnosis.

This is initially done with any one of a variety of induction methods, many of which contain similar hypnotic skills mentioned in the previous chapter. There are a wide number of means and ways that you'll be given to help you access hypnosis.

Using the word 'access' in this step could lead someone to think that hypnotising yourself is a mechanical result of the induction process, but it is not. Remember, our model of hypnosis is such that you adopt the hypnotic mindset with its inherent attitudes. The induction, this step A, is simply a cue for you to begin with the induction process. As a result, you will actually enter hypnosis just before you start with step A and not afterwards as a result of step A.

STEP B – Being in control.

This helps you to focus and keep on track, as well as develop the previously mentioned hypnotic mindset (though it will be in place prior to starting).

STEP C – Continually deepening.

You deepen your perception of your experience of self-hypnosis in a variety of ways that you'll be shown.

STEP D – Deliver your suggestions.

This is where you engage in the change work, use mental imagery techniques, apply the cognitive strategies or simply affirm suggestions to yourself.

STEP E – Exit hypnosis.

You bring that self-hypnosis session to a conclusion.

We are now going to go through the steps (A-E) one at a time in more detail, offering up options and variety for each step. Many academics tend to believe that it is much easier to access hypnosis once you have been hypnotised by a professional. If you have been formally hypnotised by a hypnotist before now, it is likely to advance your skills as a self-hypnotist.

If you have not, there is no need to worry, everything you need is explained here. However, if you wish to experiment and advance your skills, as I mentioned previously, you can download a full hypnosis session from my website for you to practice entering hypnosis: *www.adam-eason.com*.

There are a number of options and instructions given here for doing the various steps. It is not by any means fully exhaustive; that would require another full book, not just a single chapter. Do therefore consider visiting the blog of my website for more ways of inducing and deepening self-hypnosis.

STEP A: Access Hypnosis

Our first step gets a lot of attention in literature on hypnosis. It is what hypnotists refer to as the induction, whereby hypnosis is induced. This is where self-hypnotists Access hypnosis and induce hypnosis for ourselves. Please read through all the techniques in this chapter before you start practicing them. Get a general understanding and then practice them before you proceed with the applications going forward. They have a number of similar elements that require focus, attention, absorption and positive expectation, just as you have been shown with our hypnotic mindset.

Principles of Inductions

With regards to the upcoming range of ways to complete step A, prior to explaining the inductions themselves, there are some core principles to bear in mind.

1. Expectancy

Clark Hull *(1933)* stated that "anything that assumes hypnosis, creates hypnosis", and so being beholden of the belief that hypnosis is going to happen, will serve you well. Be expectant: expect to go into hypnosis and 'know' it is going to happen for you.

Irving Kirsch *(1985)* believed expectation was the dominant factor in hypnosis.

Kirsch has argued that the response expectancy (or "response set") created in the hypnotic subject by the hypnotist and the environment, are the very essence of hypnosis itself. As author of the book that you are reading, you could think of me as adopting part of the hypnotist role in which I have explained the model of hypnosis and developed a certain degree of expectancy here.

Kirsch has suggested that hypnosis can be seen as a "non-deceptive mega-placebo", insofar as it operates in a similar, but more powerful manner, than placebos in medicine. Know what your outcome is going to be: that you'll enter hypnosis. The more of a positive expectancy you have, the better your self-hypnosis experience will be.

2. Attitude

You adopt a progressive, receptive and appropriately motivated attitude throughout the induction (step A) that carries on through your hypnosis session. Have a progressive tone with yourself: communicate in a way that you find convincing, assured and with an appropriate, useful level of enthusiasm.

Create trust with yourself by believing in yourself and adopting a trusting attitude towards your own ability to do this. Also remember our five key attitudes that make up the hypnotic mindset, as laid out in chapter one too. Here is a recap:

Recognition.

You recognise the induction as your cue to initiate this progressive and favourable hypnotic mindset. You recognise how important it is to focus deeply, to absorb yourself in the process.

Attribution.

You accurately attribute your hypnotic responses to yourself, your own imagination, your own suggestions you give yourself and your own expectations. Attribute the elements of each induction to being a result of what you do in your mind.

Appraisal.

Appraise your self-hypnosis skills and the upcoming session in a favourable way. Appraise self-hypnosis as something that is serving you well. Appraise the induction process as something you are very capable of and that is leading you into and through a beneficial session of self-hypnosis.

Control.

Realise that you are in control, so encourage yourself throughout and consider yourself capable.

Commitment.

Commit the right level of time and effort into the induction process. Be patient for the responses without deliberating for too long.

3. Simplicity

Keep things simple where possible. I know that there is plenty for you to consider right now, but I assure you that inducing self-hypnosis is a simple process. Just having the attitude, the expectancy and the belief is going to develop your self-hypnosis.

Additionally though, although we'll look at the language you use in self-hypnosis later on, keep the language simple, obvious and direct. There is no need for things to get too complex.

4. On The Ball

Pay attention throughout your hypnosis sessions, and especially during Step A, when you do the inductions. Be attentive throughout. Many hypnotherapists use the term 'ratify' to describe how they feedback on what they notice is happening with the client. You can do this yourself too. Almost as though you are commentating on your ongoing experience, tell yourself the things you notice. If you notice your eyelids fluttering, or your breathing rate slowing down, or a twitchy movement of some kind, you can be aware of it.

Be tuned in to your ongoing experience throughout.

5. Non-Verbal

Have a positive intent throughout your self-hypnosis sessions. Have a positive regard to your self-hypnosis procedure that you are following. Likewise, behave as if you are hypnotised. Adopt the behaviour, fill the role of someone who is hypnotised. Act like you are hypnotised and convince yourself throughout the induction process that it is having the desired effect upon you.

This is a facet of the socio-cognitive theory of hypnosis and Sarbin's *(1950, 1954 and 1967)* social role theory, which we can utilise to advance your hypnotic responsiveness in line with a range of other facets mentioned already. Behave like a hypnotised person, adopt the position and posture of a hypnotised person and let it enhance your belief that you are hypnotised as a result.

To reiterate then, keep these five facets in mind:

E – expectancy.

A – attitude.

S – simplicity.

O – on the ball.

N – non-verbal.

These are five principles to remember and consider when you are inducing hypnosis in Step A. Now let me offer you a number of different ways of actually doing this Step A. Here are a number of different ways of accessing hypnosis, inducing hypnosis, or more simply your cue to actively engage in the hypnotic mindset.

1. Using Eye-Fixation to Induce Self-Hypnosis

On my hypnotherapy training diploma, the eye-fixation induction is kind of the "hypnosis 101" induction that all students learn before any other inductions and here, I want to show you how to apply it to yourself rather than do it with another person.

This method of inducing hypnosis was originally developed by James Braid, the aforementioned founder of hypnotism as we know it today. As well as being a medical man of the day, James Braid specialised in eye treatment, and as a result, having coined the term 'hypnosis' and moved the understanding of hypnosis away from the field of Mesmerism, it was natural that his initial methods of inducing hypnosis would involve the eyes and fixing their attention. What's more, there is a great deal more research that has been conducted on this induction method, and more research conducted using this induction than other methods used.

The basic premise is to attempt to produce a level of strain on the eye muscles by looking upwards with the eyes and without moving the head.

After trial and error with a variety of ways of doing this, Braid used an object, such as his lancet case and elevated it in front of the individual to the point where it would be a strain to continue looking at it. If such an object was not used, an individual could be asked to look at a point on the wall or ceiling, without moving their head, which caused them to slightly strain their eyes if the gaze was fixed for a while.

Here, for the purpose of using this technique for inducing self-hypnosis, we tend to suggest that you look up at your own forehead, though again, picking a spot on the wall or ceiling to create strain can be done too.

The reason that the gaze is pointed upwards in this way is of course to advance and enhance the tiredness felt in and around the eyes in a fairly speedy timescale. Importantly, you do not tilt the head backwards at all, otherwise you assist the eyes and just end up staring upwards with a bent neck. You move the eyes only, with the head in its usual, balanced position upon your neck.

With the eyes fixed in this way, creating some minor strain, the individual induces a slight sensation of the eyes being sleepy as they close in this slow manner. Importantly though, this process gets the individual to concentrate in an intense fashion by staring at that point.

Braid called hypnosis 'monoideism' at one stage because of the importance he placed upon getting some focus and attention to achieve it. When doing this with an individual in my consulting rooms, guiding them into hetero-hypnosis, they tend to close their eyes after around 30 seconds or so. When using this to induce hypnosis in yourself, you should consider aiming for a similar timescale to close your own eyes.

Once you have adopted a comfortable, seated position, with your head facing forward, without moving your head you move your eyes to the elevated position, whereby it is a slight strain to hold them there. You then need to employ your imagination to make your eyes feel like closing. This is incredibly important. You must help the process along with your thoughts: imagine that your eyelids are getting heavier, tell yourself that they want to close and that it will be so nice and comfortable when they do so.

All the time that you are communicating with yourself in your mind in this way, ensure that you keep your gaze fixed in that same position without wavering or moving or allowing your eyes to relax by compensating in some other way. Keep your head and eye position in a way that ensures the eyes become tired. Then, once they are ready to close, you let them close, and that is the initiation of your hypnosis session. You then proceed with the subsequent steps B through to E that follow.

Some theorists of hypnosis would also offer some ways of advancing the success you have with this process, which I have also added. For example, you could adopt the behaviour of someone who is in hypnosis. That is, act as if you are hypnotised to enhance the fact that you are enhancing your openness to it. Take on the posture of someone who is initially concentrating very hard, who then falls asleep as the eyes close. You've seen what happens when someone is fighting sleep. Like when I am sat in front of the open fire after my dinner in the evenings, and I get that sensation in my eyelids where they start to close and I keep snapping them open to regain my focus. Adopt that same behaviour: let your eyes close slowly and adopt the posture of someone drifting off in this way.

To further complement this, you can let your body relax deeper when you close your eyes as you proceed on to whatever deepening strategies you are going to use in latter steps of this A-E protocol.

As you purposely take on this behaviour, the idea is that you'll start to take on some of the things you are acting – in the same way a method actor takes on the characteristics of their character – you then notice how you actually start to feel slightly drowsy as your eyes flutter perhaps, and slowly close.

As I alluded to earlier, it is also important how you communicate your thoughts throughout the process. Use your imagination to advance the process and make it more effective. For example, you can simply tell yourself you are feeling more relaxed and that your eyelids are feeling heavier, using your internal dialogue. You could imagine them closing and getting heavier during the straining process. You can imagine them closing and imagine how much more relaxed they'll be when closed. You might remember times when you have been drowsy or sleepy and your eyelids felt heavy and wanted to close. As you remember that sensation, tell yourself that this is the same.

You might imagine a light shining in your eyes or a gentle breeze blowing toward your eyes, exaggerating the desire to close them and let go. Use a gentle, relaxing assured tone when you communicate with yourself. Offer encouragement by telling yourself how well you are doing, and use your imagination and cognition in whatever way helps advance the overall process.

As with any self-hypnosis process, repetition makes it better, so practice this over and over to get really good at it. Use your thoughts, expectancy and posture in line with the structure and become really good at using this method.

2. Heavy Arm Self-Hypnosis Induction Method

Here is our second way of doing step A and accessing hypnosis.

This is a self-hypnosis induction technique that engages the imagination and makes use of nature's law. Many hypnosis professionals refer to it as a 'biological' induction, or it is known as 'coupling' (whereby the suggestion is coupled with a law of nature, in this case, gravity helping the arm get heavier) and inherently includes a convincer; that is, it convinces you that self-hypnosis is occurring by the way it is carried out.

Important reminder: Excuse me sounding like a broken record. The people who benefit the most from this type of self-hypnosis induction are the ones who engage their imagination, focus on the instructions and absorb themselves in the process.

Throughout this book, I use a step-by-step method of explaining many of the processes. That starts now. Follow these simple steps to induce hypnosis using the heavy arm method.

Step One:

Get yourself comfortable and be in a place where you will be undisturbed for the duration of the session; ideally sat up in a chair with your feet flat on the floor and your arms uncrossed and ready to begin. Adjust yourself so that your head is nicely balanced and comfortable upon your shoulders and your body is at a most comfortable posture.

Throughout this hypnosis induction process, you may notice certain changes happening immediately, whereas others might take a few moments. Trust that you are doing this in the way that is right for you, you are unique and respond in your own unique way. Then take a nice deep breath and as you exhale, allow your eyes to comfortably close, and begin.

As I say in many of my audio programmes and to my clients, you don't have to sit perfectly still throughout the self-hypnosis induction processes, but the more still you are, the less spatial awareness you'll start to have of your physical body and so, the deeper your subjective experience may well appear. Therefore, experiment with stillness as much as you find it comfortable to do so. Stillness means that you tend to get less distractions, and so do consider the benefits from incorporating stillness into your sessions.

Then move on to the next step.

Step Two:

Ensure you are in a nice seated posture, with the crown of your head pointing to the ceiling and your shoulders relaxed.

It is an attentive posture you want to have, with your feet flat on the floor and your hands by your sides or on your lap, but not touching each other. I prefer to be attentive than too slouched and relaxed which tends to encourage people to wander off, lack focus and even fall asleep, which is not all that useful – unless you want and need more sleep.

With your eyes closed, hold your right arm straight out in front of you, palm facing down. Simply hold your right arm and hand straight out in front of you, palm facing down with your fist clenched. Be aware of the feelings that you are having in your right arm and hand at this time, while it is being held aloft.

Imagine that you are holding the handle of the bucket in your hand, and every relaxed breath you breathe from here onwards and for the duration of this induction process, fills the bucket with more water, making it feel as if it is getting heavier and heavier.

Get truly mindful of the sensation that exists within the arm, become aware of your arm as much as you possibly can. Scan along it and within it with your mind.

Start to notice what you notice. Is there tension anywhere? Are any (even tiny and subtle) movements occurring? What else are you noticing? Tell yourself and feedback to yourself what you notice as you hold your arm out. Become as aware of the entire arm as possible in these moments. Imagine the bucket continuing to fill with water with each breath you breathe, getting heavier and heavier, and harder to keep in that position and move on to the next step.

Step Three:

Now continue to pay attention to the arm, because this is the stage when all the fun is going to start happening.

Imagine your arm is beginning to feel heavier and heavier, imagine it is getting heavier and let it feel heavier and heavier. This is made easier by the fact it is being held out and gravity is naturally pulling on it, but start to let it take over a little by advancing that sensation of heaviness using your imagination.

As you imagine the arm getting heavier, notice that thinking about the heaviness creates a tendency for your arm to become heavier, feeling as if it is getting heavier and heavier. Affirm this by repeatedly saying to yourself those words "heavier and heavier", as you continue to let your imagination make the arm feel heavy.

As it starts to feel heavier and heavier, also imagine the arm starts to very slowly, but surely move downwards. Tell yourself what that feels like, tell yourself using your internal dialogue in your own head, feeding back as you did earlier. State to yourself that your arm is moving downwards.

The heaviness in your arm grows with your continued imagination of such, and as it grows and feels heavier, you also want to become more relaxed, more comfortable and at ease. So imagine that each movement of your arm going downwards starts to make every other muscle in your body more relaxed and comfortable.

Continue paying attention to your arm while it feels as if it is getting heavier; imagine it getting heavier, as it moves downwards, so you relax and now start to tell yourself you are going deeper into hypnosis.

Tell yourself this with volition, do not allow other thoughts to distract you. Repeat that sentiment, relax with the sentiment (too much effort or stress can impede the progress you make) and repeatedly tell yourself you are in hypnosis as you focus on the arm moving downwards and the body relaxing everywhere else. You might notice your breathing changing as you relax more, if so, enjoy that and tell yourself that it is happening.

You are to create a chain of progressive things that will occur: Imagine your arm is moving lower and feeling heavier in order to show you how deeply hypnotised you are becoming and how much more relaxed you are now.

Just as you think your hand is going to reach the chair or your lap or anything else, move on to the next step.

Step Four:

When your hand reaches your lap, it rests, it relaxes and flops into a comfortable position where the relaxation continues to spread through your body. Imagine the newly experienced relaxation in the resting arm spreading to everywhere else. Maybe even let out an audible 'sigh' as the arm reaches the lap or chair, and then enjoy the relaxation developing from it.

Use words like "relaxing" and "comforting" to describe your ongoing experience, and enjoy the arm no longer being heavy, just relaxed and feeling so good. Continue to affirm that you are drifting deeper into hypnosis, and you can commence with the latter stages of the self-hypnosis session.

You then follow the other steps from B through to E as explained later.

3. Using Magnetic Palms to Induce Hypnosis

This is our third way of inducing hypnosis, still on step A of our A-E steps of self-hypnosis session protocol.

Many street and stage hypnotists use this process for inducing hypnosis and preparing people for hypnotic induction. I have seen many professionals use this kind of process when hypnotising others. Here, I'm explaining how to use the same process to induce self-hypnosis.

This is all about 'magnetic palms.'

Before hypnosis was officially even called hypnosis, before it existed in the way we know it today, mesmerists used to believe that there was an invisible magnetic energy that flowed through each and every one of us. Out of that era came a number of tests that are used today within the field of hypnosis, and though they have nothing to do with actual magnetism, they are really useful in developing hypnotic responsiveness, and tuning self-hypnosis skills.

This process of 'magnetic hands' is very simple to do, you just hold your hands out in front of you with your palms facing each other, just 10-20 centimetres or so apart. The aim is to then use your imagination and self-hypnosis suggestions to get the hands to move together, without actually closing them in a usual deliberate manner.

It won't happen magically and there is not actually a mesmeric 'magnetic force' pulling your hands in towards each other. Your muscles do that for you. It is just that instead of you moving them in a voluntary, deliberate fashion as you usually would, you are now using your imagination and a number of different sensations instead of conscious control. As with the vast majority of self-hypnosis skills, this requires some practice to help develop fluency and overall betterment of your self-hypnosis.

Firstly, on a physical level, if you position the hands 10-20 centimetres apart and have your arms relaxed and at ease, with your eyes fixed on the space in between them, gravity will help them to feel as if they are drawing in that direction.

If you rub the hands together immediately prior to doing this, really rub them together fast and generate some heat in the palms, then the heat in the hands and the 'energy' created from that movement will enhance the physical tendency for them to feel as if they are drawing closer together. To advance this in order to subsequently advance your self-hypnosis skills though, you need to engage your thoughts and imagination.

This can be done in a wide variety of ways, but I recommend you start by imagining that there is a magnetic force pulling your hands together. Imagine that you can feel it happening, as if it is a distinct sensation all of its own that is drawing the hands in. You might also say to yourself the words "my hands draw closer together with each breath I breathe" to advance the essence of the action happening in response to your imagination. When you say it to yourself, absolutely convince yourself of the hands being drawn together, say it to yourself in such a fashion that makes you believe in it 100%.

For those that prefer something more visual, you might like to imagine the 'magnetic force' as a light or a colour that aids the process of drawing the hands in together. Or you may wish to imagine that string is tied around the hands and is being pulled tighter as the hands draw closer. You could imagine someone pressing the backs of the hands and they are getting closer. Basically, anything that you can imagine that will force the hands closer together, make it as vivid as you can and let the process happen.

Keep the remainder of your body relaxed and be fascinated in the process, enjoy it and it'll be much more effective, as you will not be clouded with any unwanted feelings or thoughts.

Expectation is incredibly important with this self-hypnosis induction. If you expect certain outcomes, they are more likely to occur. If you expect the hands to move closer together, then they will. Be positive about it, expect it to happen and engage your imagination as best as you can, and then you'll start to develop your self-hypnosis skills for use in a wide variety of other ways.

When the hands touch together, then let them drop into your lap and you proceed with steps B through to E that are coming up.

4. Hand to Face Induction

This induction process for self-hypnosis is actually a great one and is a bit more advanced than the previous three; it is also more demanding. The reason is that often we use nature to advance our imagination. For example, imagining your arm is getting heavier when you hold it outwards is easier to do, as it would perhaps feel heavy anyway as a result of gravity and the slight strain of doing so. The same goes for imagining your eyelids getting heavier when you use an eye-fixation process. This technique involves some fixation, it eventually utilises nature, but importantly requires some really purposeful use of your imagination.

Within this process, you are required to engage your imagination and to elicit some 'hypnotic phenomena' within yourself. If your internal dialogue or belief starts to defy your imagination, then quiet it by imagining a volume control of your internal dialogue (and turning it down), or simply dominating your cognition with progressive, supportive thoughts and ideas, as you have been repeatedly encouraged to do already. Follow these simple seven steps for the hand to face induction method:

Step One:

Of course you want to be in a place where you are going to be undisturbed for the remainder of the session. Be sat in a comfortable, upright position, ideally with your feet flat on the floor and your arms uncrossed. Be in a receptive posture, and not slouched, your posture will help you to engage with the process and be attentive to it.

Have your hands resting in your lap, upon your legs with the palms facing upwards. Once you have got yourself into this physical position, then you keep your eyes open and proceed to step two.

Step Two:

Keep your head in the same, still position while you look at your hands. While keeping your head completely still, just moving your eyes, focus all your attention, all your awareness and gaze attentively at the palms of your hands resting in your lap..

As you look at them, start to be mindful of your hands. That is, notice any sensations within them, which there are likely to be more of when you really focus and heighten your awareness. Notice the temperature of them, are they hot or cold or somewhere in between? Are they perfectly still or is there the tiniest fraction of movement within them? Notice the details of the lines in the hands.

When you are truly mindful of your hands, move on to the next step.

Step Three:

Now focus your attention upon your dominant hand and the expectant idea that the arm will rise. Let that thought dominate your mind and expect it to rise.

Behaviourally, consciously press the back of the hand down against the leg (or whatever surface it is resting upon) and then as you start to truly imagine the arm lifting up, stop pressing down and focus all your attention on the initial sensations of lightness, naturally created when it is slowly released and allowed to rise. Stare at a fixed point on that palm, the palm of the hand that now feels lighter than the other. Enjoy the fact that it feels lighter than the other for a couple of moments.

Now start to imagine it is feeling lighter with each breath that you breathe. Almost as if each inhalation is making the hand and arm feel as if it is getting lighter and lighter. You have to truly engage your imagination and believe that this is absolutely the case. Each breath you breathe in, let the hand draw closer to you.

Use your internal dialogue and cognition to dominate your thoughts while you imagine this and say to yourself with real purpose and volition, *"my hand is feeling as if it is lighter and lighter",* and keep repeating it as you imagine your hand moving toward your face. Keep repeating the phrase with real meaning, keep engaging the imagination, and as soon as you get a tiny movement of any kind upwards with the hand, then move on to the next step.

Step Four:

Now engage your imagination further by imagining that in the palm of this lighter, slowly moving hand is an incredibly powerful magnet. A really incredibly powerful magnet. Imagine a second magnet is on one of your cheekbones and that it is attracting the palm of your hand closer and closer.

Watch as the magnet pulls the hand toward your face. Stare at the palm of the hand, imagine it is moving more purposefully towards your face as the magnet pulls the hand to your cheekbone. Some people like to imagine that they can see some sort of magnetic force that is present and is drawing the hand closer to the face. You can do this if you want to.

Now start to engage your internal dialogue, again suggest to yourself an affirmation, "the magnetic force is pulling my hand to my face", and repeat it with meaning, say it to yourself like you really believe in it 100%. Over and over in your mind as you imagine that magnet and the magnetic force pulling the hand to your face in easy movements, at a pace that is right for you.

This is key: Now make an important distinction, think carefully as the hand moves closely towards the face; work out if the hand is being pulled more strongly by the magnet in the palm or the magnet on your cheekbone. Make sure you can tell where the magnetic force is stronger. When you know that, move on to the next step.

Step Five:

Continue to engage purposefully with all the above steps and watch the hand move closer to the cheekbone. As you watch it arrive beneath your eye line, let your eyes continue to look downwards and then close them as any part of your hand gently touches your face. As your eyes close, take a deep breath and imagine the magnetic force is cut. Imagine that as your eyes closed, the magnets were switched off in some way.

With them switched off, notice how your hand and arm feel heavier and heavier. Tell yourself that the arm feels heavier and heaver and imagine it floating slowly back to its original position on your lap. Imagine it drifting back down and as you imagine that, let it relax, feel heavier and tell yourself, "as my arm drops, so I go deeper and deeper into hypnosis." Keep repeating the words "deeper and deeper" as the arms floats all the way back down to the lap.

Let each exhalation increase the heavy sensation as the arm drifts to your leg where it began the exercise. Once it reaches the lap, as it touches, exhale deeply and let the relaxation in that arm spread throughout the body, and then move through steps B to E that follow later in this chapter.

5. The Coin Drop Self-Hypnosis Method

Although I'd recommend you start practicing by using the eye fixation process, as you practice, you might like a bit of variation and likewise, when we have some choice, it may be that we enjoy certain processes more than others.

Here I offer you another lovely methodology of inducing self-hypnosis that I have been practicing with for a number of years, and that I have used with clients in my consulting rooms too. It is entirely inspired and based upon a technique shown in *The Oxford Handbook of Hypnosis (2008)*, and I have tweaked it for use in self-hypnosis sessions instead of hetero-hypnosis situations.

To hypnotise yourself this way, you'll need to have a coin of some kind and then follow these simple steps.

Step One:

Get yourself seated in a balanced position with your arms and legs uncrossed and your feet flat on the floor. Be in a relaxed, but attentive posture.

Hold the coin in your dominant hand, then take a couple of deeper breaths and on any subsequent exhalation, allow your eyes to close. Be truly aware of the sensation of the coin in your hand, then let your breathing happen all by itself without you interfering with it and move on to the next step.

Step Two:

With the coin in your hand, hold your arm out straight in front of you.

Engage your imagination and start to tune into the warmth of the coin in your hand. As explained earlier in this book, start to use your internal dialogue throughout this process to create a running commentary of what your ongoing experience is. Tell yourself that you are aware of the warmth surrounding the coin.

Throughout this process make sure that you absolutely convince yourself of each step before proceeding. Noticing the warmth of the coin, move on to the next step.

Step Three:

Convince yourself and truly allow yourself to believe that this coin is magical in some way and has the same properties as a balloon. Imagine that each breath you breathe is inflating this 'balloon coin', and it is expanding more and more surely. Truly imagine it inflating in the palm of your hand, so that your hand starts to open and unwrap. Imagine the coin balloon is getting comfortably warmer and is expanding more and more.

Notice that your fingers begin to open up and tell yourself that you can feel them opening up all on their own. The more you imagine it and tell yourself, convincing yourself, the more it happens naturally. Imagine the pressure building in the palm of your hand, and as you start to notice the changes happening and your fingers moving, then move on to the next step.

Step Four:

Now use your breathing rhythmically while you count from ten down to zero, relaxing more with each breath, relaxing more with each number you count and with each breath and each number you count, continue to imagine the balloon coin expanding, inflating, getting warmer and your fingers opening, your hand opening more and more.

Tell yourself that all the time it takes for you to count down to zero, is all the time it takes your fingers to fully open and for the coin to drop on to the floor.

Once you have started to count, start to also think and let yourself be aware that the coin may drop. As soon as the coin drops, that is your indicator that you are hypnotised, you are responsive and your imagination is influencing you beautifully.

With the coin dropped, you can now move on and through steps B to E that are coming up.

You can use this situation to start to imagine that without the coin supporting your hand, it is getting heavier and more tired and wants to float back down into your lap. Much like you did with the heavy arm method; except this time you use it as a deepener, which will make more sense when we get to that part of the process (Step C).

You simply think something along that lines that all the time it takes for your arm to drift and float back down into your lap, is all the time it takes for you to go deeper and deeper down into hypnosis. Tell yourself you are going deeper and relaxing more as your arm gets heavier and floats back to your lap. Once it reaches your lap, you might like to sigh or imagine the relaxation spreading from the arm into the remainder of the body, and then engage in a progressive relaxation if you require it.

6. Chiasson's Induction Method Applied to Self-Hypnosis

Many of the previous five processes have shared underlying themes of attention fixation and ideo-motor responses, and so having developed hypnotic skills, techniques like this one should slot in nicely with your other methods. I'd recommend that you start with more basic and fundamental processes before moving on to a process like this one.

While researching for an article some years back, I was directed to a chapter in a book by Golden, Dowd and Friedberg *(1987)* which fell open on a page about hypnosis inductions. I fell in love with this technique for a number of reasons.

Firstly, it includes what Barber *(1974)* would refer to as 'coupling', as it uses natural physiological responses to gravity, and naturally occurring physical reflexes alongside imagination and self-suggestion to reinforce the response you are after. This will become more apparent when we get on to the technique itself. This technique utilises the fact that your fingers tend to spread apart when they are being held together tightly, and that when you breathe, your arms move in line with it, which this technique uses for aiding arm levitation.

As always, you must be responsible for engaging your own imagination, and being assured of yourself throughout, expecting the outcome without putting too much effort into it: convince yourself of the process occurring. This sixth technique also has an inherent deepener so step C may not be necessary if you used this particular induction method. Simply follow these steps:

Step One:

In a place where you will not be disturbed for the duration of this session, sit upright, with an attentive posture. The crown of the head should face the ceiling, shoulders relaxed, feet flat on the floor and hands not touching each other resting on your lap.

We are now ready to begin, so proceed to step two.

Step Two:

Hold up your dominant hand, bring it closer to your face (i.e. do not lean your head towards the hand) until it is a distance of approximately 12 inches/30 centimetres away from your face. Pick a point on the back of the hand to look at and fix your attention upon. Notice how your vision can alter when you focus it, and also notice the tiniest of details of the spot your are focused upon.

Squeeze the fingers of the hand tightly together (close them as tightly as you can) while you fix all your attention and focus upon the point on the back of the hand. Make sure there are not any spaces in between your fingers and they are being held tightly together (as much as is physically possible). Once you are tightly holding all the fingers together with your gaze fixed upon that point, then move on to the next step.

Step Three:

As you keep your attention fixed upon that point, imagine that your fingers are spreading apart. Convince yourself of it happening; as you concentrate on the back of your hand, imagine the fingers are spreading apart.

Stop holding them tightly in together, let the movement start to happen naturally, watch the spaces between the fingers begin to widen and the fingers spread more and more, almost as if it is happening all by itself. Tell yourself it is happening using your cognition, believe in it happening, let it become your reality as you imagine it happening and watch it happening right before your very eyes.

When the fingers are moving, then move on to the next step.

Step Four:

You now start to imagine that each breath you inhale, your hand moves closer to your face. Every breath that you inhale, notice your hand coming a little bit closer. Getting closer, being pulled inwards with each breath that you breathe in. Again, you imagine it happening, you convince yourself it is happening and just let it happen naturally. It is almost as if a force of some kind is pulling your hand towards your face.

Let the movements happen as you imagine it occurring with each breath you breathe, then as it gets closer, move on to the next step.

Step Five:

As your hand draws closer, imagine your eyes getting more and more tired. Imagine how lovely it is going to be to simply relax your eyelids and let them close instead of focusing on the point on the back of your hand. Imagine your eyelids getting heavier as your hand moves closer and you are trying to keep focused on the spot that is drawing closer to you. It becomes more and more difficult to keep focused on that spot on the back of your hand, tell yourself that your eyelids are feeling as if they are heavier.

Then whenever you are ready to do so, let your eyes close. Notice the wonderful sensation of relaxation in the eyelids, and the relief it brings. Imagine the relaxation in those eyelid muscles now spreads through all the muscles of your face and through the muscles of your body, softening the muscles and relaxing your entire body. Once your body starts to relax more with your eyes comfortably closed, move on to the next step.

Step Six:

With your body relaxing so comfortably, start to imagine how good it is going to feel when you allow your arm to return to your lap and relax too. Imagine it is getting heavier as the rest of your body is relaxing deeper.

Now let your arm start to drift back down to your lap. Let it happen slowly and gently. Tell yourself that as it moves towards your lap, so you go deeper into hypnosis. Every breath that you exhale makes the arm heavier; you imagine it getting heavier and heavier and convince yourself that it feels as if it is getting heavier. As it drifts and moves to your lap, so you go deeper and deeper into hypnosis. Take all the time you need to complete your relaxation throughout the body, let the arm lower to your lap before you then move on to the final step.

Step Seven:

You now follow steps B through to E as per the rest of the protocol (though with this technique, it has a deepener within it, so you may dispense with further deepening if you are happy to do so).

These are six fairly simple methods to practice step A and access hypnosis. Remember, step A is our cue to fully engage in our hypnotic mindset, we get focused, absorbed and begin our self-hypnosis sessions with the induction. Do not expect lightning bolts to fire from the sky and give you some definitive sign that you are hypnotised; remember, it is a mindset that you actively engage in, not something that happens as a result of the induction. As you practice and get persistent with it, you'll start to notice the qualities of self-hypnosis, and the signs will demonstrate to you that you are getting better and more adept at inducing hypnosis. Now once you have done step A and induced hypnosis, you move on to step B.

STEP B: Being in Control

With this step, you signal your intentions to yourself, you develop focus and you reinforce the hypnotic mindset. This is done very simply and quickly by using your internal dialogue and acknowledging that you are in control of the session. We are taking a couple of moments to consciously develop our hypnotic mindset now. This gets you receptive and also has you taking charge in a progressive, determined way.

Simply affirm to yourself, something along the lines of the following:

- *I am hypnotised.*

- *I am in full control.*

- *I respond to my intended suggestions.*

- *I expect my intended outcomes.*

- *I am protected from random thoughts, sounds and images.*

- *I am focused.*

- *The hypnotic responses are a result of my imagination, thoughts, expectancies and attitude.*

Say these things to yourself in a way that you believe. Convince yourself of the words and what they mean.

You acknowledge and impress upon yourself that you are indeed in hypnosis. You remind yourself that you are in control of the session. You give authority to your intended suggestions (or change work, as per the array of techniques and strategies following in this book), you reaffirm your positive expectancy and you state that you are protected from random thoughts, sounds and images that may occur while you are engaged in this self-hypnosis session. By protected, we mean that you are not distracted by other thoughts that could interfere. It would be unlikely that other thoughts will not enter your mind, accept them and do not let them irritate or upset the process, let them pass and get focused on the tasks at hand.

Now that you have induced hypnosis with step A, and taken control with step B, you move on to step C.

STEP C: Continually Deepening

There are a very wide range of deepening methods. The idea here is to deepen your perception of your hypnotic experience. Please note, you are not actually going deeper in a measurable fashion; it is a concept, a metaphor or a level of perception. Traditionally, it was suggested that the deeper you were, the better you would respond to suggestions or change work. However, it is very difficult to measure actual depth of hypnosis beyond individual responsiveness to suggestions.

Some of the techniques that you are going to be using in later chapters of this book will enable you to dismiss using a deepener as suggested here. That is because the technique itself has a structure that can substitute a deepener; you'll be advised if that is the case.

This step is referred to as 'continually deepening' because at times, when you are engaged and focused within a session, it might feel as if your hypnosis is getting lighter, or was less profound. If so, you can administer a deepener at your own discretion to deepen your focus accordingly. You can re-establish your focus and get the session back on track if distracted for a moment. Thus, you continually manage your self-hypnosis session, by continually deepening as you see fit. You'll learn to recognise when you might need to do that.

Many self-hypnotists that are just experimenting and exploring self-hypnosis often write to me or comment in class "I don't think I'm getting deep enough into hypnosis." In reality, this is probably a red herring and the real problem is not the "depth of trance" but the lack of understanding by the individual. Virtually anything you attempt to do "in hypnosis" should work, albeit to a lesser extent, without the aid of self-hypnosis. Evidence shows this to be the case, as previously mentioned *(Barber, 1965).*

If self-hypnosis is not working at all then there's more likely to be a problem with the technique or the way it is being applied, or the absence of the hypnotic mindset. In brief, you should be flexible, and adapt your approach to your own preferences and requirements without becoming overly fixated on the notion of "going deeper" into a 'trance.' Using the hypnotic skills training and inductions that include convincing elements will provide much of what deepeners do anyway.

As we have abandoned the outmoded notion of "the hypnotic trance state" what exactly is being "deepened" in hypnosis, if not a hypnotic trance? In real-life terms, or if you look at a dictionary definition of 'depth' or 'deep', it is primarily an actual measurement or dimension downward, and that is not the case with hypnotic experience: you do not go anywhere that can actually be measured in those same terms. In the context of hypnosis and self-hypnosis, it is more the perception of the individual that is being referred to when it comes to depth. The "deepeners" that I'll be offering up for use in self-hypnosis sessions can be put into one or more of the following categories:

Role Involvement.

This is whereby you simply tell yourself you are going deeper into hypnosis. When you tell yourself this, it implies that you should increasingly adopt the role of a more responsive person. We have looked at adopting the role of a hypnotised individual in earlier parts of this book. An example of this is simply giving yourself direct suggestions such as "I am going deeper and deeper into hypnosis and respond more to my intended suggestions."

Relaxation.

These are techniques and processes to follow which deepen physical or mental relaxation. For example, the upcoming progressive relaxation techniques.

Mental focus.

These are techniques and strategies that deepen mental absorption by focusing your own attention as much as possible. For example, truly engaging with the mental imagery content of a session, and even telling yourself that you are becoming more engrossed. For example, you might engage in the colours of the scene that you are imagining and tell yourself the same thing: "I notice the details of shade and light, the colours and distances of the things I focus upon."

Dissociation.

These are techniques and strategies whereby you subjectively experience (as suggested) a deepened sense of dissociation. For example, imagining that you are floating out of the place you are in, or suggesting that you are floating out of your body etc.

Expectancy.

These are techniques which deepen your expectancy and your belief in the overall process. This might include, for example, the types of convincers mentioned in our hypnotic skills and inductions sections, such as the heavy-arm or eye-fixation technique.

With the model that we adhere to throughout this book, applying our hypnotic mindset, the need for a major distinction between the inductions and deepening techniques is not really necessary. To be honest, most of the deepeners can be used as inductions and many of the induction methods in step A could easily be used (or adapted) for deepeners. Additionally, research suggests that deepening techniques seem to have similar levels of effectiveness across the board *(Lynn and Kirsch, 2006)*.

Here are a number of ways that you can deepen your subjective experience of self-hypnosis.

1. Progressive Relaxation

Before I explain how to use progressive relaxation as a deepener, I wanted to mention that this type of process can easily be used as an induction i.e. used as step A. As long as you have the hypnotic mindset and have a progressive attitude towards the process, it is fine to use this type of process; especially if you are going to be using the self-hypnosis for reducing anxiety or stress. For example, whereby the deepener becomes a healthy contributor to the therapeutic aim of the session.

There is a popular misconception that you need to be highly relaxed and 'tranced out' or 'feeling sleepy' to fully respond to hypnosis or to gain the most benefit from it. This is simply not universally true. Evidence has shown that people can be just as receptive to hypnosis when they are not at all physically relaxed *(Banyai and Hilgard, 1976).*

Lots of people I have encountered over the years tend to believe that if they felt 'zonked out' or were so sleepy during a session that they drifted off and did not remember anything, then this is somehow a good thing. They believed that this was evidence that they were hypnotised. Yet this is the stuff of myth and misconception. If you get yourself so relaxed you can hardly move a muscle, it is very unlikely that you are going to be able to respond impressively to suggestions of taking action, being energised, enhancing levels of motivation and increased enthusiasm. Whereas, if you are receptive, alert, attentive and focused, you are going to find it much more effective altogether to achieve that sort of outcome.

The literature shows that using hypnosis in an alert, upbeat and attentive fashion is often preferred by modern hypnotists when motivating depressed clients or enhancing sporting performance *(Golden, Dowd and Freidberg, 1987)*. The same is true of the choices you make for your self-hypnosis sessions. If you are 'zonked out' and slouched, slumped and resembling a dribbling man who fell asleep on the train home, then you are unlikely to have the physiology or the mental capacity to derive the inspiration for taking action to overcome a depressing episode in life..

Despite so many self-hypnotists thinking that their level of relaxation is somehow indicative of them being responsive to hypnosis, it is simply not the case *(Golden, Dowd and Freidberg, 1987)*.

However, if your aim is to be really relaxed, then knowing that and believing in your ability to do so, could well contribute to you being more responsive, because of your level of belief in your skills.

As a deepener and/or induction you can engage in progressive relaxation in a number of ways:

- You can simply breathe and say the word 'soften' to yourself as you think of the muscles of your body. Work your way through your body, using your awareness, starting at one end of your body and moving all the way through to the other end. This is a process I learned from Richard Bandler, one of the co-creators of the field of NLP (neuro linguistic programming), when attending a seminar of his.

- You can imagine a relaxing colour, and then spread that

colour through your body, one muscle at a time. Tell yourself that as the colour spreads, it relaxes the muscles.

- Imagine light and/or heat spreading through you, relaxing you deeply.

- Imagine that you are a rag doll and that your muscles are loose, limp and dormant.

- Imagine being close to a heat source that spreads throughout you.

- Imagining tensing specific muscles as you inhale and then relaxing them as you exhale. Doing this systematically starting at one end of the body and finishing at the other end.

There are many, many other ways to use progressive relaxation. Just use whatever process you know of to deeply relax and allow your body to be more and more relaxed. In a later chapter in this book, we focus on relaxation and you'll be shown how to use a very particular method of relaxation for desensitisation purposes that can also be used as a deepener.

2. Imagining Going Deeper

The most obvious way to deepen hypnosis is to use the classic types of means and use mental imagery that involves going deeper: skiing or trekking down a mountain, going down stairs, drifting into outer space, diving deeper into the sea, walking deeper into a landscape of your own design.

You could simply spend time imagining being in a favourite place, or you might also imagine watching the numbers in your mind as you count downwards and backwards from 100 down to 0, telling yourself that each number takes you deeper. Counting backwards is used within a lot of research.

3. Quiet The Mind—Bubble Time Deepener

Simply follow these steps:

Step One:

Induce hypnosis and take control as we did in steps A and B.

Step Two:

Now imagine a large body of water of some kind. This can be an ocean, a sea, a lake, a river or even a large pool of some sort. A lake would be ideal for the first few times you use this process, as it is more still and has less movement occurring within it, which lends itself well to the very nature of this type of session.

As you imagine that large body of water, imagine being sat on the bed of it, the floor of it, and use your imagination to let you breathe easily and comfortably.

Just be mindful at this stage. Observe yourself, your breathing and don't try to change anything and don't try to stop anything from changing. Sometimes things change just by being observed. Enjoy some quiet. Just be comfortable imagining this rather unusual idea that you are breathing comfortably and easily while sat at the bottom of a large body of water.

When you have got comfortable with that notion and are

imagining it as clearly and vividly as possible, move on to step three.

Step Three:

After any period of mindfulness and quiet reflection occurs, eventually a thought is likely to cross your mind. As soon as any thought enters your mind, watch and imagine a bubble rising out of the ground, rising up to the surface of the water.

So, if and when any image, sound, dialogue or thought comes into your mind, you watch and see a bubble rise up out of the water bed; it then floats up and up and you watch it go out of view as it reaches the surface of the water.

Imagine that the bubble is the thought and that you simply let go of the thought as the bubble drifts and floats far away. The thought then leaves your mind quiet and peaceful again. Continue doing this for a few moments. As you continue to do this, tell yourself that with each bubble that floats up, with each thought that dissipates, and with each breath you breathe comfortably at the foot of this body of water, you go deeper and deeper into hypnosis.

You might simply say the words "deeper and deeper" (for example) to yourself as a deepening mantra, and a means of keeping the mind still while letting go of any other thoughts that float up and away as bubbles. Once you have got comfortable doing this, move on to step four.

Step Four:

Let the bubbles rising and floating away be mirrored with your breathing rate. That is, create the bubble and get it rising as you inhale. Then as you exhale push it all the way out of the water and into the air to dissipate. Some thoughts may persist and continue, in which case, be patient and accept the repetition and keep repeating the process gently and easily as you breathe gently and deeply.

Do not judge or try to interfere with the thoughts you have. Just notice them, watch them happening, accept them and then let them go by imagining the bubble. Allow each facet of this mindful bubble process to take you deeper into hypnosis. As you go deeper and once you have done this for a comfortable period of time, move on to the next step.

Step Five:

Once you feel that your hypnosis is of a sufficient depth, then you continue with your change work or self-suggestion, as you would do usually before moving on to the final step. This entire process can be done simply to derive the benefits of mindfulness and enjoying a quiet, relaxed and peaceful mind for the duration of the session (we discuss mindfulness in more depth later on in this book too).

You then follow steps D through to E

Open your eyes to bring the session to an end.

4. Mind's Eye Deepener

One of my favourite deepening processes is one I first read about in the book *Trancework* by Michael Yapko, and is called the mind's eye closure. I like it because it is fairly quick, really does the job of deepening well and helps in a variety of ways with the session. The technique involves imagining the presence of a "mind's eye" as the (albeit metaphorical) part of our mind that thinks and imagines things, even when our body is relaxed, comfortable and still.

This imaginary mind's eye also has imaginary eyelids that we imagine closing (similar to an imaginary version of the eye fixation we learned earlier in this chapter). For example, you guide yourself and imagine the mind's eyelid getting heavier, and you then extend the metaphor so that this imaginary eyelid closing also helps the mind to go quiet and be less distracted. It is great to use if you are about to engage in hypnosis following some time in a busy environment, or if you are a little fidgety at the beginning of a session, for example.

Following steps A and B you then imagine that you have a mind's eye that is responsible for your mental imagery and thoughts. You imagine that this mind's eye has an eyelid, and just like your physical eyelids, it can also close. You then imagine it getting more tired and gradually closing. You tell yourself that as it closes, it also closes out stray thoughts and images that may have distracted you, and allows you to focus on the important aspects of the session. You tell yourself that you mind is getting clearer and more peaceful.

I think it goes well following an eye-fixation technique, as you will have an orientation of the eyes throughout.

5. Hypnosis Revivification - Revivifying Previous Hypnosis

Revivification remains a very powerful and simple way to deepen or induce hypnosis. Let me explain the meaning of 'revivification' in more detail. The word revivify in my dictionary means: *To give new life or spirit to; revive.* This beautifully explains the notion of using revivification for the purpose of deepening or inducing hypnosis. Revivification utilises a person's previous experiences of hypnosis or other similar types of experience, such as times when you have been highly focused, absorbed or progressively expectant.

The classic experiences you can choose to elicit are those that are predisposed to have hypnosis present. For example, experiences that are similar to hypnosis that you have been in before; times of great fascination/absorption, times of intense learning and so on. Of course, if you have experienced hypnosis formally on one or more occasions before, then you can use that previous experience of hypnosis to revivify in the future self-hypnosis sessions too.

Step One:

Having gone through steps A and B, now have a think and tell yourself how you know when you have been totally absorbed in something? Or simply remind yourself of what you like to do to relax. If you have experienced hypnosis before (hetero-hypnosis or self-hypnosis) then you can recall an occasion when you experienced hypnosis.

Step Two:

Now start to imagine that occasion, and narrate it. Simply describe when, where, with whom, what happened and so on: giving a detailed account of it happening as you imagine it in as much detail as possible. This in itself can begin to deepen your experience.

Step Three:

Now start to move the scenario from the occasion 'then' and move it to 'now' with your commentary. Instead of describing that past experience by saying things like – *'I was sat with my attention fixed on the telly, and I felt connected with the characters'* – you now start to bring it into the 'now' and describe (you are actually suggesting it to yourself) the same feelings as occurring right now, made relevant to your self-hypnosis session. For example, if you had used the previous sentence about being sat fixated on the telly, you could now say *'I am absolutely absorbed and fixated on this self-hypnosis experience and really feel connected to it.'*

To move the focus inside of you and point your attention inward, you also start to shift the focus of your words from external descriptions of the setting and situation, to internal elements, sensations and thoughts. For example, "So as I was sitting on the sofa, watching the television listening to the music on the show, I am now feeling deeply relaxed and absorbed in this self-hypnosis session."

Step Four:

You can then start to give suggestions to build, develop and magnify those feelings you experience, and tell yourself you are going deeper as those feelings increase. Remember to add belief and maintain your hypnotic mindset and those attitudes throughout.

That is revivification: a complex name, but a very simple process.

6. Perfect Hypnotist and Mirror

One of my favourite ways to deepen hypnosis when working with clients is this process. It is a great self-hypnosis induction or deepener, as it requires the imagination and personal interpretation of the individual. It is best used when you have some experience of hypnosis, as you'll benefit from being able to refer to previous experiences and understand what your own experience of 'deep hypnosis' actually means to you.

Once you have gone through step A and B, then you imagine being sat opposite a mirror and you look into that mirror and see your own reflection. I recommend that you allow yourself enough time to imagine the reflection in as much detail as possible. As you see yourself in that mirror, imagine and notice the things that tell you that you are deeply hypnotised. What is it that tells you that you are going deeper and deeper?

The beauty is, that as you see yourself in the mirror going deeper and being more absorbed in your self-hypnosis, you can further realise that state by using the mirror as a confirmation of your hypnotic experience. With that realization, start to behaviourally and cognitively adopt those things you see in the mirror. There you have it, you have very simply deepened the hypnosis. You choose whatever is convincing to you. You then generate the observable signs in the mirror reflection.

I often taken this notion a step further. For example, having induced hypnosis, you can even imagine that you are in the company of the perfect hypnotist for you in every way. The hypnotist speaks in a way that resonates best with you, that you find easiest to connect with. See the scene and the hypnotist in as much detail as possible to advance your focus and absorption. The nuances, tone and language you observe and notice, all enhance your absorption, and you expect desired outcomes as a result.

Basically, you construct and create your ideal hypnotist, and use your imagination to transfer those qualities onto what you are doing and how you are conducting the self-hypnosis session. Let it enhance the already much mentioned hypnotic mindset. One might imagine that you have a fabulous rapport, trust and expectancy with the hypnotist, but all the time remembering that you are the one responsible for generating the hypnotic effects.

If you do not have a good idea of what this would be like, then you could go and have a look at my YouTube channel, and use some of the one-to-one clips that I have there as material for your imagination.

7. Posthypnotic Suggestion and Re-Induction

Additionally, I wanted to add one more thing before we get onto step D.

The means of deepening hypnosis that I am writing about today is referred to as *refractionation*, and also goes by other names. It is particularly useful within a hypnotherapy session, as we hypnotherapists tend to work with people whose presenting issues can detrimentally affect their ability to concentrate or focus well. This process enhances concentration and focuses attention very well.

This type of deepening process is virtually the same as the

induction process often referred to as fractionation, the kind cited in a Dave Elman *(1984)* style of induction: a very popular form of induction used by hypnotherapists in clinical practice.

The process of refractionation is whereby the hypnotherapist or hypnotist delivers a suggestion to the client who is already hypnotised. The suggestion is that they can be hypnotised quicker and deeper. That individual is then brought out of hypnosis, fully emerged, and following a brief chat is hypnotised again. The ideal response is that they are now hypnotised quicker than before and have a perception of it being deeper. This process is then repeated a number of times with each occasion of being hypnotised lasting slightly longer than the previous one.

Each period spent in hypnosis teaches and demonstrates to the client how easy it is to be hypnotised, and it trains them to get better and more effective at it. On occasions, some stage hypnotists have used similar notions as a means of being able to click their fingers, while directly suggesting the person "sleep!" The person being hypnotized immediately responds and goes into hypnosis, giving an impressive display for the audience to be wowed by (sometimes not knowing that the process has been practiced and re-induced to reach this speed, prior to the show beginning in earnest).

Many hypnotherapists set up and use what is referred to as a "cue word". This kind of a cue is associated with the rapid entering of hypnosis and applied over and over, so that being used in future sessions, the client can immediately go to the level of hypnosis previously attained. The hypnotherapist then has a posthypnotic suggestion that can be used in future sessions and can spend a lot less time inducing hypnosis, and more time engaging in the hypnotherapy.

I would hasten to add that many cues actually exist inherently anyhow. I find many of my clients simply react a certain way to sitting in the chair in my consulting room. Or if I change my voice or dim the lights in a way that indicates the hypnosis part of the session is going to occur, this acts as a cue, in line with previously used words when the client was hypnotised.

This is basic stuff as far as hypnotherapy goes, but as with so many things in life, the simple tend to get overlooked and not appreciated enough when so much time is spent being in awe of the complex alternatives. For a self-hypnotist, entering and re-entering hypnosis repeatedly, telling yourself you are going deeper each time, telling yourself that it is easier each time, helps develop the skill and ability to enter hypnosis in a way you perceive to be deeper. When you are in what you consider to be deep hypnosis, setting up a 'cue-word' is just as easily done: Each time I repeat the words 'deeply hypnotised' I return to this depth of hypnosis. Then, each time you enter hypnosis, you simply use those words that you have become conditioned to, to go deeper into hypnosis. Use your own preferred words or phrase though.

8. Dissociation Example

With this deepening process, we are going to use self-hypnosis to imaginatively enter realms such as space. It is just one way of using dissociation and you can adapt the rationale and apply it in other ways too.

I recall one of the first times that I had the age-old notion of 'The View From Above' shown to me within the *Meditations* of the Emperor Marcus Aurelius. I often use it in therapy sessions with my clients to help them get a sense of perspective.

Though this process can be used for therapeutic gain, it is really being used here as a deepener.

Step One:

Having gone through steps A and B, develop a heightened awareness of yourself. Become aware of your body, the sensations within it, your breathing, and just observe yourself in this moment. Don't try to change anything, just watch and observe yourself in this moment. Become so aware of yourself that you can imagine what you look like in that position that you are in.

Then imagine that you are watching yourself as you relax in that position. When you are aware of watching yourself relax in that position, as if you are seeing yourself from the outside, then move on to the next step.

Step Two:

Now as you look at yourself start to float upwards and away from your body, leaving it there in the chair. Leave the building your body is in, and as you float up, imagine going deeper inside your own mind and all the time going higher. Start to notice the surrounding area, notice the life going on and the movements of traffic.

Then start to notice more of the landscape as you travel higher. Start to see the larger land mass and even the coastline. As you travel higher, you see less detail of the streets and more of the general surrounding area.

As you float higher, move through the clouds and beyond the atmosphere, and take all the time necessary to float up and into space, until the entire planet Earth is there in front of you, so that you can look at all of its beauty and magnificence.

Notice the colours of the planets, the clouds around it, see it from outer space. Spend all the time necessary to do this step in a thorough and enjoyable way, making sure that you notice the different perspectives as you move further away from that point where your body remains.

When you have done this, move on to step three.

Step Three:

From the place in space, totally removed from the planet Earth, viewing the earth and all the life that exists within it from outer space, start to imagine you are sharing and benefiting from the wisdom of the universe. That you are gaining insight, wisdom and perspective from being here in space for a while.

There are more advanced ways of using this process for therapeutic gain, but as a deepener, that is all that you need to do. When you are about to exit hypnosis, to help you reorient, you may want to include a journey involving you floating back down to earth.

You can use a combination of these deepening methods. Understanding the principles of the processes recommended here will enable you to create and develop your own ways of deepening too. There are going to be some mindfulness processes recommended later in this book, which could also be used for enhancing your awareness of the moment and enhancing absorption. They do have a good deepening effect that could be employed at step C stage of your self-hypnosis sessions.

Having adopted our hypnotic mindset, induced hypnosis, taken control and then deepened, we now move on to the next step in our five-step self-hypnosis protocol.

STEP D: Deliver Suggestion or do Change Work

Throughout the remainder of this book, you are going to be given a wide array of techniques, methods, strategies and processes to do at this stage of your self-hypnosis sessions. Once you have induced hypnosis, taken control and deepened (if you needed to) you then get to the important part of the process, which is the change work, the process that is going to advance and contribute to your well-being in some way.

This is going to include self-suggestion, affirmation, mental imagery, cognitive strategies and a range of other processes and protocols supported by evidence. For now, it is important to simply know that you do this in a way that adheres to the hypnotic mindset, and in a manner that has an appropriate level of enthusiasm.

STEP E: Exit from Hypnosis

E stands for Exit or Emerge. It is not referred to as awakening because you have not been asleep and we want to make a distinction from sleep altogether.

The exit process given here should be done at a pace slow enough for you to fully reorient yourself. Probably the most important part of this process is actually telling yourself you are coming out of hypnosis and having an obvious intention to come out of hypnosis.

As we have distanced ourselves from the notion of a 'special hypnotic trance state of altered consciousness' you might wonder what it is that we are actually exiting here, what are we emerging from? Throughout a self-hypnosis session you will possibly experience a range of different physiological sensations and other changes as a result of the suggestions given and the use you have made of your imagination. If you have used dissociation deepening methods, or imagined being in a different place, then you will benefit from reorienting yourself to your actual surroundings. Even if you've been greatly relaxed, you want to then reorient to being your usual, alert self as you go about your day.

You conclude the self-hypnosis session by simply counting from 1 to 5. You can count aloud or in your mind. Whichever way you do so, when you count 5 and open your eyes, you signal the end of that self-hypnosis session.

Each of the numbers can represent a number of different things, so you might like to consider that the first few times you exit hypnosis, try telling yourself the following:

As I count from 1 to 5 I am coming out of hypnosis. I am emerging and exiting this self-hypnosis session.

When I count 1, I have full control, flexibility and coordination throughout my entire body, from the tips of my toes to the top of my head, from the tips of my fingers and thumbs to my shoulders. Any feelings of lightness or heaviness return to their true and correct perspective.

Here we have put all our bodily sensations back as they should be. Sometimes, prolonged stillness in hypnosis can, for example, alter our sensations of lightness and heaviness in our limbs, and some of the inductions we use may have altered sensations and perspective that we want to return to normal.

When I count 2, I position myself back in the place where I entered hypnosis, remembering and recalling what was to my left and right, above and below, remembering and recalling some features of the place.

This is important if you have spent some time in a favourite place or used your imagination vividly to evoke being somewhere else. Some of the mental imagery techniques we use later in this book require you to imagine rehearsing coping skills when being somewhere else in your mind, for example. Therefore, you need to ensure that you reconnect with the place that you are actually in once again.

When I count 3, all sounds return to their true levels of importance and have the correct perspective.

Some people find that, while in hypnosis, their hearing can become altered slightly. For example, a lady I once hypnotised commented that my voice seemed like it was background noise, even though I was sitting right next to her and the traffic outside seemed louder. Our focus can sometimes make sounds seem different. Likewise, a strong imagined experience can potentially have our hearing tuned differently, so we like to make sure that it is all back in place.

When I count 4, I am keeping and bringing with me all the wonderful benefits of this hypnosis session.

All the good stuff that you have worked on in the self-hypnosis session can now be brought back with you into your real life. Make sure it is integrated and is not left in the domain of hypnosis. Evidence suggests that you'll enhance the suggestions used in the session, if you tell yourself that they'll be effective when the session has come to an end.

When I count 5, I open my eyes to be fully emerged and out of hypnosis.

You then count from 1 to 5 and open your eyes. That particular session is completed. I strongly suggest that you revisit this chapter now and run through the A to E protocol, practice the various inductions and deepening skills, then you are ready to start using it for the upcoming ways of advancing your wellbeing.

This chapter has explained the A-E step-by-step protocol:

- *access hypnosis,*

- *being in control,*

- *deepening,*

- *delivering suggestions (or engaging in mental imagery or other cognitive strategies) and then*

- *exiting.*

Remember throughout to apply your progressive hypnotic mindset, and we are then ready to start applying self-hypnosis for beneficial and therapeutic change, and enhancement of well-being.

I'd recommend that you do not continue with subsequent chapters until you have practiced with the previous two chapters, developing your hypnotic skills and running through the A-E self-hypnosis protocol.

Chapter Five:
Using Suggestion in Self-Hypnosis

First and foremost, when I refer to suggestion, we are talking about an instruction or a dominant idea that you give yourself, that in turn you want to have a subsequent beneficial effect upon you. We concern ourselves with suggestions while hypnotised. Though, of course, we are giving ourselves suggestions all the time with our thoughts, sometimes leading to negative suggestions or negative self-hypnosis, whereby limiting thoughts or negative cognitions of some kind have a detrimental effect upon us.

At the most basic level when hypnotised, if you wanted to stop smoking, you give yourself the suggestion of "I stop smoking", and that becomes the dominant idea focused upon, which you hope will impact upon you. You imagine being a non-smoker in line with that suggestion too. There is slightly more to consider though, as we shall see in this chapter.

The cognitive-behavioural model that we are adhering to here, considers suggestion to actually be "imaginative suggestion." This refers to the fact that suggestions we give ourselves are probably better understood as the self-hypnotist imagining the required experience *(Lynn, Kirsch and Hallquist, 2008).* With our stop smoking example, the self-hypnotist may say, *"I am a non-smoker"* and thereby think and respond *as if* they are now a non-smoker; or they imagine being in a particular environment and behaving *as if* they are a non-smoker.

We do not respond literally to suggestions as per the common hypnosis misconception. If we revisit the notion that 'all hypnosis is self-hypnosis' we are again made aware that it is us creating the responses and reactions to suggestions. Hypnosis is not a tool for mind control, it is a tool for willing imagination.

There are some basic rules of suggestion that are prevalent in hypnosis literature. They may well appear to be no more than common sense to you. They are guiding principles that can help you to get the most beneficial response to your self-hypnosis sessions when using suggestions. These basic rules of delivering suggestions are as follows:

1. Make your suggestions meaningful and evocative

The suggestions you give yourself when doing self-hypnosis must be meaningful and evocative. Use language and words that elicit emotions within you. We shall be coming on to the use of words much more specifically later. However, think about what words you really like, which ones appeal to you, or words that have certain positive feelings and associations when you hear or think of them. How would you describe the most enjoyable experiences of your life? Use those words in your self-hypnosis sessions. The more good feelings that you can induce within your suggestions, the better.

It is worth bearing in mind that words like "confidence" or "enthusiasm" tend to be understood intellectually by some of us, and might not actually evoke any emotion or stimulate the imagination. Therefore, use words that create a feeling within you and *not* words that you think *should* create a feeling within you.

Use clear language, free from ambiguity, in terms that you understand the best and are most comfortable with.

2. Make your suggestions happen in the now

Even if you want results for your future, phrase your suggestions in the present tense; make them happen right now. Your suggestions flow better when phrased in the present tense, and tend to be more meaningful and evocative, as per our previous rule.

3. Ask for what you want, not what you do not want

It is better to suggest to yourself that you *feel more confident* rather than you *feel less shy*. State your suggestions, goals and objectives in the positive. It is best to move towards and suggest the things you want and not try to drive yourself away from the things you do not want.

There is a train of thought that believes that whatever you focus on the most will be what you'll get more of, regardless of whether it is positive or negative. It is the content of your imagination and suggestion that will sink in and dominate your thoughts. Someone may want to reduce weight by no longer eating cream cakes. They may tell themselves, over and over, not to eat all those lovely cream cakes. They are painting their awareness with the message of the cream cakes. It is like driving towards a lamppost in a car, staring at it, accelerating and saying, *"I hope I don't hit that lamppost."* Whatever you focus on you tend to 'stick to'. If you keep focusing on what you don't want, even if it seems that you are pulling away from it, you may be pulled back towards it.

For example, in terms of weight loss, it would be better to focus on achieving and maintaining the size, shape and weight that pleases you, and moving towards the goal of how you want to look and feel for your ideal weight.

4. Keep it simple

I giggle when I read hypnosis text books referring to this rule as the 'law of parsimony', which strikes me as an oxymoron. A common mistake is that you want to make things simple, but you use a non-simple word to describe it, a word that hardly anyone recognises.

Be direct, specific, concise and precise. Let your suggestions be simple and immediate..

5. Want your suggestions to work and expect them to work

You need to want the suggestion to work; it is no good trying to get something to happen in your life that you don't really want to happen. If you don't want it to happen, you'll not have the belief, positive expectation or any of the attitudes required to attain the hypnotic mindset to be responsive to your suggestions. Any suggestion that you deliver to yourself will be rendered impotent if you do not want it to work.

It has been referred to a great deal already in this book, but it is fundamental to have the highest expectations for your suggestions; this is like sunshine and rain upon your seeds. Truly wanting a suggestion to be effective and expecting it to be effective is a powerful combination.

When you expect success and certain responses to your suggestions, and believe in your suggestions, this is an indicator of how effective that suggestion is likely to be. They are correlated.

To utilize this process, we can use some of our convincers and induction methods to couple with our suggestions. When you engage in a heavy arm induction, you might say that as your arm gets heavier, so you are letting go of your unwanted habit. You might suggest to yourself that as your eyes close, your confidence grows. You might say to yourself that as you unstick your hand from your leg, you let your suggestion be achieved. I think you get the message.

If you attach a suggestion to the hypnotic skills and 'phenomena' we used in earlier chapters, it can enhance the effectiveness of the suggestion, with the use of expectation and belief attached to the ongoing phenomena that is occurring.

6. Ensure your suggestions are relevant to you and your desired outcomes

The suggestions you give yourself should be relevant to your own circumstances, your own goals and your own values. This will make them far more inspiring and ensure that you are motivated by them too.

7. Avoid ambiguity

Some Ericksonian-styled hypnotherapists use ambiguity a lot to help other people to enter hypnosis. The Erickson model of hypnosis does not fit well with the cognitive behavioural model of hypnosis that this book adheres to. There are many reasons, and none are really relevant to this book about learning self-hypnosis, so I shall not go into any more depth with that. However, with self-hypnosis, it is more important to be precise with meaning. There is no point in having a term or a phrase ambiguous, if it is yourself that you are communicating with. You know what you want to achieve and so that is precisely what you focus on.

When I say avoid ambiguity in your self-hypnosis sessions, what I mean is avoid phrases that could be interpreted in a way or ways that you were not intending.

In addition to that, referring to "tomorrow" or "the day ahead" (as we have already discussed) is also ambiguous. This is because you are experiencing *now* and "tomorrow never comes" when you are experiencing *now.*

8. Use repetition and different words

Suggestions are often repeated for hypnotic effect. Repeating suggestions is a great way to get them to be effective. However, on occasion repeating a word or phrase could render the message boring and could lead to it losing its evocative power and its emotive presence. Therefore, you can repeat the underpinning theme in a variety of different ways, using different words to vary the way the message is delivered to yourself.

You can continue to use words that keep you interested and engaged.

9. Use your senses and imagination

I was running a training course a little while ago and I had asked all the delegates to go and get into groups to do an exercise involving using the imagination. As is often the case, I had a gentleman who told me that he could not make pictures in his mind, and he carried on making himself believe that he could not do it. I asked him if he could remember a time in his childhood when he was happy and he replied that he could remember a time. I asked where he was on that occasion and he told me he was in his bedroom playing with his model airplane. I asked him to describe the room and he told me that it had blue walls, and he began to explain the room in detail. He got so into his description that he even fashioned shapes with his hands during his description. When he stopped with his description, I asked him if he still believed he could not make pictures in his mind. I think you know what the answer was. He carried on happily with the exercises from there on.

If I were to ask you what colour your front door is at your home, when you answer, how do you know it is true? How did you arrive at your answer? A natural way to do this is through imagery in our minds, and by using our imagination and range of senses.

We often do not realise how much we use our senses with our imagination, and I suggest that using your senses and imagination with your self-hypnosis is a sure way to increase the effectiveness of your sessions.

Imagery is far more than just pictures. We often use imagery to recreate and remember emotions, as well as using imagery with our senses of smell, touch, hearing, and even taste. Have you ever been hungry and imagined what it would taste like to have your favourite food at that moment? Your imagination may be so vivid that you can almost taste it in your mouth.

You learned the importance of engaging your imagination when developing your hypnotic skills earlier in the book. Use your imagination within your suggestions. Convince yourself of the effectiveness of your imagination. Believe in it and you'll derive much benefit with your suggestions.

To help his students understand the importance and power of imagination, Emile Coué *(1922)* would use a number of examples to support his argument that the **conscious will is weaker than the imagination**. When teaching, he would point to the common experience of someone who was struggling to get to sleep. When they try to use their will to get to sleep, they end up achieving the opposite, keeping themselves awake by their efforts. He would also use a forgetfulness example; when people forget a name or a key piece of information (like when a song comes on the radio and you try to remember the artist's name) they often find that the more they try to remember it, the more frustrated they become. However, when they stop making the effort, it seems to pop into the mind (perhaps when it is no longer needed).

Coué would also use the "walk the plank" example that is still used in workshops today to illustrate the influence and powerful effect of our imaginations. Coué would ask his students to imagine walking across a long plank of wood placed on the floor. Most manage this with ease. When he then asks whether we would be able to do so with the same ease, if the plank were balanced on two skyscrapers spanning the length of a street, often it is more of a challenge. The anxious imagination of falling interferes with our conscious intention to perform an act as simple as walking in a straight line! He used many other examples to illustrate the power of the imagination, which needs to be incorporated into your self-hypnosis sessions.

In addition to this, be aware of the difference between association and disassociation in your imagination. If you imagined seeing yourself riding on a roller coaster, it would be a very different experience compared to if you imagined **being on** the roller coaster and going along in it. To add or desensitise from an experience in your mind, consider the difference between associating and dissociating with what you are imagining.

If you are engaging your imagination and using the hypnotic mindset correctly, you can deliver your suggestions to yourself with ease, applying what you have learnt up until now. We can just say them to ourselves, think them, imagine them and engage with them.

Couéism

We have already looked briefly at the 1920s work of Emile Coué: when we were developing hypnotic skills in an earlier chapter and when referring to the power of imagination within this chapter. Emile Coué's "Conscious Autosuggestion" method is considered by many to be the main historical precursor to modern self-hypnosis, and though Coué did not choose to call it self-hypnosis, his method includes many facets of what has been recommended here so far:

> *Every morning before getting up and every*
> *evening as soon as you are in bed, shut your eyes,*
> *and repeat twenty times in succession, moving*

your lips (this is indispensible) and counting
mechanically on a long string with twenty knots,
the following phrase: "Day by day, in every way, I
am getting better and better." Do not think of
anything particular, as the words "in every way"
apply to everything. Make this autosuggestion
with confidence, with faith, with the certainty of
obtaining what you want. The greater the
conviction, the greater and the more rapid will be
the results obtained

(Coué, 1922).

You can see how this excerpt from his classic text has influenced what you have learnt here already. Coué abandoned classical hypnotism in favour of this technique of *"conscious autosuggestion",* in which subjects are taught how to use suggestion and imagination for themselves. He was part of the Nancy school of hypnosis, which made a substantial contribution to the field of hypnosis. The reasons Coué gave for abandoning the field of hetero-hypnotism were that he found not all hypnotic subjects responded to the suggestions they were given by the hypnotist, and as a result, he became disillusioned with it.

Born out of this disillusionment, Coué wanted to address the two most fundamental misconceptions about hypnotism:

Firstly, that the client is normally conscious and not asleep, unconscious, or in a "trance". These are subjects that we have addressed in this book already and are adhered to accordingly in this book.

Secondly, that the client is not under the hypnotist's control or power, but responds primarily because he voluntarily accepts suggestions in the form of autosuggestion.

It made sense to him therefore, to create a way of using self-suggestion, or as he termed it *"conscious autosuggestion."* Despite many self-help books being written long before him, he is considered by many to be the father of modern *"self-help"*, because his process was used by so many people worldwide.

Just as we have basic, common rules to consider when using suggestion, Coué outlined a number of laws of autosuggestion. The two main fundamental principles of Couéism were that *"all suggestion is autosuggestion"* and that *"internal conflict occurs between the will and imagination, but the imagination is always stronger"* *(Coué, 1923, p.19)* which are both very relevant to anyone learning self-hypnosis today.

Coué had other famous laws of autosuggestion that included the **law of concentrated attention**; this referred to the notion that the more attention you give ideas, the more their effect is magnified. Therefore, conscious autosuggestions should be repeated with focus and with a level of belief in them, just as discussed within our rules regarding expectancy earlier.

Another one of his well-known laws is also relevant to us. The **law of auxiliary emotion** states that when suggestions are combined with powerful emotions, they will be more effective. This helps illustrate negative self-hypnosis, whereby negative ideas can get stuck in our minds because of the powerful emotions attached to them, especially the emotion of fear.

The other of his famous laws that is relevant to the model of self-hypnosis adhered to in this book, is the very well-known **law of reversed effort.** This law referred to the fact that the harder we try to do something, it is often harder to do successfully. Likewise, with suggestions, we need to remove anxiety caused by too much effort in trying to achieve the outcome we desire. Coué's New Nancy School therefore stated that conscious autosuggestion should be used without any sign of tension caused by too much effort, and with an accompanying sense of belief in the desired outcome making it easy to accomplish.

About negative self-hypnosis and negative thoughts, Coué says:

> *"If unconscious and bad suggestions are so often realised, it is because they are made without effort"*
> *(Coué, 1922, p.36).*

Therefore, the message to us all is clear. When we give ourselves suggestions, we believe in it, we believe it is easy to accomplish and that we are going to accomplish it. Excessive conscious effort tends to presuppose failure and tends to evoke feelings and thoughts of failure that will impede progress with suggestions.

Central to Coué's approach was the idea that we should believe that change is easy, and this attitude should be inherent when giving ourselves suggestions. Therefore, no effort is necessary, if we truly believe that change is easy to achieve. He stated that effort and willpower just interfere, but belief and faith in oneself were key to success:

> *"Make this autosuggestion with confidence, with*
> *faith, with the certainty of obtaining what you*
> *want. The greater the conviction, the greater and*
> *more rapid will be the results"*
> *(Coué, 1922, p.94).*

There are many parallels with this notion that I have encountered many decades later. Today, I receive emails from people all over the world who are not getting the results they are after when using self-hypnosis, and very often it is because they are 'trying too hard' which is something Baudouin *(1920)* pointed out with students of autosuggestion at the time. When they free themselves of the effort and start to believe in their ability, the results they get improve greatly.

Coué believed that preparation for using autosuggestion was key, much like what we have discussed already with the establishment of the hypnotic mindset and the rationale underpinning it before engaging in self-hypnosis. Following the preparation, Coué really only instructed on two methods of giving yourself suggestions.

Firstly, Coué's **General Method** which centred around the use of the very famous phrase "every day, in every way, I am getting better and better." This phrase was to be repeated at least 20 times every single night, eyes closed, spoken monotonously in a whisper, as one relaxed before drifting off to sleep.

An emphasis was to be placed upon the words "in every way" and when you said it, you were to have an awareness of referring to both physical and mental improvement of well-being. The author Baudouin *(1920)* probably wrote more on Coué's method than Coué did, and often actually referred to the use of self-hypnosis *(Baudouin, 1920)*. Baudouin stated that this generic phrase being repeated was most effective when the individual had previously reflected upon their own therapeutic goals, and were mindful of the details of their own desired outcomes and their own well-being. This would then give the generic phrase some specific meaning (as we discussed previously, suggestions are more useful if they are meaningful and evocative).

The second method Coué taught was the **Specific Method,** whereby the specific formula involved used the words, "it is going", when faced with pain, distress, anxiety, discomfort, etc. These words were to be said quickly to prevent unwanted or detrimental thoughts from entering the mind.

Coué *(1923)* rejected the label "self-hypnosis", but would end his seminars by asking the group to close their eyes, and what ensued was virtually identical to a group hypnosis session for ego-strengthening (something we'll be learning more about later on). There is much we can learn and apply from the work of Coué.

Using Written Suggestions

Next, we'll look at how to combine numerous suggestions together and formulate them into full-blown **written** hypnotic programmes of change. This is whereby you'll write up a system that will consist of many suggestions strung together to form a written self-hypnosis programme. If you are not writing them, then you can simply apply what you have learnt so far. Before I go into more detail on creating written hypnotic programmes, let me first address how we actually deliver these written suggestions.

Other Ways of Delivering Suggestion

Aside from giving yourself suggestions in the way previously described, I am going to show you three other methods of entering written, more complex, lengthier programmes of suggestions. You may develop other ways for yourself in addition to those that you learn here.

Method 1: Pre-session entry

With this first method, have your written programme nearby (on paper, for example). You initially have your hypnotic mindset and ensure that you are in a safe place in order that you can proceed with step A for accessing self-hypnosis.

Then, immediately prior to step A, read the programme aloud and with enthusiasm. Reading aloud makes it more real and tangible than reading it to yourself silently in your own mind. Again, be (appropriately and congruently) enthusiastic, let yourself know that you mean this and want it to work.

Then you go through step A, take control as per step B and deepen hypnosis as per step C. Then you simply give yourself this type of suggestion:

> *"The programme entitled*
> *<programme title/name>, which I read out*
> *immediately prior to this self-hypnosis session, has*
> *full hypnotic authority and effect upon me."*

Or you can use your own words to have a similar effect and meaning. Then proceed to step E by counting from 1 to 5 in your mind or out loud to signal the end of this hypnotic session.

Method 2: Open eyes

With this method, simply enter self-hypnosis by going through steps A, B and C. Again, have your programme written up and nearby. When you are happy that you have deepened enough, say to yourself in your mind:

> *"When I open my eyes, I remain in deep hypnosis and read my suggestion. This suggestion has full hypnotic authority and has full effect on me as I wish it to. After reading my suggestion, it is fully effective."*

Then open your eyes, remaining in hypnosis and read your suggestion to yourself or out aloud. Then, you just Exit as usual with step E counting from 1 to 5.

Method 3: Record your programme

The majority of my own written programmes are recorded so that I can listen to them whenever I like, and relax while doing so. Here is a simple way of doing so.

When putting the audio track together, leave your first 60 seconds of the recording blank. You will see why shortly.

Secondly, you then record steps A to E, which includes your written, scripted programme. When you record your written programmes remember to use the second person tense For example: "*Adam, you are in deep hypnosis*", and **not** "*I am in deep hypnosis.*"

Usually during self-hypnosis you use the first person tense, as you are talking to yourself. However, when recording, you use the second person. This is because if you settle down to listen to your recording and the voice started saying, "*I am in deep hypnosis and I am relaxing...*" You will think to yourself, hmm. That is nice for you. What about me? In other words, the second person tense appears to address you directly.

When you are ready then, press play and let the recorded track start. Use that 60 seconds to get into your hypnotic mindset prior to following step A. Then, you can just lie back and enjoy the ride!

This has explained how to deliver the programmes once you have written them. We are now going to examine the best way to write them and how to make them as effective as possible.

Writing Programmes for Change

What is meant by self-hypnosis **programmes**?
What I am talking about is a script that you write, that you can then deliver to yourself during a self-hypnosis session.

Out there in bookstores around the world, there are lots of books filled with scripts, and I have included a sample script or two in this book. However, I highly recommend that if you are going to use suggestions in your self-hypnosis sessions, then use the information in this chapter to create your own scripts, your own self-hypnosis programmes for change, rather than use someone else's generic approach.

If you have invested the time and energy in doing that (writing your own programmes rather than using someone else's), you will know that this is important for you when you want to make a particular change. Also, my scripts or the scripts of another writer may not be the kind of language or expression that resonates with you; its components may not be congruent with you, if someone else has created the script. We are all unique individuals and respond to things differently, and you are the one person who knows how to push your own buttons and what you respond to the best and most powerfully.

You are going to forge these programmes like a piece of prose that you deliver (as previously instructed). Here are some guidelines for you to follow when creating your own written self-hypnosis programmes for change. Please do remember, this is not the law. You do not have to follow everything here to the letter. Your programmes will be most successful when they are congruent with you and your style. All I am suggesting is that the guidelines that follow may well enhance the effectiveness of the programmes and are things to be aware of.

If you want to have a scripted programme for weight reduction, or for more confidence, or to enhance your performance in some way using just suggestion, then you may wish to write a full-on programme. You'll be given evidence-based protocols, techniques and interventions in the second part of this book, but for now, you can write programmes just for suggestion with imagination. Here are some guidelines for doing so:

1. Write it down and read it through several times

Once you have written out the programme, put on your editing hat. Have any words entered without your intention? (We will be coming on to use of words later).

Are you happy with the finished result?

Do you get a good feeling about it?

Remember that during the early period as a self-hypnotist, a few suggestions per hypnosis session can be more successful than giving many. Then work your way up to more complex programmes of change.

2. Set a time to start and finish

Programmes should all have a time to start and in some cases, a time to finish. For example, if you are writing a programme for dealing with driving test nerves, for enhancing mental calmness during your driving test, it can have an end when the test has finished. You can suggest that the success generalises into future exams, but if you have specific elements pertaining to a particular date, be aware of using the date as the start and finish time.

When do you want it to begin? Most of my programmes have the beginning and ending in the first sentence, I often write "from this moment and lasting throughout my entire lifetime…" I often want that programme to last my entire lifetime, so the sentence is sufficient.

We are also going to be learning about how to use self-hypnosis for pain relief. Again, you will want that pain relief to end after a period of time. Pain is there for a reason, it is a signal, you do not really want to be pain free for longer than a set period of hours at any one time.

3. Label your programmes: Give them a title.

Title your programmes. This makes altering, boosting or removing them easier. You can then refer to them when you use your self-hypnosis to alter an existing programme. This is much better than going into self-hypnosis and saying to yourself, "ok, that programme I delivered a few weeks ago, about excelling in my exams.. erm… that programme is now changed to… er." You can understand where I am coming from with this can't you? If for any reason a programme is no longer valid or it has expired, then it can be removed if it has a title and a way of removing it.

After my first training course learning how to use self-hypnosis, I wrote loads of programmes, put them all on disc and had them filed with their titles, and I always tell the students on my self-hypnosis seminars and courses to do the same. On one such course, I had a lady who was not thoroughly impressed with this notion and she asked me: "Adam, are you not worried that with all this programme writing and installing that you are doing, that you are just becoming robot-like and too programmed?"I replied instantly with a smile: "No, I am not worried, if that ever concerns me, my programme for spontaneity just kicks in." As Kryten from Red Dwarf would say, "smug mode."

4. Reward yourself

Give yourself the rewards you deserve. Include rewards in your programmes by thinking about the gained benefits. For example, as a result of stopping smoking I am healthier. As a result of having more confidence, I enjoy social occasions more. When I stop biting my fingernails, I feel more beautiful. When I achieve and maintain my ideal weight, I can wear those clothes that I have not been able to wear for years.

You get the idea. Think about how you will benefit from achieving your goal.

5. Provisional clauses

If I was to include within a programme something to do with having better quality sleep, I might want my sleep to be more and more undisturbed. However, I would want to put in a provisional clause, something along the lines of:

"My sleep is more and more undisturbed. Undisturbed unless there is an emergency and an emergency as I know is anything that requires my immediate attention. Should en emergency exist or occur, I awake and deal with the emergency in the most appropriate way. In the absence of such an emergency, my sleep continues to be so wonderful and deeply refreshing and invigorating."

I add a provisional clause where necessary to cover eventualities.

6. Be progressive

At the end of your self-hypnosis programmes, state that you are becoming better at self-hypnosis, and that each time you use self-hypnosis you derive more benefit. Enhance your belief and tell yourself that practice is making you better, more fluent and more effective with your use of self-hypnosis. Tell yourself that you are a good self-hypnotist, that you are responsive to suggestions and that you are going deeper and getting better results.

Looping and Quantum Looping With Your Self-Hypnosis Programmes

"Thy firmness makes my circle just, and makes me end where I begun."

– John Donne

Now, this is a sure fire way to rocket fuel your written self-hypnosis programmes. Think about the power of a circle. I am sure you have seen the symbol of eternal life with the snake consuming itself in a circle by eating its tail. Circles are powerful but we often utilize them in the wrong way. For example, think about when someone has found themselves in a vicious cycle; someone who is, in their own opinion, overweight. They eat more because they feel lonely or bored or in need of comfort, or for whatever reason. Shortly afterwards they feel worse as they are contributing to their own condition of being overweight, and often end up eating more to feel temporarily better. It is a vicious cycle.

With the self-hypnosis programmes that you write, create and formulate for yourself, you want to create a virtuous circle. You can create a virtuous circle so that each element of the programme leads to the next, and then the last element of your programme leads to the element that the programme began with. This might sound confusing, so I have enclosed an example to illustrate this idea of looping programmes.

Here is an example of a programme that loops.

This programme is very one dimensional, it is just prose, but it is here for illustration purposes. This programme is for enhanced mental calmness and developing inner strength. It is very generic and non-specific. The importance is to note how each element of the programme leads to the next (the transition points are in bold) and how this starts and finishes on the same theme. It is for illustrating the looping process:

This is my programme for strengthening and enhancing my inner self. From this moment forwards and lasting throughout my entire lifetime, I find that I am feeling and being progressively more and more mentally calm. I are more and more calm in my thoughts, more and more calm in my feelings, more and more calm in my reactions, more and more calm in my responses. Progressively feeling and being more and more calm with place and person, time and event, circumstance and situation, so wonderfully, naturally and easily calm and beautifully and gently relaxed. It's like I have more time for my thoughts, more time for myself, my inner self.

And mental calmness is the ability to experience events,

155

circumstances and situations in my life in their true and correct perspective and so progressively I do find from this moment forwards that I am experiencing each and every aspect of my life in its true perspective, experiencing each and every event in my life in its true perspective, as it should be; free from distortion of events and happenings of the past.

I am so much more mentally calm and what this means is that I have the ability now to deal with and to cope with each and every aspect of my life in a more and more calmer way, having time for my thoughts and my feelings, my reactions and my responses.

And because I am more and more calm, I am more and more relaxed. More and more physically relaxed, for example, when I am walking upstairs, I am using the muscles that are required to climb upstairs, and the muscles I am not using are resting and relaxing, easily, gently and naturally. And on the occasions when I am resting all my muscles, each of my muscles in turn are relaxing easily and gently, conserving and reserving the energy and the life force that flows through my system. Giving me more natural energy at the times I require it and need it the most, enhancing my belief in myself, my enthusiasm and my motivation for life.

And I know, there is a by-product, a natural benefit of feeling and being more and more relaxed and feeling and being more and more calm. And that is that I notice, I truly notice, that I am becoming, feeling and being more and more confident, more deeply self-assured and this is natural because two of the main ingredients of increased confidence are mental calmness and physical relaxation. When I am calm mentally, when I am relaxed, physically, I find that I am naturally feeling and being more and more confident, and so I am from this moment forwards being more confident in each and every aspect of my life.

I am more and more confident with place and person, more confident with time and event, more confident with circumstance and situation, so much more confident in myself, really believing in myself and my abilities to achieve the goals I set my self in life. A deep-rooted self-belief in myself. More and more confident in relying on myself to help myself get the very best out of each and every aspect of my life, getting the most out of each and every situation. Instinctively and intuitively depending on my intuition and my instincts and my inner, natural, creative abilities to help me make the most out of each and every aspect of my life.

As I am and feel more confident, more deeply self-confident, so those around me can feel it and how wonderful that feels, how naturally my self-esteem is enhanced more and more each day and night, night and day. Growing and enhancing within me.

And because I am becoming more and more confident, so it is that I am becoming more and more competent.

More and more competent in each and every aspect of my life that pleases me. I am better and better in more and more aspects of my life, better and better at making changes in my life that please me, better and better at achieving goals. Better at relying on my self in a way that promotes, endorses and encourages the results I am looking for, the effects that I wish.

Because I am becoming better and better in each and every aspect of my life, of course, this means that I am becoming better and better at using hypnosis.

I find that my hypnosis is of a better and better quality. Each and every time I choose to enter hypnosis I find that it is easier and easier and more natural for me to enter into hypnosis. I find that I go deeper and deeper so naturally and easily. As a result of this I find that my hypnosis sessions are more powerful and beneficial for me and to me.

As a result of my continuing better quality hypnosis, I find that the quality of my sleep is also becoming progressively better and more natural.

Each and every time I choose to sleep, I drift easily and simply into sleep, each and every time I choose to enter into sleep I enter into a deeper and deeper, more natural, more beneficial, refreshing, invigorating and relaxing sleep. I find also from this moment forwards and lasting throughout my entire lifetime, my sleep is progressively more and more undisturbed. Undisturbed, of course except in case of an emergency and an emergency, as I know, is anything that requires my immediate attention and should such an emergency occur or exist, of course, I wake and deal with it in the most appropriate way.

*In the absence of such an emergency my sleep continues to be so
wonderfully refreshing and relaxing that I wake at the time I set
myself, feeling and being so wonderfully calm, refreshed, relaxed
and at ease, often waking with enthusiasm, sometimes with
excitement, and always, always with this wonderful, gentle
beautiful mental calmness.*

**(Remember, this theme of mental calmness is the theme we
started with at the beginning of this programme. The end of the
programme leads to the beginning.   It loops and empowers
itself.)**

*This is my programme for strengthening and enhancing my
inner self. It is a natural hypnotic programme always working
effectively and efficiently for me and to me, each breath that I
breathe and with each beat of my heart, I am strengthening
and enhancing this programme, ensuring that it is working
even more beneficially and progressively for me.*

You can see, if you continue to loop the content of your
programmes, you can make them more and more powerful. You
use the power of the circle to your advantage. The simplest way to
do this is to get the last line of your programme to relate with and
lead into the first line of your programme (as illustrated in the last
programme for mental calmness).

The above script is also an example of an ego-strengthening
routine (ESR). An ESR is simply a string of positive and
progressive suggestions designed to advance general well-being. An
ESR tends to contain elements, such as mental calmness, physical
relaxation, confidence, competence and so on. You may want to

write up your own ESR that is tailored for your own specific requirements.

The Language of Suggestion

We are going to discuss self-talk and cognitions in more detail later on in this book. For now though, when engaging in some of the earlier self-hypnosis sessions, be aware of how you use your language when talking to yourself in hypnosis.

I encourage you to use language in a progressive way to ensure your internal dialogue can be as useful as possible within your self-hypnosis sessions. You do not have to be sickly sweet or incongruent, just be as progressive as you in an appropriate way.

Think about an occasion in your life that was a wonderful occasion: maybe a happy birthday, the birth of a child, a wedding or a celebration, or maybe a time when you achieved something, when you succeeded, or when you felt the full force of joy or love. Really think about that experience. Remember what you saw, remember and think about the sounds that you heard, and think about how you know and how you knew you felt so good then. Whereabouts in your body were those good feelings? Now, as you think about that memory and immerse yourself in it, think about the words that you would use to describe that experience.

These are the words that are going to elicit the most powerful response from within you when you use them in self-hypnosis sessions, and when you communicate with yourself at any other time. Have a think about these questions: what words make you feel good? Which words give you good feelings? These words will serve you well when used appropriately in self-hypnosis sessions.

Words in Self-Hypnosis

Now, I am going to add a couple of words here for you to think about. Think about the words more and more and increasingly. These words are going to be important to create growth, power and fluidity in your mind. Let me explain how.

Consider the sentence, *"as a result of achieving my ideal weight I am happy."* This is a nice way to remind yourself that achieving this particular goal (whatever it might be for you) you are happy. Great. However, we can make that more powerful by changing a rather static happy to *more and more happy*. I don't know about you, but I would never want to think that I ever reached the pinnacle of happiness and could not go any further.

Happy is static. In order to supercharge your self-hypnosis sessions and the way you utilise language in self-hypnosis, you can mobilise the words and get them moving onwards and upwards for you.

You can change **happy** to

- happier and happier,

- more and more happy

- increasingly happy

- progressively more happy

- more and more appropriately happy.

Use whatever feels right for you, the words that help develop and empower you. Make sure you do this appropriately and usefully of course, certain words may not always be right for you or your outcomes.

Words to Avoid in Self-Hypnosis

Some of my suggested words may seem fine and feel fine for you to use. I am just giving you ideas and considerations to use in a self-hypnosis session. When communicating with yourself , my recommendation is that you consider avoiding the following words and types of words:

Words that elicit bad feelings. Words that are ambiguous. Words that are limiting, restrictive or disempower you. Words that you are uncomfortable with.

Words That Elicit Bad Feelings in Self-Hypnosis

Firstly, I want to point out some words that can elicit bad feelings: Try, can't, won't, don't, should, shouldn't, must, mustn't, jealousy, temper, no, lose, will, sad, difficult, but. I want to point out a couple of these words in particular.

The word **try** is limiting for some people. When you are trying to do something, you are not doing it. You may be building in failure by using the word try.

The word **will** is another one to avoid if you can. Will is not actually happening, it is something you *will* do rather than actually are doing. It never occurs. You can put almost any sentence together with the word will in, and simply remove that word to make it more progressive and positive for your self-hypnosis requirements.

Here are a couple of examples:

As a result of stopping smoking I will be healthier.
Now becomes:
As a result of stopping smoking I am healthier.

I will successfully achieve my goals
is transformed into:
I successfully achieve my goals.

Here we have just removed the word 'will' to make the sentence more progressive.

We are going to examine some thinking errors and distortions later on in this book. We'll look at *musterbation*; using the word must implies it is an obligation to do that thing, rather than actually wanting to do it.

Likewise, the issue of *shouldism* is whereby you feel you should do something rather than actually wanting to. Therefore, be aware of some of those types of words for now. This might not always be the case for you, but it helps to consider your own language when using self-hypnosis.

Put Down the Put-Downs

I recommend that you avoid using words that are putdowns. They don't have a place in self-hypnosis or your mind at all. Avoid the following words and words like them:

Untidy, Dirty, Smelly, Ugly, Stupid, Lazy, Hopeless, Disliked, Unkempt, Smelly, Idiot, Embarrass, Ridiculous.

I know you know lots more.

I don't really like even having to write these in this chapter. Your internal dialogue and self-hypnosis sessions are better without these words. You can allow yourself to find the right solutions and methods for you. As you get more and more used to being in self-hypnosis, or just communicating with yourself more progressively and discovering the kind of suggestions and words that have the most powerful effect for you, then you can fine tune your use of them.

In this chapter we have looked at how to make the most out of our suggestions, how to write longer hypnotic programmes, using language effectively within our suggestions, and a number of key principles and rules to apply throughout.

So far in this book, we have learnt the theory underpinning the model of self-hypnosis, how to enhance responsiveness using hypnotic skills, how to structure our self-hypnosis sessions using the A-E protocol, and how to deliver suggestion during self-hypnosis sessions.

Now that we know how to do these things, let's look at some applications of it. The second part of this book will now focus upon using self-hypnosis in the areas that have the most evidence to support successful outcomes, and whereby the techniques and strategies can be applied to a wide range of facets of your life: relaxation (and stress management), anxiety, depression, sleep, pain and habit control.

There are also some specific techniques looking at helping with IBS, hypertension and anger, but these can also be applied to other aspects of life.

PART TWO

Chapter Six: Introduction to The Applications of Self-Hypnosis

I want this to be a practical book, a book that you can use. At times, I'll need to contextualise and illustrate the techniques, but there'll be less theory and far more applications for you to follow in this second part of the book.

The vast majority of it will be a step-by-step process for you to follow. Lots of people find it a challenge to remember all the steps, especially in some of the lengthier processes. For that reason, I wanted to explain that you do not have to do each exercise completely and utterly as laid out here. Get a good understanding of the process and then adapt it to your own preferences and make it relevant to you, then start with it. You can always return to the written notes of the process afterwards and make changes should you wish to.

Many of the processes in the upcoming chapters will be applicable for all kinds of uses, and can be used with a wide array of issues. Therefore, do not just limit yourself to using techniques in the applications I have suggested or the chapter title that they feature in.

A couple of other points I want to make:

With the areas that we focus upon in the coming chapters (stress, anxiety, sleep, pain, anger etc.), self-hypnosis should ideally be used as an adjunct and not as a complete solution. Self-hypnosis is best woven into a gamut of approaches, lifestyle amendments, conventional medical advice and so on.

I have put the chapters in an order that I believe makes logical sense. The earlier skills are ones that can be applied throughout the latter chapters, and some of the initial learned coping skills and applications of self-hypnosis form a repertoire of fundamental flexible skills to apply in a variety of ways: hypnotic relaxation, mental rehearsal, imaginal exposure, self-monitoring and cognitive restructuring are all good examples of these (you'll become familiar with all these notions as we proceed).

Each of the following topics of focus have had many books written on them. A book dividing these subjects into chapters cannot be wholly exhaustive. This book focuses on how self-hypnosis can help with that subject matter. You are advised to explore other avenues of assistance and to seek out professional advice if you are dealing with a serious issue.

I have attempted to offer as wide a range of techniques and strategies as possible, which can be applied to a variety of issues (as already stated). There is a great deal of theory attached to these subjects that I cannot possibly include. My aim is to show you relevant research to support the use of hypnosis to deal with these issues, then to give you some general ideas for approaching them, before offering up step-by-step applications for you to use . I think this strikes a fine balance of theory and key understanding with practical, tangible and useful tools that you can apply straight away.

It is my opinion that the practical tools and techniques described in this book are all advanced by having an understanding of the underlying rationale. When you understand the theory underpinning the approaches, you are likely to derive better gains from them. This is my way of suggesting that you do not simply skip to the step-by-step applications without doing the initial reading.

There follows, a very large number of techniques and step-by-step strategies for you to follow and use, according to your desired outcomes. The first step is usually telling you to induce hypnosis, and then you do the remainder of the steps while hypnotised. You absolutely must remember that the induction is simply a cue for the session to start, it gets you focused, but that prior to the induction you should engage in the hypnotic mindset. This is key. From here onwards it is assumed that you do that for each exercise that you engage in.

Using Cognitions to Enhance Imagery

You are going to be required to engage in mental imagery within most of the upcoming chapters. One way to advance your mental imagery skills is to combine your cognitive skills and internal dialogue when using the mental imagery processes.

I was recently having a discussion with a client of mine (who is a runner) about the importance of being able to engage our imagination. This particular person, like so many others that I encounter, stated that they struggled to visualise or even to get any modicum of stability in the images that were in their mind. They got flashes and had distractions and found it thoroughly frustrating.

That frustrated sense is going to impede the ability to visualise during hypnosis sessions; it is what we often refer to as the 'the effort error' (see chapter 3 of this book) and which can obstruct us greatly, not just with visualising, but in also in using self-hypnosis with any degree of success. Throughout our hypnosis sessions, we do need to avoid any excess mental or physical effort that can frustrate and hinder our progress. Therefore, using the progressive relaxation techniques discussed in previous and upcoming chapters, in conjunction with self-hypnosis, can actually be incredibly useful.

If we have any anxiety, concern or even a fear of failure, any one of these things can obstruct the progress we desire with self-hypnosis and mental imagery processes. Practicing relaxing throughout is one particular means of helping providing a solid foundation for the use of mental imagery. In line with autosuggestion pioneer, Emile Coué, and his law of reversed effect, we want to stop trying to exert ourselves too much, as that obstructs our progress.

Everyone is capable of visualising and using mental imagery to great effect in conjunction with self-hypnosis. When we have a positive expectancy, correct expectations and engage our imagination, the process can and does become smooth with practice.

I thought I'd highlight a very simple, but often overlooked way to practice getting better at visualising, which involves the use of cognitions to direct, guide and keep you on track. You'll be incorporating verbal affirmations that accompany your visualisations, repeating the process over and over. What tends to happen is that the cognitions keep the focus, block out potential distractions and engage the mind in order that you learn (with repetition and over time) how to focus on the images, and your mental imagery prolongs and becomes more vivid. Simply follow these steps:

Step One:

Induce hypnosis using any of the processes you have learned so far.

Step Two:

Firstly imagine yourself in a favourite place. It can be somewhere you have been to before, or somewhere you are creating and imagining in your mind. Let it be a place where you feel safe, secure and at ease.

Start to get a sense of the scenery of this place; notice the colours, shades of light and textures of what you see. You can notice sounds too, and enjoy the comfortable feelings, but primarily we are working with your visualisation here. Just get as much detail as you can for now, and then move on to the next step.

Step Three:

Now begin to state clearly to yourself using your internal dialogue to describe the scene that is around you. Use statements that affirm what you are visualizing, and include the fact that you are seeing and visualising these things within your statements:

For example,
"I now picture the trees being blown slightly by the breeze",
"I notice the green colour of the leaves of the trees",
"I am imagining the trees to be 20 metres away from me",
"I am visualising the trees to be in a group, clustered together."

The above was fairly tree-centred. However, you can then move on to other facets and aspects of the scene around you, just stating and repeating that you are seeing XYZ happening, and that you watch ABC in detail. When you have done this for the entire scene, then move on to the next step.

Step Four:

Now think of some desired outcome that you have for yourself in your life. Whatever it is that you wish to achieve, start to have a think about yourself successfully taking the actions required, and start to think of that goal situation. As you imagine and visualise the scene with you fulfilling the successful outcome, again, start to use your cognitions to affirm your visualised scene:

For example, *"I now picture myself proudly achieving that outcome." "I see myself being happy."* And so on.

While you repeat these statements, let your internal dialogue be calming, soothing and enjoyable. As you do this, let it enhance your relaxation. Remember that remaining relaxed and positive throughout, with peace of mind, is important to help you develop proficiency with the process. Then move on to the next step.

Step Five:

As you continue to describe what you see, using your cognitions to keep your mind focused, gently repeat those cognitions and statements over and over. As you focus upon the scene, using your cognitions, keep telling yourself that you can see more detail and picture things more vividly.

Step Six:

When you have practiced and repeated the cognitions for this scene to the best of your ability, then take a couple of nice, big, deep energising breaths, wiggle your toes and fingers, and come out of this session by counting from one through to five.

This practice depends on repetition for your visualisation to get better. If you practiced this process a few times and start to use it with the other techniques in this book, you'll start to notice distinct results with your own visualisation skills.

Before moving on, I thought I'd offer up a psychosomatic technique that will test and advance the ideo-dynamic reflex that you practiced in earlier chapters; it is a valuable technique in itself. I would have liked it to be a pre-cursor to the pain management chapter (I think you'll realise why once you have looked at this technique and then read the analgesia protocol), but could find no logical way to incorporate it. I offer it here instead, then as a self-hypnosis technique and as part of your advanced hypnotic skills training, prior to moving onto the second part of this book.

Using Self-Hypnosis For That 'Deep Heat' Effect

In my work in this field, I have had the absolute pleasure of seeing some truly remarkable applications of hypnosis. On my self-hypnosis seminars, when people create self-induced anaesthesia, we often notice a difference in colouration in the localised area. It happens as a bi-product of the other aims of the session, however, such things can be done volitionally too.

One of the other ways to control the flow of blood, is to control, to some extent, body temperature. This is an application I have used a great deal within my marathon running training and recovery. We have all experienced this kind of body temperature fluctuation effect on an involuntary basis: perhaps you have blushed, or when you got sexually aroused, or as a response to something fearful (cold response).

This is an area that benefits from a good level of research, which has shown that anybody can gain a pretty impressive level of control over body temperature in a fairly brief time, and without much difficulty *(Barabsz and George, 1978; Clarke and Forgione, 1974; Dikel and Olness, 1980; Wallace and Kokoszaka, 1992).*

The key here is to practice and condition the response before you start to use self-hypnosis to advance and get it to become a cue-controlled skill to use whenever you choose. I'll come to that shortly.

Even though I stated that I use it for enhancing recovery and relieving pain in joints and muscles, I have also used it to warm my throat when I have had a cold or flu. This process can be used by anyone wanting to warm parts of the body that feel cold, for safely warming the entire body in cold scenarios, or for enhancing the healing of wounds and other injuries by increasing blood supply to the affected area. I have also seen this kind of application used in studies for shrinking warts and tumours, by restricting blood supply to a specific area. It also has applications for enhancing sexual response or controlling a migraine headache. What's more, and as crazy as it sounds, hypnotically suggested hyperthermia has even been used to control cancer metastases *(August, 1975).*

Preparation

Before you start using hypnosis, a neat trick to develop your skill is to practice the response you wish to experience in real-life terms and allow your mind to record it, register it in detail. You might use the warm water in a bath, or washbasin. You might use a fireplace or heater of some kind. You might use the sunshine on a hot day. You might use close proximity to an oven when cooking or baking.

Get safely seated or in close proximity to the heat source. Move your hand close to it as you start to notice the increase in temperature. Notice the tiniest of details as your hand gets warmer due to it being so close to the heat source. Once you have done this a few times, remaining safe and careful, start to move your hand closer, while using your internal dialogue you tell yourself that your hand is getting warmer. In a relaxed, simple fashion, advise yourself that your hand gets warmer as it moves closer to the warm area. Repeat this several times (5-10 times) and each time you do it, commentate to yourself in your mind about the many sensations that you notice.

All the tiniest of sensations, record and be aware of them.

Get every detail of this scene vivid in your mind. Watch the hand going closer to the heat source, notice changes in colour and really be sure you notice as much as you possibly can. Once this has been done, then proceed with the remainder of the self-hypnosis process. Adopt your hypnotic mindset in a place where you'll be undisturbed, sat upright, in an attentive posture with your feet flat on the floor and your arms and legs uncrossed. Then follow these steps.

Step One:

Induce hypnosis using any method of your choice. Once you have induced hypnosis, move on to step two.

Step Two:

Now imagine being in the scene where the heat source was. Notice the colours, the sounds, and all the details of the place as vividly as possible.

Imagine moving your hand closer to the heat source (you can move your hand towards the imagined source if you want to, but it is not essential) and then imagine the hand getting warmer and warmer. Notice and imagine all the sensations happening that you experienced earlier. Use the same internal dialogue and tonality, and repeat the same words to yourself that you used previously (when prior to this technique, you told yourself that your hand was getting warmer in the real-life scenario).

Imagine your hand getting warmer, imagine all the qualities of the hand changing to really be a warmer hand (colour, sensation etc.), and start to notice it getting warmer. Tell yourself that it is feeling as if it is getting warmer – convince yourself, say it as if you truly believe it 100%, undeniably convince yourself by imagining it so realistically that it becomes your reality.

Once you have done that, once you have truly generated warmth in that hand, move on to step three.

Step Three:

Now move your warm hand toward your face and right up to your cheek. Imagine that all the warmth is draining out of your hand and into the cheek. As you exhale, imagine the heat growing and leaving the hand and moving into the cheek.

At this stage, whether you can actually feel the increased temperature is not the most important thing. Just imagine that you can. Pretend and convince yourself that your cheek is getting warmer. The more you practice this, the more you'll notice it in real terms.

Now move your hand away from your face and start to imagine that the heat in your cheek is intensifying. Imagine it becoming warmer, stronger and more noticeable.

When you truly notice it, move your hand back towards your face, touch your cheek again. This time as you inhale, imagine that you are drawing in all the warmth—real and imagined—back into your hand. Imagine that with every exchange (from hand-to-face or face-to-hand) you can feel the warmth increasing and intensifying.

Step Four:

Repeat step 3 as many times as you like and really develop and build this skill. Each time imagine the heat getting stronger and more intense. Convince yourself in a gentle, assured way. Do not grasp at the effect you want, just trust yourself and make your imagined responses as vivid as possible. Once you have repeated this several times, once you have developed this skill, move on to the next step.

Step Five:

Now move this hand that is experiencing the warmth hand to any other part of your body where you wish to increase temperature. Then repeat the process as you touch that area; as you exhale, let the warmth transfer from the hand into the other part of the body. You can be as precise as you like and really imagine the warmth going to that area. Take your time and let the warmth really spread into that part of the body. When you notice the warmth, move on to the final step.

Step Six:

Finally, move your hand away from that area, breathe comfortably and deeply, and exit hypnosis.

Open your eyes as you count yourself up and out from 1 through to 5.

Now respond as if you can actually feel the warmth, and go about your day. Behave as if the area is warm, think as if the area is warmed. Do note that at times, it might take a short while for the warmth to be truly noticeable in the new areas you move it to.

Trust yourself, trust that it will happen, be assured without pushing yourself or grasping at the response you want.

You will also benefit by using your internal dialogue to remind yourself of this ability and congratulate yourself, as well as affirming your ability to do this. Do tell yourself that each time you practice this, it works better and better, and is more intense and effective. The more you help yourself to believe in your ability to do this, the better it becomes.

Once you have done this a few times, you'll find that it happens quicker. You may also develop the skills so well that you can start to do it out of hypnosis altogether. Many people get so good at it, that they simply imagine the area warming, spread it to whatever body part you like and notice it working and developing.

The more you practice, the better it becomes. It is another skill that will enhance self-efficacy with self-hypnosis. Now let's move on to specific areas of application with the second part of this book.

Chapter Seven: Hypnotic Relaxation

Many people in the field of professional hypnosis and hypnotherapy get worried, concerned, and sometimes even frustrated by the similarity between hypnosis and relaxation. I say 'frustrated' because some people assert that hypnosis and relaxation are totally different and quite rightly so. There are, however, a very large number of studies out there, in particular the work of Edmonston *(1981 and 1991)* which demonstrate that relaxed clients in the therapeutic environment are just as responsive to suggestions as clients who are hypnotised and given suggestions.

Relaxation is going to be useful for us self-hypnotists.

Banyai and Hilgard *(1976)* showed that by having an individual exercise vigorously for a period of time prior to a hypnosis session, the individual could still be hypnotised, but would not be at all relaxed. In fact, they would be alert and focused and have a heart rate and pulse that was very active and alive. A patient undergoing relaxation training in any form of psychotherapy would not gain the benefits of the relaxation in the same way, making the two quite different. This study has been successfully replicated *(James, 1984)*.

As often seems to be the case, many people wrongly suppose that hypnosis is simply relaxing, and many people perpetuate the myth that relaxation is inherent within hypnosis. This is not the case. Hypnosis can be used to develop relaxation though, and it can be used to enhance relaxation to ensure we derive much benefit from relaxing. In fact, studies have helped us to recognise how a profound physiological state of deep rest can be created by suggestion and hypnosis. This is particularly interesting and important when you consider that, as Platonov *(1959)* showed, that natural sleep does not always completely rest all of our bodily functions and organs.

When we look at the origins of hypnosis, James Braid originally termed it, "neuro-hypnotism", meaning "sleep of the nervous system." Braid's early use of hypnosis was to induce a deeply relaxed state, which vaguely resembled sleep, but the individual being hypnotised had a conscious awareness of it.

When we see that some individuals derive a seemingly more profound benefit from the relaxation achieved during hypnosis sessions, it makes sense to learn how to do this and benefit from it ourselves. That is what this chapter is all about.

Lots of people I have worked with report that they find the process of structured self-hypnosis sessions, and everything involved within it, to be quite stimulating. Likewise, a number of researchers have also noticed that many of the processes involved in self-hypnosis can have a stimulating effect on the self-hypnotist – such as mental imagery, focusing, making suggestions using internal dialogue and so on.

Many of the elements of our hypnotic mindset require effort and too much effort can create an impediment to successful self-hypnosis; it can even sometimes cause anxiety, which impedes progress greatly.

The previously mentioned Edmonston *(1981 and 1991)* published a very thorough review of hypnosis and relaxation. Edmonston wrote about the use of hypnosis without any specific suggestion or mental imagery or cognitive strategies, which is sometimes termed, "neutral hypnosis" and is ideal for generating a profound level of hypnotic relaxation, due to the absence of stimulation or distraction that these things can sometimes present.

Platanov and other former Soviet Union researchers made a major contribution to this topic . Relaxation was often synonymous with hypnosis, and in some cases, formalised hypnosis was preceded by an hour of lying down to relax in a darkened room – which really curtailed distractions and stimulation, but may not win favour in therapy rooms of today. (I don't think my therapy clients would be prepared to start their therapy sessions off by sitting in a darkened room for an hour on their own before we started). Sometimes after treatment, having given corrective suggestions, they would then instruct the client to drift off to sleep again and leave them for another hour.

Platanov *(1959)* discusses conditioning in hypnosis, as influenced by much of the earlier work of Pavlov. He showed that the activity of the cortex and subcortex are different during the states of waking and suggested sleep. Here, we are going to build upon the notion of "suggested sleep" to advance our relaxation skills, which are going to prove useful in a number of ways and techniques used later in this book. I am going to refer to this as progressive relaxation. When I refer to progressive relaxation, I am referring to relaxation advanced by the adjunctive use of hypnosis and hypnotic suggestion.

Prior to starting with the step-by-step process, make sure that you frame the hypnotic relaxation session in such a way that you are aiming to relax deeper than you are usually capable of doing. Platanov suggested that in some ways, hypnotic relaxation offered up more health benefits and usefulness than natural sleep. It is certainly going to offer up a variety of health benefits if practiced regularly.

You should aim to have a minimum of 10 minutes to invest in this, though ideally a fair bit longer as you practice more, aiming to gain major benefits from it (20-30 minutes). You'll also want to make this part of a regimen that you put together and practice daily for at least 2-3 weeks to derive the benefits, and to build up the ability to do this for longer thereafter.

Find a comfortable seated position to be in with your feet flat on the floor and your hands not touching each other. If your intention is to use this to drift off to sleep, then you'll want to be lying down in bed. However, to gain the full benefits of hypnotic relaxation, you do not want to fall asleep. You associate lying in bed with sleep, so unless that is your aim, do this seated.

Throughout the upcoming process, remember your goal is to relax deeply and ideally deeper than usual. Make it your aim to learn how to induce deeper levels of relaxation within your self-hypnosis sessions. Therefore, whenever possible, gently convince yourself that you are relaxing, adopt the position and behaviour and thought patterns of someone who is deeply relaxed, and help yourself along with the process – without trying and without exerting effort – just gently assuming you are relaxing and doing this beautifully well. Imagine that you are completely relaxed throughout and let your imagination help you along.

The steps given here are very similar to the relaxation process involved with the hypnotic systematic desensitisation that we'll be learning more about in the next chapter, and that I use in my clinical practice. The steps are supported with research to support their efficacy and benefit to the recipient.

Engaging and Practicing Progressive Relaxation

With all that understanding and preparation complete, now follow these simple steps:

Step One:

Induce self-hypnosis using your preferred method. Ideally use a method that is going to lend itself well to relaxing, or a technique that you are used to doing and feel good using.

With hypnosis induced, move on to the next step.

Step Two:

Once you have induced hypnosis, you want to initiate the relaxation response. Whatever active component you used in your induction (eyelids, arms etc.) you can imagine that area becoming totally relaxed. Start to let your breathing happen automatically; that is, stop interfering with it, just observe it and let your body breathe by itself. Don't try to change it and don't try to stop it from changing.

As you relax, your body will require less oxygen, so your breathing may become lighter and shallower, just let that happen.

Using your imagination, just imagine your entire body settles and relaxes with your breathing for a few minutes. Keep allowing a gentle, relaxing mindfulness to of yourself to form and you can return to this mindfulness at any stage throughout the process again. Just let thoughts happen, let your breathing happen, imagine relaxing and gently settling and then move on to step three.

Step Three:

Now you are going to use a progressive relaxation process.

The aim here is to spread relaxation into various parts of your body. As you get better at doing this, you can start to imagine more specific parts of the body relaxing (rather than generalised areas), something referred to by hypnotherapists as fractional relaxation, that I'll describe in more detail shortly. With all of these ideas, you can also assume that they deepen your self-hypnosis too, and let them become an inherent deepener.

Here are some ideas of how to engage in a progressive hypnotic relaxation process:

a) Use your internal dialogue and simply tell yourself that each part of your body is relaxing. For example, *"my toes are relaxing deeper... and now my ankles... moving into my lower legs..."* and so on.

b) As you work your way through your body, you may like to use a colour or light or imagine a warming sensation;

spread that through the muscles and imagine the colour (ideally one you associate with relaxing) spreading through the muscles as you reach each part of your body.

c) Additional cognitions can be used. The co-founder of the field of NLP, Richard Bandler, uses the word "soften" in one of his audio programmes to relax parts of the body. He focuses on each muscle and then says, *"soften"*, as he moves the awareness through the muscles of the body. You might like to do the same or perhaps use the word *"relax"* (or any other suitable word) if that soothes and helps you more. Remember to believe in the word you repeat to yourself without using too much effort.

d) You may imagine a relaxing sound moving through your body. This could be the sound of music, or even a gentle relaxing sound from nature, or a comforting sound that is personal to you.

e) You may imagine the muscles limp, loose, dormant; maybe like a loose rubber band, or a rag doll, or whatever else you can imagine indicating the relaxation spreading. I learned a great technique from Terence Watts, who suggested imagining the body as a candle and as the candle softened and got warm and started melting, so the muscles of the body got warm and softened and so on.

Ideally, use a combination of these elements. Bask in the relaxation you create, enjoy it and enjoy this time as well spent. You may like to repeat this step a couple of times to make sure you develop the progressive relaxation as much as possible. Once you have done so, move on to the next step.

Step Four:

Use your internal dialogue and start to count downwards with each breath that you exhale. You might imagine the numbers in your mind, or simply say it with your internal dialogue.

After each number, say the words *"relaxing deeper"*. Say it in a highly relaxing tone and manner to yourself, so there is no hint of effort, just gently assume it is happening, counting downwards as you exhale and all the time focus on being deeply relaxed.

Tell yourself and imagine that on each number you count, you are relaxing deeper into profound hypnotic relaxation. This process works well if combined with breathing. You can breathe outwards with each number that you count.

Make it your aim to be very deeply relaxed by the time you reach zero. I have seen it suggested that you count from 10 to 0 and then perhaps repeat if you want to, which encourages mindfulness and so on. I have also seen people count backwards from 100, and even stop if they are relaxed enough by the time they have reached a particular number. You get to choose which, and you might benefit from experimentation in this regard. When you reach zero, move on to the next step.

Step Five:

The next step is to fix your attention and focus onto a single ongoing and repetitive train of thought. You will use the idea and belief of being highly and deeply relaxed.

You can do this in a number of ways:

a) Continue to say certain words upon each breath you exhale. Such as *"deeper"* or *"more relaxed."* Use whatever word you find to be most relaxing to you.

b) Focus on your breath; you might count your breaths and keep going. Do not alter your breathing, just count each breath as it happens. If you lose track of your counting, simply start from 1 again and see how long you can continue to be aware and tuned in before your mind wanders. Do this without challenging yourself, and without effort. Just accept it calmly if you lose count and start again. Enjoy the counting.

You can also simply follow the movement of your breathing, maybe just watching the ribs expand, or the chest rise or noticing the change of temperature in the nostrils as you inhale and exhale and watch your breathing that way instead. Tuning into it and letting it consume your attention and train of thought.

c) Enjoy the relaxing sensations. Simply notice somewhere on your body that is relaxed, notice what tells you it is relaxed, and then watch those sensations start top spread to other parts of the body. Again, bring your awareness back to focus, if it wanders.

Whichever of these you use, keep a fixed train of thought for the remaining time you have allotted to this. Keep encouraging yourself, keep assuming it is working, being progressive and positive with yourself, and engage in a gentle, easy approach without ever 'trying' or getting anxious or worrying about anything. Simply enjoy it lazily with utmost relaxation of the body, keeping your awareness and focus in place.

When you have done this for the remainder of your allotted time, move on to the final step.

Step Six:

Take a couple of deeper, energising breaths, wiggle your toes and fingers, then count from 1 through to 5 and open your eyes to bring this session to an end.

As with so many of the processes in this book, you'll derive more benefit from focused practice and developing your skill (and thus your self-efficacy) with these relaxation techniques. Be aware that you can be physically relaxed while your mind races, and you can be physically active while your mind is still and quiet (I swear I am at my most peaceful when running marathons) – this process addresses both: you get to relax the body first, and then ease the thoughts and feelings by engaging in the continuous train of thought, engaging in repetition to still and quiet the mind and relax.

Practice and enjoy getting some deep hypnotic relaxation into your daily routine, the benefits are vast and you'll be pleased you did it. Plus, these relaxation skills are going to be required in a number of other chapters of this book.

Further Considerations For Hypnotic Progressive Relaxation

As well as some of the fascinating observations made with EEG, PET scans and fMRI, regarding what happens in the brain during hypnosis and hypnotic relaxation, there are a number of more easily observable physiological and psychological changes of note too. We are all different and respond differently on different days to different techniques. However, there are some commonly reported responses, and these are not just anecdotal, they are also reported and recorded during research studies in controlled conditions.

Some people notice a gentle tingling sensation similar to light "pins and needles" in the limbs, which can be attributed to a change in circulation that occurs when engaging in progressive hypnotic relaxation. This happens as blood flows to the hands, feet and surface of the skin. Some people notice a change in their breathing. As you relax deeply and your body requires less oxygen, the heart rate slows, your breathing becomes gentler and more rhythmic. The breath may seem more shallow and light due to you inhaling less air and may slow slightly too.

Within many of my audio tracks I refer to little twitches that we get within our limbs or facial muscles, which are sometimes referred to as "hypnotic jerks". They can be quite amusing, though they can also give us a jolt of surprise if experiencing them for the first few times under deeper levels of relaxation.

Relaxation is varied. As well as relaxing our body, as this chapter has mainly focused upon, we can also relax our thoughts, feelings and general levels of mental activity. We come to deal with this in more depth in the next chapter. It is worth bearing in mind that you can still derive a great deal of benefit from physical relaxation if you still have an active mind, and you can also relax your mind while your body feels tense. If you wish to derive the most benefit, learning to relax it all (as much as possible) is desirable. With practice it becomes a lot easier to do.

As well as the progressive relaxation techniques you can use and practice, I thought I'd offer two specific mental imagery processes that also aid relaxation. They provide some variety and a different approach. You can, of course, develop these ideas and build upon them, using scenarios that suit you. You might simply like to imagine being in a safe, relaxing place that lends itself well to you relaxing. This could be a familiar place, or an imagined one. Using imagery and suggestion throughout to advance them, these two processes can be used for purely relaxation purposes or for restorative benefits too.

The Hypnotic Mud Bath

When I was younger, I lived for a few months on a Kibbutz and have written about some of my experiences during this time and my other travels. After living for a while in Nacscholim, Israel, I got to travel to the Dead Sea in Jordan. If you have ever floated in the Dead Sea for a while, you appreciate that whether it is because of the minerals, or because so many people told you it was good for you, you feel good being there.

It led me to fancy going and plunging myself into one of those mud baths. So I went to a local one and I have since been to others; one in particular was on the periphery of the volcanic Greek island of Santorini. You get to wallow in mud and minerals and sit with it on you before you swim into the sea and wash it all off. Again, it feels good I have to say. I have only fond memories of hanging out in mud, mud, glorious mud.

When your weight gets suspended and you firmly believe in the healing properties of that thick, gloopy, gooey, brown stuff you are in, then you respond accordingly. It is this premise that I am relying on for this next self-hypnosis process. I would like you to believe that you are gaining all the benefits of a mud bath, without the actual mud. Many believe that mud is good for the skin, good for the joints and for aching muscles and much more besides.

Step One:

Induce hypnosis using an induction of your choice. Once you have done that, move on to step two.

Step Two:

Imagine you are in a natural environment of some kind. A favourite place in nature. Notice the sights, colours, sounds and how wonderful it makes you feel to be in this place of your own choosing. Truly get a vivid notion of the surroundings. Imagine that the temperature is just right for you and create in your mind the most perfect day. Notice the air around you, how it smells and seems, really tune in to this place in nature. Only move on when you have got that firmly and vividly in your mind.

Step Three:

Look all around you and notice and locate a pool of water. See the light glittering and glimmering on the surface of the water. Watch the surface of the water, notice how calm it is and allow yourself to relax in response to it.

Start to imagine that the water is just the right temperature for you. That it looks inviting, clean, beautiful, revitalising, and you anticipate how it is going to feel to get in.

When you are certain that you have imagined exactly how you'd like it to be, then dress accordingly and take a step into it.

Be assured that this is your own creation, your own private place that only you can attend. You can just be at one with yourself here and enjoy it deeply. Imagine stepping deeper and comfortably deeper into the water; it is the right temperature, it feels wonderful on your skin. Engage in this for a while in your mind until you are at a comfortable depth to just relax and be calm as you are supported by the water.

Notice and imagine the various parts of your body relaxing. To enhance your relaxation while you are in this pool, spend some time using whatever progressive relaxation technique or process you know. When you are suitably relaxed, then move on to the next step.

Step Four:

Look deeper down and around you, and start to notice that in places there is a soft white mud. Put your feet into it and feel the sensation in your toes. You may even place your hand in and notice how smooth, soothing and nice it is.

With the initial touches, start to notice your body relaxing further. Then in your own time and in your own way, start to allow yourself to sink slowly and easily and comfortably into the mud. Deeper and more enjoyable, it is a delight to the senses as it starts to be felt all over your body. Notice the feel of the mud around your joints. Notice how your muscles respond and react to the depth of relaxation that the mud instills. Imagine the goodness of the mud starts to find its way into your muscles and joints, as it soothes, relaxes and comforts deeper and deeper.

You may even like to imagine being cleansed deeply in whatever way you find to be useful and beneficial. Now take this relaxation and soothing quality a step further and imagine that the mud draws out any discomfort from your muscles and joints. Imagine that it absorbs any discomfort and takes it away, lost in the pool. Let the time you spend here be one of healing. Whatever that may mean to you personally, imagine yourself being healed and rejuvenated, and bask in this glorious sensation for as long as it takes for you to notice some tangible difference in how you feel as a result of the healing mud.

Relax in the mud. Just be at one with yourself in the mud. Wallow and love it.

Step Five:

Once you have spent enough time enjoying the healing sensation, then start to move up and out and away from the mud, into the clearer water that cleans off all the remaining mud, leaving you feeling more refreshed and invigorated and comfortable.

You might like to dry yourself naturally with the warming rays of the sun, or towel yourself down. Let the sensations of well-being stay with you, notice the difference in how your muscles and joints and body feel, and encourage these feelings to stay with you for longer. You can then dress and prepare yourself for bringing this session to an end, and engaging with the world once again. Remind yourself that each time you choose to do this, it works better and more powerfully and progressively.

Step Six:

Exit hypnosis by counting from 1 to 5 and opening your eyes, remembering to bring all that lovely relaxation with you. As much as is appropriate to what you are going to do next.

Relax, Aid Recovery and Enjoy The Benefits of a Massage

At the time of writing this, I had been aching all over. Yes indeed, my marathon training miles had been upped greatly in the previous couple of weeks. One of the biggest challenges I face is recovering. I am no longer a twenty-something whose body responds to exertion with the greatest of ease. I am at that age where I get up to use the toilet in the night, and yes my legs tend to feel sore after my weekly long run, and they scream at me during my speed sessions.

I do go and see a sports massage therapist and other great people who tend to me, but I never lose track of what my own mind is capable of, and do use self-hypnosis at any and every opportunity to help along the way.

Here is another simple, relaxing and restorative self-hypnosis process that anyone can run through to help ease aching muscles and speed up healing. Or it can simply be used to enhance relaxation, as we have been focusing upon in this chapter.

Step One:

Induce hypnosis using any induction of your choosing. Then move on to step two.

Step Two:

You are going to engage your imagination in a number of ways now. Firstly, we want to warm you and your muscles up.

Imagine you are in a natural environment of some kind. A favourite place in nature. Notice the sights, colours, sounds and how wonderful it makes you feel to be in this place of your own choosing. Truly get a vivid notion of the surroundings. Imagine lying with a balanced and comfortable posture, in a position that you feel relaxed in start to imagine the sunshine naturally and gently warming your legs, your back, your shoulders. The heat is so softly warm, at exactly the right temperature for you.

When people ask me to imagine lying on a beach, I tend to think, "No! When I am at a beach the sun burns me!" So, at this stage, you need to adapt this notion to your own level of comfort and suitability. Just imagine and feel the sun warming and easing your muscles. Take some time to let the sun's rays work their way into your muscles; imagine them relaxing and softening, and do take some time to consciously let go of any lingering tension. As you relax deeper, imagine and sense that the rays of the sun are directed to those places on your back, shoulders and legs (and/or any other place where they are needed) that need it the most.

You might start to notice that as you focus your attention on relaxing and warming the body, that you start to develop some mental calmness too, and notice your breathing relaxing. As the sunshine continues to warm and soothe you, imagine that it is slowly and deeply easing and allowing you to let go of any discomfort. You might imagine a change in colour to represent this happening, you might imagine a sound soothing your discomfort, or you might just notice a change (however subtle) in actual sensation in those areas.

As you imagine being warmed, soothed, and letting any discomfort ebb away, spend as much time as it takes for you to notice something tangible (as above) to enhance the experience. Once you notice that difference occurring, then move on to the next step.

Step Three:

Now imagine that the goodness and benefit of the sunshine is moving deeper and into your bones. Imagine them moving gently and feeling soothed, and feel a shift in how you hold your body in the most optimum and balanced posture. Imagine this happening beneficially to gently enhance your comfort.

Let the light move towards the source of any previous discomfort, warming and soothing and working into those places, relaxing and loosening.

This is the start of the deeper relaxation and healing. Let yourself relax and warm-up deeply, and allow your mind to become more calm and focused. As you heighten your awareness of how much good you are doing yourself, allow yourself to smile and get ready for the next, even more progressive step.

Step Four:

Continue to engage in the surroundings: smell the air, let it soothe your senses and enhance your calmness, notice the sounds and enjoy basking in the relaxing position you are in. Now imagine that a number of beautiful looking hands appear directly in the space above your back and legs. Sense that you are comfortable with them, imagine the number to be the amount that will help you the most. Imagine them to be magic, healing and beneficial to you and your recovery and healing.

You can watch and feel what happens now as the hands start to gently and deeply work on your back, legs, shoulders, and anywhere else that requires it. Notice the hands going to the areas that need it the most. Notice them massaging gently but deeply; it is almost as if they know the perfect pressure to apply for you to sense that it is really doing you some good.

You might imagine each warmed muscle now feeling as if it is melting and letting go of any traces of tension and discomfort. The heat remains and helps the process. Imagine that the hands are absorbing any discomfort, removing it and letting it go. Imagine a sense of relief as the hands move along and through the muscles.

Let the massage benefit each muscle, tendon, fibre, and then let every bone get a sense of relaxing and letting go. As you engage your imagination with this step, spend as much time as necessary for you to notice a difference in sensation. When you are truly noticing the benefits, then move on to the next step.

Step Five:

Now let the hands start to manipulate a bit more and mobilise, not just the soft tissue of the body, but also flexing the joints and allowing everything to slot into its correct place, making any beneficial adjustments. Allow each muscle and bone to find its correct place and enjoy the sensation of knowing things are healing.

Imagine repairs starting to happen more rapidly than usual, and notice a continued sense of relief at letting go of old, lingering discomfort. All the time you enjoy this calming your mind, and allow yourself to continue with a satisfactory smile that tells you and your mind that you are benefiting from this process beautifully. Let any last remnants of tension leave the body; let the hands continue until that happens, and then let them disappear and spend some time basking in a sense of weightless, soothing, warming comfort. Bask in that for as long as you feel you need to get the maximum healing and enhanced relaxation benefits.

Step Six:

You can return here whenever you choose. Tell yourself that each time you come here and run through this process you relax deeper, it works even better and the benefits increase.

Then you exit hypnosis by counting yourself up and out from 1 to 5. Go about your day feeling better and letting the feelings continue to be felt as much as is pertinent to do so.

Using Fireworks For Mental Calmness

In addition to the main strategies of physical relaxation, I wanted to offer up a simple mental imagery strategy that is designed to relax your thoughts and help increase mental calmness. You can do this in all manner of ways: with physical relaxation that relaxes the thoughts (sometimes as described previously), with direct suggestions (as we have already learned), by imagining being in a safe place, and also with some of the many other techniques and strategies offered up later in this book (in particular the thought controlling section in the next chapter).

Every November here in England, we have 'bonfire night', or 'fireworks night', which is lots of fun and I do love watching fireworks. I have a slight gripe and that is that aside from the impressive displays that go on, organised in public places for large numbers to watch, lots of neighbours now also let off loads of fireworks late into the night, and without any prior warning. Which is a problem for our cat, who gets terrified by them. That said, our cat deals with it in a very intelligent manner. He finds a spot behind the sofa, sits there calmly and waits for the fireworks to end. When the furore, noise and flashing lights are all over, he decides to go about his business of being a cat. I have encountered a number of people who react to fireworks in a less than enjoyable fashion, so why on earth am I suggesting that imagining them could be beneficial in calming and relaxing our mind? Sometimes life gets a bit like a firework display and I see a metaphor here with some parallels to be drawn. It is summed up wonderfully by Rudyard Kipling, in the brilliant poem - *If*:

> *If you can keep your head when all about you*
> *Are losing theirs and blaming it on you*

I once made a joke on my diploma course when someone questioned something I said. After questioning me, the person attempted to get others to join in and agree to support the argument. We had a lot of fun discussing it, but what I observed from this was that very often, when someone really believes in something strongly, those in close proximity get drawn in to agreeing without needing to be asked.

For example, look at big sporting events where the same team supporters all rise up in protest of something in unison. There are many other similar examples. In life, often if a crisis ensues, some people react in a particular way and others automatically respond to the contagious state of mind, or develop the same feelings and all hell can be unleashed upon the world.

Sometimes, we need to be able to find ourselves a protected spot to make intelligent decisions and react in our own way, rather than being dragged into feeling and responding according to the way of others. But rather than sitting behind the sofa next to a lovely warm radiator (as my cat does,) this 'firework' process equips you with the ability to find space, quiet and calmness of thought; it relaxes the thought by using an initial stimulus (of fireworks) in which the subsequent contrast aids the relaxation.

This is not just useful for calming the mind and relaxing thoughts, it is also useful for keeping calm and maintaining a progressive mindset in a range of life's circumstances. Before you begin with this process, ascertain a colour and sound in your mind that you find to be truly calming. Just get them firmly lodged in your mind: a colour and a sound that you consider to be calming. Then begin.

Step One:

Induce hypnosis using any preferred method. Once you are hypnotised, move on to step two.

Step Two:

Imagine and find yourself in a room, an empty room. A shell of a room that feels safe and secure, and at ease to be in. There are just the plain walls and a door. Establish this image in your mind in the way that is best for you. Once this is established and vivid in your mind, move on to the next step.

Step Three:

You can stand in the centre of the room or sit comfortably within the room, and as you do, start to notice that fireworks begin to be displayed on the walls and ceiling of this room. Notice all the variety of colours, the variety of effects, the variety of noises and sounds that they create. Watch this exciting, noisy and bright display on the walls and ceiling all around you, and tell yourself that with each light, with each sound, you go deeper inside of your mind, and use this time to deepen your self-hypnosis for a while.

When you feel that you have sufficiently deepened your hypnosis and watched the impressive variety of fireworks for a few minutes, then move on to the next step.

Step Four:

Now start to imagine all the fireworks turn to the colour that you thought about prior to starting with this session. Let that colour deeply dominate all the fireworks, and start to imagine that colour filling the room around you and being absorbed by your body and mind. Notice all the sounds changing into the sound you thought of prior to this session, and let that sound softly and gently begin to resonate in the room, and be heard and felt by your mind and body.

Now notice the calmness that develops as you focus on this colour and sound. Imagine spreading the calmness through your body so that it feels as if you are deeply calm and soothed. Absorb the colour and light to the point where you imagine you are glowing with that colour, glowing with that coloured light, with a faint hum of that wonderful calming sound. Bask in the calmness as pure calmness emanates from you, around you and all through you.

Imagine your muscles softening, your nerves doing nothing more than is absolutely necessary, and your entire being feeling centred and at ease. Importantly, notice the clarity of thought that you have, feel the intelligence that you have available to you while you remain in this space, enjoying the calmness. All the time, tell yourself that this takes you deeper into hypnosis. When you really feel like you are emanating this sensation, then move on to the next step.

Step Five:

Now as you continue to enjoy that feeling of calmness, notice that the fireworks start to get noisy again, and that they turn into a multitude of colours again; yet you remain calm, balanced and at ease, glowing with your calmness, retaining a clarity of thought. Start to notice that however loud, exciting, distracting and colourful the fireworks become all around you, however much they dominate the walls and ceiling of the room, you remain calm, at ease and with a clarity of thought. You choose how you feel and how you think, you retain that clarity and your thoughts stay relaxed.

Do this for a while longer and tell yourself that you start to react and respond to life's situations, circumstances and events in the same way. That regardless of what goes on around you, you are able to think intelligently, to reason well and keep your head calm, and to make the best decisions about how to respond and react.

Step Six:

When you have repeated those ideas enough times, count yourself up and out of hypnosis. Remind yourself of your ability to react well to life's situations and go about your day keeping that in mind.

This chapter has shown you how to develop your own relaxation skills and derive the inherent mental and physical benefits that are to be had as a result of developing those skills, learning to relax more deeply and more often in this amplified hypnotic way. Relaxation is often the ideal antidote to anxiety, and so some of the things you have learned here will be very relevant to the next chapter too.

Chapter Eight: Overcoming Anxiety

Anxiety is defined by clinicians as "a fear that persists even when a salient threat is not present" *(Nash and Barnier, 2008)*. 'Anxiety' is such a broad-ranging category of issue that covers fears, phobias, generalised anxiety disorder, post-traumatic stress and many other conditions too. If you look at the section of the DSM (Diagnostic and Statistical Manual of Mental Disorder used by the psychiatry profession) you'll see a large number of variants of anxiety-related disorders.

The Evidence for Using Hypnosis to Deal with Anxiety

There is an incredibly impressive body of evidence supporting the use of cognitive behavioural therapy (CBT) to reduce and alleviate anxiety, which tends to make it the first choice of therapeutic intervention within most countries and their healthcare services *(Chambless and Hollon, 1998)*. As previously mentioned, there is evidence that when hypnosis supplements CBT, it has led to greater clinical gains than when CBT is used on its own *(Kirsch et al., 1995)*. Therefore, when dealing with anxiety, it makes sense for us to make use of combining some CBT methodologies within our self-hypnosis sessions.

The limited studies that have been conducted comparing CBT with hypnotic techniques have shown that hypnosis compares as well or very slightly better than CBT *(Van Dyck and Spinhoven, 1997; Schoenberger at al., 1997; Brom et al., 1989)*. There have been a moderate number of studies that have shown certain stand-alone hypnotic techniques resulting in anxiety being reduced too *(Boutin and Tosi, 1983; Stanton, 1992).*

There are schools of thought, particularly prevalent in academic circles, which state that hypnosis in and of itself is not a therapy; it is actually a tool that can be used in combination with established evidence-based treatments. This is probably not a debate for this book, but either side of the debate, we can benefit from the gains of hypnosis and other techniques from other evidence supported fields to help deal with anxiety (considered in the subsequent chapters of this book).

Ways to Use Self-Hypnosis to Overcome Anxiety

Before the specific step-by-step techniques in this chapter, I want to give you an overview of the classic ways in which we can employ self-hypnosis for reducing anxiety. This is essentially a self-hypnosis book, so I won't be including more information on how to use other techniques from other therapy modalities (if they do not require any self-hypnosis for their effective use) such as, for example, behavioural exposure therapy and the use of thought forms used in CBT. These interventions are likely to be suggested by a therapist and are things you can research or work into your own self-hypnosis sessions if you feel they are of benefit (once you have explored them).

Let's have a look at 3 ways that self-hypnosis can be used to help reduce anxiety then: with physical relaxation, mental imagery and controlling thoughts.

1. Physical Relaxation

A range of relaxation techniques are used when treating anxiety. According to Taylor *(1982)* this is because such relaxation techniques reduce tension in muscles along with accompanying anxiety.

The previous chapter showed how to develop your relaxation skills, which can form the basis of any use of self-hypnosis for reducing anxiety. There are a number of ways that relaxation is categorized therapeutically.

Firstly, there is basic generalised relaxation, which is one of the main benefits of practicing the processes from our previous chapter. When people learn how to deepen their experience of relaxation and practice relaxation skills regularly, they become more relaxed in general in their lives. According to Golden and colleagues *(1987),* the benefits derived from generalised relaxation are not as impressive as those derived from the following two applications of relaxation.

Secondly then, cue-controlled relaxation was mentioned at the end of the previous chapter in a roundabout way. This form of relaxation benefit occurs when people regularly practice relaxation and become so adept at it that they can relax at will ('on command') and with more ease. This is very useful if you wish to apply relaxation when you are in different environments that trigger stress or anxiety: for example, waiting to go into a job interview, during a performance, or in a public situation of some kind.

Thirdly and finally, we have systematic desensitisation. A classic and highly evidence-based technique of psychotherapy that is a central component of early CBT. The aim of systematic desensitisation is to prepare the mind in advance to face adversity. Basically, you learn to imagine being in the stressful or anxiety-inducing situation while maintaining your physical relaxation. You then mentally rehearse being relaxed in that situation which helps you to condition yourself to relax in those real-life situations in the future. There is a step-by-step guide on how to do this with self-hypnosis later in this chapter.

2. Mental Imagery

Research suggests that hypnosis advances our belief in mental imagery *(Sheehan and McConkey, 1982)*, which can be used greatly for our benefit as self-hypnotists. Imagery tends to be used by therapists for dealing with anxiety in a couple of ways.

Firstly, mental imagery can help facilitate relaxation. As mentioned in our previous chapter, imagining being in a safe or comfortable place can enable us to relax more readily. If you hypnotise yourself and then take yourself to a place that you associate with being relaxing, calming, safe and comfortable, then it aids your ability to relax greatly, and you already know how relaxation benefits us. While imagining being in that safe place, the benefits are maximized by also using your internal dialogue to suggest that any tension is fading and draining away, as well as using your cognition to truly believe you are relaxed (made all the more easy with hypnosis). I think with all you have learnt so far in this book, you can do that kind of session without a specific step-by-step protocol to follow.

Secondly, imagery can be used when it comes to imaginal exposure. As discussed already, with some techniques you are asked to imagine being in a particular situation or scenario (in this case, a scenario which induced anxiety in the past). With imagery typically being more vivid with the use of self-hypnosis *(Fromm et al., 1980)* and absorption and focus being enhanced, it is easier to recreate the situations for more therapeutic benefit. You are then required to expose yourself to those situations, while engaging in a number of different therapeutic techniques. One such technique, the already mentioned systematic desensitisation is coming right up, and there are others in the later chapters of this book for you to work with..

When it comes to using evidence-based imaginal exposure techniques, some believe that hypnotherapy should be the number one therapeutic choice, because it helps break down barriers to creating anxiety inducing imagery in the mind that is subsequently used for therapeutic gain *(Spiegel, 1996).*

Another way of utilising mental imagery is to engage in mental rehearsal. One example of this is to imagine the target scenario and apply coping skills; you imagine yourself to be applying coping skills and dealing with the scenario effectively. This chapter will later set out a specific protocol for achieving this.

Systematic Desensitisation

Before we get onto our third central method of reducing anxiety, I want to show you how to use systematic desensitisation with self-hypnosis to reduce anxiety. It incorporates our previous two central methods of mental imagery and physical relaxation.

Although CBT pioneer, Joseph Wolpe, tends to take a great deal of credit for the creation of systematic desensitization as we know it today, there are earlier citations of similar techniques to be found. Wolpe even *(1990)* states that he was influenced by Wolberg's 1948 text book, Medical Hypnosis, which was originally written 10 years prior to Wolpe's 1958 book on the subject, and included Wolberg's techniques of reconditioning and desensitisation. There are citations found earlier than Wolberg too *(Jones, 1924; Herzberg, 1945)* describing exposure and desensitisation. Today, this process has been used in clinical practice for well over half a century and is proven time after time to produce results.

Anyone that has experienced anxiety in the past needs to know that it is most likely a learned response, an old habit. Just like any other habit, physical tension and emotional anxiety can be learned over time and become associated to certain circumstances, events or situations in your life that stimulate anxiety.

It is a core and fundamental belief inherent within modern therapy, and certainly within my consulting rooms, that anything that can be learned can also be unlearned. That is, all habits can be broken. I am not saying that it is easy to break an established habit. However, it can be made easier by a practicing process.

When my wife first took in our cat, Spooky, because he had been abandoned by his previous owners and left without food or shelter for a long time, he mistrusted humans. He actually feared people, which we suspect was due to his poor treatment. You see, even animals can learn to be anxious when they do not necessarily need to. Our own experience, as well as much documented and researched evidence, shows that animals can also be trained to overcome their anxieties. Spooky now loves the affections and attention of humans, and loves being around people in general. So much so that when I am working from home, he jumps all over me and my computer's keyboard to get my attention.

One way to break an old habit is by replacing it with a new habit. Anxiety and relaxation are two mutually exclusive states; they cannot dominate the same body at the same time, the stronger one tends to progressively cancel the weaker one out. By training yourself to relax very deeply, and by facing the things that used to cause anxiety, gradually and systematically, you can use your relaxation skills to cancel out anxiety; in steps and stages, you can replace your anxiety with feelings of calm. All it takes is a little patience and focus.

You'll begin by easily and simply rehearsing some basic relaxation skills, and then facing your fears in the safety of whatever comfortable room or place you choose at the same time. You just use your imagination to picture the things that you want to overcome and dissipate. By running through such a process, you then find that the same feelings of relaxation remain with you outside in the real world, when you have finished the process. Adopt your hypnotic mindset, be expectant with this, encourage yourself throughout and then follow these seven steps.

Prior to beginning, think of something you'd like to have less (or no) anxiety about. On a scale of 0-10, how anxious do you feel about it? With that situation at the back of your mind and that number at the forefront of your mind, proceed with the process. Get in a place and position that will ensure you are undisturbed for the time that you are engaged in this process, and with your arms and legs uncrossed, then begin.

Step One:

Induce hypnosis using any method you choose. Make it a fairly swift process and not one that involves relaxation, as there is much of that within the steps that follow. No deepening process is required here either, as the process itself deepens greatly throughout. Once you have induced hypnosis, proceed to step two.

Step Two:

Run through a progressive relaxation process. Any of your choosing. The one that is used most frequently when this process has been standardised and researched is to imagine tensing muscle groups in turn, then relaxing them. You don't actually tense them, you just imagine tensing them. As you imagine letting go of the tension, you breathe out and notice the relaxation more profoundly.

The key is to go through your entire body systematically and thoroughly and develop a very deep level of relaxation. Tell yourself that you go deeper into hypnosis at the same time. When you are at a very, very deep level of relaxation, move on to the next step.

Step Three:

Now, before we progress to the main crux of this process, scan through your entire body. If you notice any last tiny traces of tension whatsoever, just imagine the feeling turning into a cloud of coloured mist or something similar that appeals to you. Maybe you can just imagine it all relaxing away, melting into nothingness. This is just letting go of any last remnants of anything unwanted and leaving you deeply relaxed before moving on.

Step Four:

Now just imagine the scene you thought about prior to starting with this session, that used to make you feel anxious in some way. While you think of it, remain nicely and deeply relaxed. Think of relaxation, imagine relaxation, focus on letting go more deeply. As you relax, you are neutralising any tension or discomfort that you used to associate with that old stimulus, instead allowing those peaceful feelings to spread into your life and into future situations. Truly get that lodged into your mind as you relax and think of that situation at the same time.

Truly imagine that you are in that scene right now; see it through your own eyes, as if it is actually happening right now, make it seem real, all the time remaining wonderfully relaxed. You are facing those things, being in that place, hearing those sounds and continue to let go and relax deeply.

Now fade that scene completely for a few moments, continue to relax. Calm your mind and smile to yourself inside. As we did right at the very beginning, just before step one, on a scale of 0-10 what was your level of discomfort as you imagined that scene just now? Tell yourself that number and when you know it, move on to the next step.

Step Five:

At this stage, deepen your relaxation by using whatever progressive relaxation method you prefer. Maybe count your breaths from 10 down to zero and saying the word 'soften' again as you drift deeper. Or maybe imagine walking down some stairs while your muscles relax as you go deeper, or imagining all your muscles relaxing again.

Once you are really nice and deeply relaxed again, imagine the very same scene again and as you imagine that, concentrate and focus on remaining beautifully relaxed and at ease. Run through the scene in your mind, the scene that used to make you feel anxious. As you continue to relax, truly imagine that you are in that scene right now, as if it is really happening and continue to let go and relax completely.

Then give yourself a score of 0-10 to rate your discomfort again. Ideally repeat this process over and over until you reach zero. It is recommended that you persist with it and do it a couple more times after you have reached zero.

Step Six:

Imagine that this is going to spread into your real-life scenarios and situations, and tell yourself so. You might also like to do a small ego strengthening routine here that advances your belief that you are reducing your anxiety in that situation (as learned in the first part of this book, include elements about being more mentally calm, confident, competent and so on, as a result of this technique).

Step Seven:

Exit the session by counting from one through to five and opening your eyes.

Practice this process repeatedly for a few days before you then start to place yourself into those situations to see how much you've progressed. You can also use the same relaxation skillset in the actual situation. When you go into those situations, do stay there and really see it through. If you 'escape' from the situation, this negatively reinforces the fact that you feel better by running away instead of facing the situation, and you do not want that.

3. Controlling Thoughts

Following on from our other two central themes for dealing with anxiety using self-hypnosis (with physical relaxation and mental imagery), we now come on to the third theme, which is all about controlling thoughts.

In the next chapter, there is a process included that is referred to as "using cognitions to advance mood", which could easily slot in here with this chapter. It uses imaginal exposure again, that is, you imagine being in the problematic situation (that used to cause anxiety), and you mentally rehearse using positive cognitions while imagining being there. This allows your cognitions to help you feel better and more able to cope with the situation successfully.

Problematic thoughts are very typical of anxiety issues *(Clark, 2005)*. There is evidence to suggest that simply trying to repress the unwanted or anxiety-inducing thoughts makes them more prevalent *(Wenzlaff and Wegner, 2000)*. Rather than trying to repress the thoughts, you are advised to attempt to restructure thoughts. There are a variety of techniques for doing that within this book, though in addition to the brief discussion I offer about them later in this book, you may also want to investigate and explore thought forms as an aid to help you with this.

Spotting Thinking Errors and Self-Hypnosis

Later in this chapter, I will be offering up strategies for employing self-hypnosis for cognitive disputation and restructuring; in simple terms, that is whereby we catch, dispute and restructure negative thoughts, or thoughts that somehow contribute to our anxiety (or any other ongoing problem).

This is all well and good, however, many people often are not even aware that they were having the negative thoughts in the first place. Some of my clients that I work with often do not recognise the negative thoughts they have until they had experienced a number of them and looked back upon their day, thinking it was then too late to do anything about them. We are therefore now going to examine ways we can advance our awareness and become conscious of problematic cognitions in more detail, ideally before or during them happening.

One way to begin practicing becoming more aware of your thoughts is to tune in to yourself at regular intervals throughout your day. For example, as far back as the early 1950s, the book Gestalt Therapy *(1951)*, shared a number of "awareness experiments" designed to help build mindfulness and is often used as a precursor to more advanced mindfulness techniques.

The most basic of these Gestalt awareness experiments was entitled the "ABC" of Gestalt by Fritz Perls. It was as simple as this: "Try for a few minutes to make up sentences stating what you are at this moment aware of. Begin each sentence with the words "now" or "at this moment" or "here and now" *(Perls, Hefferline, and Goodman, 1951 p.31)*.

It is incredibly simple, but encourages the individual to start tuning in and being aware of their ongoing experience.

There are many, many techniques and strategies used by therapists of different backgrounds, designed to help individuals spot unwanted thoughts, which they can then apply thought stopping and restructuring techniques to – the likes of which I shall be sharing later in this book.

First of all then, I offer up a self-hypnosis process that draws upon a number of different therapeutic modalities and enables the self-hypnotist to rehearse the awareness skills within a self-hypnosis session, and then apply those skills in real life. This is going to help you become more aware of problematic thoughts in which to later deal with in a variety of helpful ways.

Think about a typical situation in your life where in the past you may have had unwanted thoughts that you wish to be more aware of and deal with in a more constructive fashion. Or this can be the same anxiety-inducing situation whereby you want to feel relaxed and calm instead. Then keep it in mind ready to use later in this self-hypnosis session. Ensure that you are in a comfortable positive setting, ideally sat, with your arms and legs uncrossed, feet flat on the floor in a place where you'll be undisturbed for the duration of this session. Then proceed with these steps.

Step One:

Induce hypnosis using any method of your choice. Once you have induced hypnosis, move on to step two.

Step Two:

Now imagine being in that target situation. Really imagine being there, seeing through your eyes, noticing the sights, colours, shades of light. Engage with the sounds, those that are near, those that are further away.

Start to feel how you would feel in that place, behave as you usually do and engage with this place just as you would any other time. When you truly feel that you are fully immersed and you have engaged your imagination fully in this place, then move on to the next step.

Step Three:

Continue to imagine being in this place, and while you are really there in your mind, fully engaged and tuned in, use your cognitions (your internal dialogue) and tell yourself what it is that you feel, think and desire in this situation. Just state to yourself all the things that you are noticing and experiencing about yourself in this situation.

Run a commentary to yourself of everything that is going on inside of you: all the stuff that anyone else would not be able to see from the outside. Tell yourself and give yourself an accurate, detailed account of everything.

For example:

> *"I am aware of the urge to leave."*
> *"I am aware of criticising myself."*
> *"I feel inferior to the people I am with."*
> *"I want to shout at the driver of that car."*

Start to notice all the things you say, do, feel, and state it to yourself in your mind, using your internal dialogue. Run through it methodically and in depth and detail, go through it all thoroughly step-by-step and state to yourself everything that is going on within you.

Acknowledge and label all of these habitual experiences that usually go on beneath the surface. As I said previously, give yourself a running commentary on everything that goes on within you. As you give your commentary, start to imagine all the words drift away from you. Imagine they take a physical form and the words drift away, they are distanced and float away from you. Once you have done that in detail, move on to the next step.

Step Three:

Start to imagine that all those words that you told yourself have floated away, and all the feelings, old behaviours and associations that used to be attached to them, have also floated away. Imagine feeling lighter and better, and smiling to yourself.

As you noticed your ongoing experience in that situation (while you commentated on it), realise that by acknowledging and noticing all those things, you let all the feelings go. When you are sure they are all gone, then take a couple of nice deep breaths, as you exhale you may even wish to sigh. Remain in that situation, continue to imagine being there, and then move on to the next step.

Step Four:

Having run through this, having let the feelings go, having tuned in to your thoughts, start to adopt an alternate perspective on the entire situation.

As you look at the situation, explore it intelligently, and as you look at facets of this situation, ask what else could that mean? How else would this be viewed by someone else? See if you can be as flexible as possible, and start to think of lots of different ways to interpret the environment and the situation you're in. When you have done that thoroughly and well, move on to the next step.

Step Five:

Now you are going to distinguish between your thoughts and facts.

Tell yourself and repeat – my thoughts are not facts. Really convince yourself that all the previous thoughts, feelings and internal experiences you used to have in this situation are not necessarily an accurate account of reality. Realise and repeat to yourself that those earlier thoughts and feelings are not facts. They were just an old way of you habitually communicating with yourself.

When you think you have drummed that thought into your head properly and diligently (my thoughts are not facts), having reviewed those earlier thoughts, then move on to the final two steps.

Step Six:

Still in that same situation, still engaging with that place, imagine being there. State some new thoughts, some better thoughts, and deliver to yourself some positive cognitions. Encourage yourself, state something progressive and positive to yourself, give yourself some better thoughts that support and nurture you.

For example:

> *"I feel much better"*
> *"I am capable of change"*
> *"I have taken control"*

Or use any words and statements that are good for you and make you feel better when you repeat them. When you have repeated them enough, you will notice a better sense and feeling within yourself.

Step Seven:

Tell yourself that the more you practice this process, the easier it becomes to do in real-life situations. Then exit hypnosis in the usual fashion by counting from one through to five and opening your eyes.

Practice this process as a self-hypnosis session every day for a week, then start placing yourself in those real-life situations and run through that well-rehearsed process. You'll be spotting unwanted thoughts and removing them before you even realise you are doing it.

You may start to notice that there is a theme to the type of negative thoughts you are having. These negative thoughts are often referred to in the literature as thinking errors or cognitive distortions. David Burns *(1980)* provides us with an influential top ten list of common thinking errors (that I have related to anxiety for the purposes of this chapter, but can relate to other areas of life if you wish to use them in the following chapters:

1. **All-or-nothing thinking.** Thinking this way does not permit us to have any shades of grey; it is black and white, 100 or 0%. Someone may see themselves as a total success or a total failure.

2. **Over-generalisation.** People with anxiety can sometimes think that because a problem happened one time, it will happen every time; they have over-generalised, maybe with disregard to what is the most realistic an outcome.

3. **Mental filter.** This is where people ignore some of the facts and focus on the ones that make them more anxious. Likewise, this is the case with our general outlook sometimes, and we'll be learning a technique to install a happiness filter to remedy this kind of thinking in the next chapter.

4. **Discounting the positives.** Similar to our previous thinking error, but with this people tend to notice the positives, but discount them as unimportant.

5. **Jumping to conclusions.** Making unfounded assumptions.

6. **Magnification or minimalisation.** Exaggerating or trivialising things in a way that makes us feel more anxious.

7. **Emotional reasoning.** When people allow their heart to rule their head in a way that is problematic. As discussed already, our gut feelings are not always 100% reliable or accurate. I don't recommend anyone make big life decisions or plans when they are feeling highly emotional; it'll be much more useful to make decisions about your life when you are balanced and can think soberly.

8. **Should or must statements.** We discussed these in our language section. Albert Ellis refers to these as 'musterbation' which raises a grin with me. When we believe we should or must do something, it implies that we do not want to. We are doing it out of obligation or necessity instead of wishing it.

9. **Labelling.** People often label themselves a failure or no good at something and respond accordingly.

10. **Personalisation or blame.** People taking things too personally or placing incorrect blame upon themselves or others.

Whereby these points can contribute to anxiety, they are also relevant to general levels of happiness too, and can be applied to a wide range of areas in our life. This list is certainly not exhaustive and several overlap, but it gives a rough idea for us to apply some intelligent reasoning and logic when we start to be more aware of our thoughts.

In CBT, clients are taught to use Socratic questioning techniques to seek out the real-life evidence for such problematic thoughts: to look for logic, balance, reality and so on. However, with this being a self-hypnosis book, we're going to look at what self-hypnosis techniques we can use to diffuse these anxiety-inducing thoughts.

Updating Your Thoughts

With the awareness of our thoughts in place and developing an ongoing attitude and internal environment of awareness, the self-hypnotist's internal dialogue can then be adapted, changed and updated if necessary. We have a wide number of ways of doing that: using suggestion as we have learned about already, or simply being progressive with our internal dialogue as per our language considerations in the earlier chapters.

Thought Stopping

Stopping certain thoughts in their tracks can help limit and prevent unwanted internal dialogue *(Meyers and Schleser, 1980).* Thought stopping shows the self-hypnotist how to interrupt and stop unwanted thoughts as they happen, or prior to them happening. Sometimes this might involve using the word "stop" or imagining a stop sign flashing in the imagination, or it could involve a number of ways of getting the internal dialogue to be quiet or turned down.

With frequent and persistent use, the unwanted thoughts tend to lessen. One very practical way to do this and incorporate some of our previous themes, is to start using a thought form. There are many types of thought forms from within and outside of the field of cognitive behavioural therapy that I use within my therapeutic work to help clients update their cognitions and internal dialogue. Here with regards to anxiety (or other topics covered in this book), a very simple form can be used to heighten awareness of our internal dialogue and also to help restructure our internal dialogue.

You simply divide a page into 3 columns. You keep the form with you throughout your days, and keep vigilant and aware of your thoughts. If and when a problematic thought occurs in your internal dialogue, you write it down unabridged and unedited in the first column. You get to see it exactly as it is and the thought becomes exposed and vulnerable. It is also moved out of your head by doing this, which ceases the way the brain makes it worse and amplified by letting it rattle around in your head.

In the second column, you then write down how you think that thought can detrimentally affect you and your anxiety (or performance or happiness etc.). You are refuting the thought here and applying some rationale and intelligent reasoning, showing yourself it is of little value to continue with such thoughts.

Then in the third column you write up a replacement, progressive, beneficial thought that you say to yourself with meaning, purpose and volition. You then repeat it inside of your mind a few times for it to start restructuring your thoughts.

For example, I work with a lot of athletes. An example that I give in my Hypnosis for Running *(2013)* book, is whereby a runner may catch himself thinking, *"I can't be bothered to run today."* The runner writes that down exactly as it occurred in the first column. Then in the second column, he writes that *"by thinking this, I am talking myself out of training, which could negatively affect the goal I want to achieve of running that half marathon in June."* Then, having given it some thought, he writes in the third column, *"I really want to get out and enjoy a run today, I know how good I'll feel afterwards."* He then repeats that a few times with a sense of conviction and belief to truly get it registered.

The negative thought in the internal dialogue has been

1.   Spotted.

2.   Disputed.

3.   Restructured.

Some forms will encourage you to measure your level of belief and assess the ownership you have of your thoughts, and you may wish to explore and investigate other more comprehensive thought forms to monitor your internal dialogue. However, the method here is going to be useful, effective and simple.

Turning Negative Internal Dialogue Into Positive

With this type of approach, we aim to allow positive thoughts to dominate and prevail in our internal dialogue. However, we don't just want one set of thoughts to be shouting over another set of thoughts. Increasing the use of positive internal dialogue may well help us reduce the negative or limiting internal dialogue.

A favourite process of mine that I use in my therapy rooms often has it roots in cognitive behavioural therapy and is referred to in the field of hypnotherapy as the cognitive mood induction (already referred to in this book later titled 'using cognitions to enhance mood'). The process encourages you to accept the negative thoughts if they happen, not resist or fight them, but let them simply lead into more positive and progressive thoughts. This process is explained in depth in the next chapter.

Thought Stopping With Self-Hypnosis

In behavioural cognitive hypnotherapy, one of the stock processes to teach our clients, is to dispute thoughts that lead us to catastrophise, and we ideally then learn how to restructure our thoughts in a number of ways.

Catastrophising makes people anxious. Here though, I am simply going to show you how to dispute the thoughts effectively with self-hypnosis, and other upcoming techniques are going to help with developing some thinking skills to enhance what we do and develop cognitive restructuring.

With this process, you are simply going to run through typical situations in your life, where you have had negative thoughts leading to thinking the worse, and you are going to interrupt the thought process mid-flow with an alarming method of disputation. Before starting with the process, get a good idea of the typical situations where you might have negative thoughts that lead to you catastrophising or expecting a negative outcome. It is also important for you to accept the idea that negative thoughts are not useful and can cause problems, and that you intend and expect them to stop as a result of this session – frame things in a progressive and positive way, develop expectation, and then get stuck in to the step-by-step process that follows:

Step One:

Induce hypnosis using any process of your choice. Once you have induced hypnosis, move on to step two.

Step Two:

As vividly as you can, imagine yourself in the kind of situation where you would typically experience negative thoughts.

Really imagine being there. See the sights of the place, the colours, the shades of light and detail. Hear the sounds of the place, notice the distinctions of the sounds around you and just engage in this place. Allow being in this place to take you deeper inside your mind and when you are truly engaged and tuned in to this place, move on to the next step.

Step Three:

Start to take the actions you usually take in that situation and then pay close attention to your thoughts and how you think in that situation.

Talk to yourself and describe to yourself what your thoughts are in that situation. Start to translate your feelings into words and describe to yourself the kinds of mental imagery that happens in your mind in this scenario.

Truly explain to yourself all the thoughts, ideas, imagery and feelings that you have in this typical situation. Run through the situation in its entirety.

When you have done that in detail, then move on to the next step.

Step Four:

Here comes the fun. Run through the previous step again in your mind, but this time as soon as the unwanted, negative thought and accompanying feelings starts to happen in the slightest, you imagine wild, loud sirens going off in your head, and there right in front of your eyes pops up a bright and large STOP sign flashing noisily before you.

As soon as the old negative train of thought starts you create the most alarming noise in your mind, the most vivid, bright STOP sign that fills your entire imagination; fills it entirely. It dominates your awareness.

Practice this step over and over, making things more vivid, more real and encourage yourself to make it more forceful each time you practice doing this. Take responsibility here too, and be as creative as you like in making the stop imagery as alerting as possible to interrupt the negative thought before it gets started. When you feel that you have got a hang of stopping the old thought as it starts, then move on to the next step.

Step Five:

Following on from that rather frenetic step. Take a couple of minutes out now and engage in some progressive relaxation. Just imagine relaxation spreading through your body: you can do this with colour, you can simply imagine muscles relaxing, you can tell them to soften, you can imagine tensing muscles and letting them relax thereafter, or you can simply spread a relaxing sensation through your body using your intention and imagination. Spend some time to get your body deeply and beautifully relaxed. When you are feeling really relaxed, move on to the next step.

Step Six:

Think of a progressive, positive, encouraging statement that you can say to yourself in that same situation in the future. Word it in the present tense, make it be something you want, not something you don't want, and let it be supportive and using the words that appeal to you, get them set up in your mind.

Now run through the same situation that we began with, while you are wonderfully relaxed, run through that same scenario and repeat this new internal dialogue statement to yourself. Say it with meaning, and say it in a way that is undeniably convincing to you, say it in a way that makes you feel that you believe it to be true. Run through the scenario 3-5 times while relaxed, repeating your new positive thought, your positive statement to yourself in your mind. When you have repeated it all those times, move on to the next step.

Step Seven:

Tell yourself that you plan to bring the benefits of this session with you into real-life situations from now on. Tell yourself that you are going to STOP negative thoughts if they occur again, you are going to relax and replace them with positive statements in your mind.

This is going to stop catastrophisation, for sure. Bring yourself up and out of hypnosis by counting from 1 to 5, take a deep energising breath, wiggle your fingers and toes and open your eyes.

Practice this process daily for a week in your mind using self-hypnosis. Then go and place yourself in those situations and start to practice using this skill, enjoying taking control and stopping 'awfulising' in its tracks.

I am now going to share some further step-by-step techniques aimed at helping you reduce anxiety. These techniques incorporate a range of themes and strategies while introducing new concepts too. They involve mental imagery, mental rehearsal and thought control to some extent.

Mentally Rehearsing, Coping to Mastery

This upcoming process is aiming to overcome anxiety by engaging in positive future mental imagery: mental rehearsal. Mental rehearsal is a process that has a number of applications but usually involves running through specific challenging situations in our imagination, while imagining dealing with them well in order that we prepare ourselves for coping in real life. This particular process is certainly applicable for a wide number of applications, not just anxiety. It is actually probably better applied to other areas, however, I wanted to include it in an earlier chapter, as it gives an understanding of a number of key approaches that will be underpin others in the later parts of the book. I was originally taught this process in class by Donald Robertson whose books you can find in the reference section of this book. He has influenced my own work greatly. I have adapted it to be used with self-hypnosis.

On a plane journey to a holiday destination a few years ago, some good friends were on the same flight as us (this tends to happen when you take flights going from Bournemouth airport) and were enjoying having their young daughter on a plane with them for the first time. Many might be worried about such a thing, not these guys. As we waited in the airport, they were all excited and happy about the prospect and then when the plane took off, she was interested, excited and thoroughly loved the experience in its entirety, all the way laughing while we landed.

There was much preparation that went on for this to happen. They did not consciously choose to do what they did, but in fun they had pointed at planes in the sky and talked about being on one of those when they played in the garden. They imagined and played games imagining being on planes, and got a marvelously good level of comfortable mental association, therefore it all panned out perfectly.

Most of the people that come to see me for therapy have learned somewhere along the line to cope in some way with their issues. They have not mastered dealing with the issue, otherwise they would not need to see me. This next technique is a process that allows anyone to move from coping to mastering just by using the imagination, thoughts in combination with self-hypnosis, so that you can (albeit metaphorically) be flying without a care too.

Prior to starting with this process, for a moment close your eyes and think of a situation that you feel uncomfortable about. This is the situation that we'll use throughout this process. Ideally a situation that you'd like to feel wonderfully at ease, confident and comfortable about in the future.

With that situation in mind, imagine the situation like it is a film clip that has a distinct beginning, middle and ending. Like a scenario whereby you imagine that the scene begins at a point before anything has happened, goes through the discomfort of the situation, and ends when it is over and you feel safe once again. Run through that entirely and thoroughly in your mind before you even begin the step-by-step process.

Having done that, briefly and starting at the beginning go ahead and describe the sequence of events out loud to yourself, or someone else that you can get to listen. Just verbalise it and make sure it sounds right and is a worthwhile situation to be dealt with. Then give yourself a score of between 0-10 about how confident you feel about the situation right now having run through it. Maybe make a note of that score - this is going to help us measure your progress later on. Now you are ready to move on and get into the process.

Step One:

Induce hypnosis using whichever method you choose. Then, when you are hypnotised, proceed to step two.

Step Two:

Firstly, you are going to dissociate and distance yourself from the chosen situation that is to be worked on in this session. You do that by simply imagining that you are seated in a comfortable chair in your own private cinema. You are going to watch a film clip of that situation, the one you ran through prior to starting this. This time, it is going to be viewed in a different way though. You're going to view things from a distance, and feel more detached, neutral and objective about them.

From here onwards, you can still think about the target situation, but you do so in a way that is much more helpful, progressive and constructive. What we want to happen here is for you to be able to face those old negative, unwanted emotions, feelings and thoughts and learn from them. Heck, maybe even grow stronger as a result of them. Now bring the cinema screen to life and see yourself on the screen at the beginning of that imagined situation. Hit the pause button for a moment.

In a moment, you are going to watch the things you were worried might happen. Run it through including the beginning, middle, and end. Tell yourself that the more you watch, the more calm, relaxed and confident you feel. Face those old, unwanted fears, worries or anxieties from this distanced position, and just drain all the negative feelings away. Maybe you can imagine them as colours, or hear them, or just assume that they are draining in whatever way is best for you.

Do that right now, watch yourself going through the scenario. Once you have arrived at the end of that scene, fade the screen, blank it out, pull a curtain over it and relax. You could also use good progressive relaxation process here, just in case there was any anxious feelings creeping in. Do all you can to relax yourself more than before.

When you now think about that same situation, how self-confident do you feel about coping with it, on a scale from 0-10, what number do you have? How higher is it than it was before? Cool, eh? Repeat this process at least two more times, remembering to score yourself after each time. Then move on to the next step.

Step Three:

Having done that at least three times, you now use your imagination and actually put yourself in that same situation. This time you are seeing things through your own eyes, hearing through your own ears and feeling what it is like to be in the situation. As vividly as you can, imagine being there and it's happening here and now.

While you are there, deliver some powerful messages to yourself, affirming that *"I can do this"* or *"I feel calm"* or *"I am in control of myself"*, or whatever kind of internal dialogue helps enhance how you feel in this situation.

Imagine that you are now coping with that situation in a more calm, relaxed and confident manner. Not perfect yet, though better than before. Start at the beginning, and imagine yourself handling things in a more progressive and capable manner. Then once you have reached the end of the clip, with you in it, blank out the screen, fade the picture or pull a curtain over it all and relax, as much as you possibly can. Again, using whatever relaxation technique is best for you.

When you now think about that situation, on a scale of 0-10 how self-confident do you feel about coping with it? How much higher is that number now? Repeat this process at least two more times, remembering to score yourself after each time. Then move on to the next step.

Step Four:

This step is the climax, the crescendo, the mastery being met: the fun.

Finally then, imagine yourself having totally mastered the same situation and dealing with it in a completely calm, relaxed and confident manner. You may want to repeat any internal dialogue or messages to yourself again, saying them with vigour and with a sense of really meaning it. Imagine that you are now handling that situation to the best of your ability, as calm, relaxed, and confident as you can imagine. It is personal to you, so do this in whatever way you deem to be the best of your abilities.

Again, as before, start at the beginning, and imagine yourself experiencing things in as progressive and comfortable way as possible, as if it is happening right now. When you've reached the end, blank out the screen and relax. Take a really nice deep breath and relax. Again, when you think about that situation, how self-confident do you feel about coping with it, on a scale from 0-10, what number do you have? You can repeat this until you get to ten, if for any reason you have not already.

Step Five:

Exit hypnosis by counting from one through to five.

Practice this technique over and over again. It'll make a huge difference. Then think about going and taking some action that is undeniably convincing to you that you are making this progressive change.

Using the Worst Case Scenario for Benefit

This next technique has a similar theme. Judith Beck *(2011)* describes a process to help overcome anxiety for a wide range of situations that could cause us to worry or be fearful. The process is one of a number of mental imagery techniques that she incorporates into her work. This process again asks you to engage in positive future mental imagery. However, this process also asks you to imagine the worst-case scenario happening too. By doing so, you get to see how unlikely this is and that there is realistically far less to worry about or become anxious about. It also has a desensitising effect as a result of the exposure.

In early 2013, I had been saying it to my current students, my friends, my clients, my family, *"as soon as my cognitive behavioural hypnotherapy certificate is completed, I'll have much more time to focus on getting things straight and into a routine again..."*

The course went wonderfully well and was completed. Then, back in the office, I remembered that we were launching a new audio programme in the coming weeks, and it had not been fully written, let alone recorded. Then I also remembered I was running two marathons in less than 3 months time, which I needed to train hard for following injury. There was my day-to-day business to be run, and of course I wanted to spend time with my family too.

I knew I'd cope, I knew I had the skills to deal with such things, as I knew I had done much more than this in shorter timeframes in the past, so I was not too stressed about it. In fact, a little bit of stress keeps me firing on all cylinders and working smart. I was not imagining the world caving in, and I was not imagining the worst things that could possibly go wrong. Though I did do on Monday when I had the day off. I went to the beach with my son, we went to the Bournemouth flying club café and watched the planes, then we went out for dinner and had a lovely time. When I put him to bed, I spent some time imagining the worst-case scenario of what could go wrong with the crazy workload I had at the time. Yep, you read it correctly, I imagined the world imploding when I got to work the next day.

Let me explain.

The strategy that is coming up next involves you rehearsing your desired outcome in your imagination while hypnotised, so that you feel capable of doing the same in the real world. This self-hypnosis process works with the fact that we spend much of our time running simulations of reality through our minds. Some consider it a benefit, but it can also cause us problems, as we often react to our own thinking and imagining *about* our reality, just as we do to actual perceptions and real-life experiences.

Possibly more importantly though, as we react to our own thoughts and internal dialogue, we can become more detached from the reality we actually perceive of our life. For example, so many people tend to negatively dwell upon events and circumstances, imagining the worst possible scenario happening, or imagining that they will be unable to cope with the event, or turning it into a catastrophic in some way.

It is part of our 'fight/flight' response. Those people tend to feel anxious about and avoid situations that seem likely to turn out badly for them. Scenarios that generate strong negative feelings of this sort, tend to stick in our minds, perhaps because these feelings seem so real to us. We get snared by this way of thinking. Each time we imagine life turning out in these negative ways, we generate feelings and real physiological responses associated with danger and catastrophe. Before we know it, we may have convinced ourselves that this negative interpretation of the situation is inevitable. We'll then either avoid the situation altogether, or cause it to go wrong in the way we imagined.

This type of thinking blocks our ability to make the situation turn out in the best way and achieve a potential desired outcome. Rather than really going for it and engaging with the event to the best of your abilities, you end up self-fulfilling your worst fears. This is widely referred to as performance anxiety. Performance anxiety describes a situation where you are so fearful about how you will do, that your attention and imagination get stuck, and this results in you becoming tense or anxious, and so you prevent yourself from being able to do what you could have done relatively easily, if you had simply relaxed.

This next self-hypnosis technique capitalises on the relationship between thinking, feeling, imagining, and the resulting performance. It ends the anxiety and generates positive self-fulfilling prophecies. You'll start this process, as unusual as it may sound, by imagining the worst possible outcome, letting yourself experience all the bad feelings and negative consequences that go with that unwanted outcome.

Then you imagine a completely contrasting scenario, making everything work out well in your mind. By practicing this kind of imagined scene, you show yourself that there is nothing to get anxious about. You show yourself that the very worst that could happen is not anywhere near bad as you may have previously feared. You show yourself that you really are capable of making it work out right and of performing at your best. You don't even have to imagine the best outcome – you might simply imagine the most likely, the most realistic, and then get your mind accustomed to reality according to your intelligently reasoned thoughts.

Get yourself into a comfortable position, ideally sat upright with your arms and legs uncrossed, in a place where you'll be undisturbed for the duration of this exercise. Have in mind the situation that you'd like to feel comfortable and capable in, then follow these simple steps.

Step One:

Induce hypnosis in whichever way you choose.

Step Two:

Start to imagine that situation, event or circumstance that you want to have an agreeable outcome with. Imagine that the more vivid you make the scene, and the more you focus upon it, the deeper you go into hypnosis.

Continue to imagine the scenario progressing now. The day of the event/circumstance arrives. Imagine everything that could go wrong, does go wrong. This might involve you getting up late, or waking in a bad mood or with a headache or feeling under the weather in some other way.

Then imagine the entire day occurring in stages, and everything continues to go wrong throughout. Move through the day, all the way up to the actual event or crucial important moment for you to act, engage, perform, or whatever it is you want to do. Again, imagine that everything that could go wrong, does go wrong and turns out badly.

Add further negative details to this scenario; maybe add physiological symptoms that are evidence of you not coping well, such as your hands shaking, sweating profusely, thinking calamitous thoughts or your mind going totally blank. Maybe even imagine making a fool of yourself and any other fears you had about this scenario actually occurring.

Now start to consider the impact of this imagined failure. Let the unwanted feelings grow. Notice how other people respond and react to your failure. Colour this scenario with any relevant frustration, embarrassment, or other unwanted emotive response. When you have enough of those negative feelings as is useful for now, move on to the next step.

Step Three:

Take a couple of deep breaths. Imagine a curtain closing across your mind, or 'white out' the content of your imagination, or imagine the scene getting smaller and fading into the distance. Then focus exclusively upon your breathing. Upon your exhalation, imagine your body relaxing more and more. As you breathe out start to state some progressive, strong cognitions. Consider saying to yourself something along these lines:

> *"I don't have to feel this way. I'm free."*
> *"I'm in control of my life, I choose what happens."*
> *"I feel good being me, I know I am capable."*
> *"I am better than this."*

Say these words with belief and conviction. In a way that you find to be truly believable. State them with assurance and a sense of 'knowing' them to be true. Repeat the words to yourself as you breathe out strongly. Start to imagine you are breathing out the unwanted feelings and the last remnants of the old unwanted scenario. Let it be gone. Breathe out strongly and powerfully, relax your body, dispel the old images and feelings; this should happen completely with about 5-6 breaths or so.

If you feel a little bit light-headed, just relax, let your breathing regulate, imagine you are going deeper into hypnosis. Then once the old, unwanted feelings have fully dissipated, move on to the next step.

Step Four:

Consider how you want things to turn out, think about your desired outcome. Think about how you want to think, feel, act, and react in that situation so that things turn out as you want them to. Tell yourself that you are consciously choosing for this desired, progressive, healthy outcome to happen. Tell yourself you are taking control.

Run through events in your imagination again. Make it all as vivid as you possibly can. Imagine everything going ideally for you. It does not have to be perfect; it can be grounded in reality. See the sights (details, colours, shades of light etc.), hear the sounds (those that are near and far away), and feel how good it feels for this outcome to be happening.

Perhaps imagine waking up in the morning after a revitalising and invigorating period of sleep. Maybe you imagine yourself doing self-hypnosis before getting out of bed, imagining the day ahead going wonderfully well – plan for it and expect an ideal outcome.

Run through the day; being in a good mood with high, expectant spirits. Notice things going well and turning out right throughout the day. You might imagine that on occasions throughout the day, you prepare by using self-hypnosis and seeing things turning out right. Imagine the day working out exactly as you would realistically and ideally, hoping it to turn out well. Again, notice the reactions and responses of those you come into contact with –

notice how they respond to you in every way. Enjoy their responses and reactions, let those feed your own positive response to this scenario. Work your way right up to the action, the key point, the performance....

Then notice it going ideally and wonderfully well. Experience the thoughts, ideas and feelings that accompany your success. Let the good, personal feelings spread through your body, You might imagine them as a colour, spreading through you, building and amplifying. Feel accomplished, feel proud, feel in control and spend all the time you want just basking in these feelings, continuing to encourage and support yourself with your thoughts. Once you have enjoyed this for long enough, move on to the final step.

Step Five:

Exit hypnosis. Count yourself up and out, or wiggle your fingers and toes, breathe a couple of deeper energising breaths and open your eyes as you get reoriented to your surroundings.

This is a great process to "psych yourself up" and boost performance in a wide number of areas of your life, as well as reducing anxiety. It is best used to prepare yourself for what lies ahead by mentally rehearsing in a focused fashion. For it to be the most beneficial, you ought to practice it repeatedly for a few days or even a couple of weeks leading up to your desired outcome or event.

If you have no strong concerns, worries, or anxieties about the situation to begin with, or if you feel too tense, fearful, or uptight to feel comfortable about imagining your worst possible scenario, then you can simply omit step 2 and 3. This type of imaginative rehearsal combined with self-hypnosis is one of the most easy strategies to apply, and it can yield some of the most impressive results when it comes to overcoming or dealing with a range of anxiety-related matters. Enjoy it.

Chapter Nine: Mood Elevation

I was originally going to refer to this chapter as 'dealing with depression', but in addition to it sounding rather flat, to suggest that self-hypnosis can cure depression would probably be misleading. The evidence base is limited for applying hypnosis as a treatment for depression. Historically, using hypnosis to treat depression has been frowned upon and actively discouraged. It has not been until more recent decades that major contributors such as Michael Yapko *(1992, 2001, 2006)* have led us to think differently. However, as a result of hypnosis being traditionally discouraged from being used in treating depression, we have very little empirical evidence to draw upon for this application of hypnosis.

We can draw upon a wide range of related studies and evidence though; applications that do help depressed individuals, such as managing anxiety, feeling more capable and enhancing mood, which is the main focus of the strategies offered in this chapter *(Lynn et al., 2000; Montgomery et al., 2000; Schoenberger, 2000).* At the time of publishing this book, one single study had been conducted that specifically targeted using hypnosis to treat depression; Alladin and Alibhai *(2007)* showed that hypnosis used with cognitive behavioural therapy produced better results than cognitive behavioural therapy alone.

Many applications of hypnosis and self-hypnosis help people to feel happier. One key way of doing this is to build positive expectancy. The major therapeutic contributions of Aaron Beck

(1967, 1976, 1979), Albert Ellis *(1987, 1994, 1997)* and Martin Seligman *(1989, 1990)* highlighted that many people who experience depression (which is, according to statistics from the mental health charity MIND, one in four of us at some stage in our lives in the UK) had negative expectations and felt a sense of hopelessness in life. Therefore, targeting our self-hypnosis sessions at increasing our levels of positive expectancy is going to be useful.

Using the types of strategies and techniques that I have described in previous chapters will also help to control mood. The processes of mentally rehearsing positive outcomes, relaxing more, being progressive with your internal dialogue, engaging in cognitive strategies and using the imagery processes, all give the self-hypnotist more reason to feel good.

I do want to mention your internal dialogue here again, because that affects and influences your mood massively; the most powerful influence in your life is you. The things you allow to go on inside your head influence you far more than anything I can offer up in this book,. Therefore as we look at these ways of enhancing mood and developing a culture of happiness in your life, please be sure to incorporate as much as possible from the previous chapters, and build upon that material.

Discover How You Attribute Success and Failure

Lots of the previous chapters have offered up processes, techniques and strategies that have a bi-product of enhancing confidence in ourselves and building inner strength, along with a belief in ourselves (self-efficacy). When we are looking at taking control of our mood, many people I encounter in my consulting rooms are troubled by what they deem to be previous failures, to the point where it is out of perspective and potentially affecting their life detrimentally.

If we ever perform, behave or act in a way that is not to our liking, or even make a mistake with some part of our life, then the key is to focus forwards instead of replaying it repeatedly and letting the poor experience dominate in any way. Instead of having a simmering notion of failure, we can start to uplift and learn from those so-called failures by framing and perceiving each as a real-life opportunity to learn, and as a direct means to enhance and better our own behaviour, and in turn build our self-confidence and mood.

We need to adopt a mindset that is always encouraging us to look forward with positive expectation, rather than look back at mistakes. There is going to be time to review the failures as learning experiences. One of the best ways to help encourage this type of solution-focused, progressive thinking and to adopt an internal environment of this kind, is to adapt the work of Martin Seligman *(1990)* and his formulation of how to increase optimism.

Seligman found that upon measuring the levels of optimism that individuals had, the ones that were more optimistic tended to perform better and were happier in life. The way optimism is explained in his work is in terms of the way people respond to their own success and failure.

It is this attribution theory that states that humans need to explain why events happen. We explain to ourselves why we performed well or badly, and we attribute things to our success and failure. We find or invent causes for things that happen to us. It is not necessarily the real reason the thing occurs, but it is the way a person interprets the cause of the thing that happened.

You are encouraged to examine your own thoughts and see how you attribute certain reasons for your success or failure. Some people think they were lucky when they have done incredibly well, but, for example, to go through all the training, to build work experience that contributes to a promotion is surely not down to luck, is it? Others might say they did well because of all that effort, hours of training and dedication, which is a different way to attribute success. The simple way to enhance your awareness of how you attribute failure and success is to do the following simple steps:

Step One:

Induce hypnosis by using your preferred chosen method.

Step Two:

Deepen the hypnosis by running through a successful life experience. Imagine being there, performing in that way and run through it in detail, engaging as many of your senses as possible. As you think about the event, reflect upon it and ask yourself the reasons for your success, noticing your thoughts without editing them at all – trust your initial response.

Step Three:

Deepen further by running through an experience that did not go as you wanted, just observe the event, without getting into it too much. Note what you did and then ask yourself the reasons for the results you got, and then notice what your responses are. Again, make sure you do not edit your thoughts, let them be as authentic as possible, so that you get the honest account of what you do inside your mind.

Step Four:

Exit hypnosis and make a note of what the thoughts were. Note how you attribute success and failure.

Step Five:

Finally, now think of the kind of thoughts that you can affirm to yourself and dominate your thoughts with these as you go forward. This will help you to be more progressive and truthful about how you attribute your success or failure, and to ensure that you are not getting things out of perspective.

This is a nice and simple process to help you understand how you attribute success or failure, which is really important for developing a progressive mindset to advance mood.

Using Rational Emotive Therapy For Enhanced Optimism

Having looked at how optimists and pessimists attribute different things to their success and failure, I want to share a process that could easily fit into virtually any other chapter in this book, but I think warrants being used to build our positive, happy mindset and positive expectation in life.

The previously mentioned Seligman *(1990)* does not, of course, endorse total optimism. A total optimist would have trouble seeing and correcting problems in life. As discussed earlier, analysing a failure for its true causes can be of great help in overcoming problems. It is important for self-improvement to maintain a balance between optimism and taking responsibility for yourself. Neither a totally optimistic nor a totally pessimistic attitude, leads you to examine realistically your problems with any hope of improvement.

Using Ellis' Rational-Emotive Therapy to be More Optimistic

We looked at how to identify the way you attribute success or failure. Once armed with that information, you are in a position to work out how best to enhance your optimism – and, according to the research, being more optimistic about your life experiences, enhances your actual performance.

It was Seligman *(1990)* who took the theories of Albert Ellis, and applied them to his optimism work. Seligman suggested building upon Ellis' Rational Emotive Therapy in order to override the falsely pessimistic thought processes, and enhance the more optimistic ones.

Using self-hypnosis, we identified how to attribute a cause to our good and bad performances. When dealing with pessimistic clients in my consulting rooms, I often use the process based upon Ellis' Rational Emotive Therapy ABCDE framework, which provides us with a way to enhance optimism and move towards more successful, progressive thoughts.

This ABCDE framework states that each of us experience Adversity (A) or an **Activation (A)** of some kind each and every day. This can vary from seemingly small things to deal with, such as a light bulb needing replacing, to much bigger, more profound things, such as dealing with the loss of someone close to you, or a change of career. If I illustrate this from the perspective of a runner; a relevant example may be a poor training run, or even a skipped training run, or a race where you failed to achieve your desired outcome or set goal.

Whether these experiences are major or minor, they get us thinking about the reasons for things occurring, which then results in us developing a **Belief (B)** about the situation, the circumstances, and how we relate ourselves to that situation and occurrence. Now that we have a firmly rooted belief set up inside of our mind, there are now emotional **Consequences (C)**, which result in response to our belief. If we develop irrational beliefs about life events, then we generate irrational emotions. These are beliefs though, but not necessarily the truth. In order to deal with any irrational beliefs, we subsequently **Dispute (D)** them, using disputation methods, and once they are successfully dealt with by disputation and are seen as they are, in perspective, this in turn **Energises (E)** you.

With all this in mind, let's continue to apply this to a runner who is problematically being too pessimistic about their performance. Let's move towards being more optimistic and enhance the subsequent performance.

(A) is the Activation that appears to produce C, a Condition or an emotional consequence.

After a poor time in a race (A) for example, a runner might be disheartened (C) and even think about not running anymore. (C) is the emotional consequence and condition that is created by (B).

(B) Is the Belief, often created in response to (A). Rational Emotive Therapy suggests that it is not actually the poor performance that has caused the runner to be disheartened but (B), the Belief of the athlete.

If this belief is a negative, pessimistic type of belief, the runner is now shown how to dispute that belief and is encouraged to Dispute (D) the pessimism and negative belief, and thereby Energises (E) themself to move forward to better performances, and is energised to change the way they perceive the poor performance.

There are many ways to dispute thoughts and dispute our reasons for pessimistically thinking about our success and failure. One way of doing this was explained in a previous chapter, where you were asked to stop (STOP!) certain thoughts in your mind if they were negative. Another way is to use a thought form (as previously explained),that is noting the thoughts occurring and how they contribute to the negative belief, and then writing down a more constructive thought and belief to have.

Another way is to simply ask Socratic questions of the belief (as previously mentioned): do you have any evidence for this? What proof do you have that this is the case? Another way is to mentally rehearse success, as you have been doing with our mental rehearsal techniques. The other way is to enjoy some progressive and positive self-hypnosis sessions that encourage and help to build a positive outlook, which is what I have for you next.

Building Internal Encouragement

The marathon running bug hit me the year before I decided to run my first. I watched the TV coverage of all those people running together throughout the streets for London marathon. The City was just about closed. In addition to the thousands of people that were running in the event, there were more thousands lining the 26.2 miles of the course.

When I first started participating in races and getting into marathon training and running, someone said that it is a great idea to write your name on the front of your running vest, then throughout the race the crowds will keep on shouting your name and giving personal encouragement. It is such a wonderful tonic in busy races. It is amazing how different it is to run on a street lined with thousands and thousands of people, shouting and encouraging you, compared to running alone on a rainy, cold, dark evening ,or a grey, windy morning, with only your own internal dialogue and MP3 player for company.

I also remember when the world record holder marathon runner, our very own Paula Radcliffe, ran the London marathon for the first time - every inch of the course, she was greeted with cheers and encouragement that was unparalleled to anything I had seen before at a marathon event. She led within the first couple of miles and destroyed the field. She made the world's greatest marathon runners look ordinary and herself look superhuman. You just know that everyone watching at home was cheering her on and encouraging her too. This often happens for the home team at a football match, where the crowd supports and encourages their players so much more. The home team are said to have an advantage, as they are playing in front of more of their own supporters.

I believe that we all need some of that kind of encouragement from time to time. This is especially true when we want to make positive and powerful changes in our lives for our own betterment. In previous chapters, I have written a great deal about internal dialogue, and I recommend that your own internal dialogue supports and encourages you. Take a moment out here to imagine this scenario. First of all, think of someone that you love: a child or your spouse or best friend, or any other dearly beloved person in your life. Imagine that they were really trying to achieve something, truly trying to achieve a personal goal. Now imagine that a total stranger came and belittled their efforts. The stranger told them that they could not do it and they might as well give up. Imagine the stranger said that they should not have tried in the first place and their efforts will amount to nothing!

How would that make you feel? To understate it, I guess you would feel annoyed at the stranger's sentiments. You are likely to defend your loved one, aren't you? Maybe you'd like to box the ears of the stranger! In contrast, what would you say to that loved one to encourage them and support them? Take a moment out to think about that. How would you encourage them to successfully achieve and apply themselves?

So often the kind of thing that the stranger was saying, is the kind of thing that people say to themselves. You would not tolerate that sort of thing being said to a loved one, as you have just demonstrated, yet you may well be just as guilty and harmful in the way that you communicate to yourself. Not just with your internal dialogue, it could be with your belief about yourself and your actions in life. Encouragement should not just be reserved for sports stars, or babies learning to walk. You never hear anyone saying to a baby, that was a pathetic attempt to walk, you are rubbish at walking, just give up and get back in that Moses basket! We all need encouragement as often as we can. Even if we are not getting as much as we should from others, we can encourage ourselves.

My brother still jokes about the time him and I ran the Bristol half marathon together a few years ago. We were going for a personal best time at this race, and in the last few miles we were battling ourselves, our aching legs and lungs were readying to burst! We encountered a steep hill that most runners were groaning at the prospect of scaling at this late stage in the race. As we got over the hill and carried on speeding along the flat road, trying to catch our panting breath, my brother was laughing at me and I asked him what he was laughing at.

He said, "I was just laughing at you shouting and swearing at yourself."

I had not realised that I was so determined and was encouraging myself so much inside my head, that I had said my words out loud! I shall not repeat them here, as they are far too blue. As of this very day, begin to think about what you would say to someone else in certain situations in life if you wanted to encourage them. How would you encourage a loved one? What language and tone of voice would you use? Consider writing it all down and repeating it to yourself inside your mind to become your new, progressive internal dialogue. How do you encourage others?

Ensure that you are convincing and sincere, make sure that you really mean what you are saying. When you then communicate with yourself in that way, notice how that makes you feel. Notice what it is like to have that kind of progressive, encouraging internal communication instead. It can be like a breath of fresh air for your brain, because you are now nurturing it.

As a result of encouraging yourself so much more, each time you create some internal communication of any kind with yourself, as you are more and more supportive, this is going to naturally increase your self-esteem and your self-confidence too! In turn, that builds a stronger foundation for your success and grows your ability to achieve more as a runner.

The way in which you behave and the feelings that you have affect each other. Your behaviour often shows what your feelings are, and your behaviours also affects how you feel (and vice versa of course). Very often, people think that they have to feel different before they change any of their behaviours. However, it is often far, far easier to do it the other way around. Follow these simple encouragement steps to start helping yourself to achieve more:

Step One:

Induce hypnosis in whatever way you prefer. Then proceed to step two.

Step Two:

Have a good think about a success that you have experienced, or something that went really well in your life. If you are struggling, you can instead think of an everyday achievement. As you think about it, think about what it is that was so successful about it. Furthermore, notice that thinking about it makes you feel better.

Notice what you thought, what internal dialogue you had, where in your body the feelings were, what you saw and heard and how you behaved. With a full, sensory rich idea of your successes you can learn from them and replicate them.

Step Three:

Run through that entire process again with another occasion. Repeat it a couple of times for both events [?].Invest some energy into your success here. These are things that are indicative that you are on the right path in certain areas of your life.

Step Four:

Give yourself some praise. Go on, go ahead and praise yourself. Pat yourself on the back! This is nourishing, it is nurturing your relationship with yourself and rewarding, and it leads to you building your sense of self. Have some laughs as you do it – I know I find it hard to keep a straight face when I am doing this.

Now, start piling on the encouragement.. Give yourself some really good encouragement. Encouraging yourself gives you more and more resources for the challenges and difficulties that may lie ahead. As we did earlier, think about how you would encourage someone else, and then deliver that encouragement to yourself.

Step Five:

Next up is comfort. Now I am not talking about the kind of comfort that I get when I sit in my lovely reclining chair, although it is very nice. I digress. Comfort yourself about something that may have not gone as you wanted. Heal those old wounds that used to be there. Take some time out to nurture yourself and heighten your own personal awareness of self.

Accepting and heightening your awareness of these things, rather than resisting and fighting past things, will allow you to start to take yourself to a new place in the future. This is a different flavour of encouragement.

Step Six:

Create a time in the future when you have a darling loved one encouraging you. Imagine them telling you how amazing you are and how proud they are of you; maybe someone that motivates you or someone you admire.

You can take it up a level and imagine a small crowd of people that you know and love, all encouraging you and loving you and telling you all those wonderful things that make them sure that you can achieve what you want to achieve.

Then, you can even take it higher than that. Imagine the sights, sounds and feelings of running past thousands of people, or standing on a stage in front of thousands of people, or whatever you want to imagine, and those people are cheering you on, applauding you and showing you how much they believe in you. Soak this stuff up and enjoy the encouragement of the masses!

Step Seven:

When you have soaked up enough of these combined encouraging processes, exit hypnosis by counting from one through to five and opening your eyes.

This is fabulous stuff. Having practiced this process in hypnosis, start to encourage yourself when in a variety of areas of your life to enhance your mood and develop a more progressive outlook on life. Apply encouragement to yourself and observe what a fabulously enjoyable effect it has on your life in general. We are now going to look at a number of differing strategies for advancing mood.

Using Cognitions to Enhance Mood

In 2002, in a statement from the World Health Organization (WHO), depression was declared the leading psychological cause of human suffering, and despite a wide range of scientific literature showing how to best treat it, the WHO also predicted that the rate of depression would increase in years to come.

It also seems that increasingly more people lack satisfaction as far as their moods are concerned. Therapists of varying kinds that I encounter are reporting that more people are coming to see them and reporting being depressed or having a withering level of positivity. This next technique is a process to lift moods.

Now for some, a dip in mood could well be some sort of biological issue in the brain, the chemical make-up of the individual, or hormones of the body, so I always make sure that people consult with their GP as well. That said, there are many things we can address in addition to any therapy we have, and any medication we end up taking as a result of formal diagnosis.

There are basic things that we can all examine in relation to enhancing our moods: levels of quality sleep, regularity of exercise, the kind of diet, the amount of natural light you encounter, whether you have meaningful relationships in your life and a sense that the choices you make in this life reflect what is important to you. There are other factors that determine your general wellbeing, the stability of your moods and your levels of positivity.

Even if you have a medical condition that affects your moods (as diagnosed by a medical professional) looking at the above mentioned factors will help you. I have encountered therapists that firmly believe managing these areas of your life and incorporating relaxation or meditative practices into your life, along with some good quality therapy, is the full recipe for lifting your mood in general terms. Additionally, mastering your cognitions can vastly alter mood.

When I refer to cognitions, as stated previously, I am talking about anything inside of your head that can be verbalised: such as ideas, thoughts, beliefs etc. Those are your cognitions. More than just the internal dialogue.

This process can be used in so many aspects of life and is very simple, but incredibly effective. The vast majority of the individuals I encounter in therapy state that they feel hugely better as a result of running through this process.

Before you actually run through this process, work out, create, design and write down a statement (a positive cognition) that you think will be undeniably convincing to you to enhance your moods in certain situations and circumstances of your life. You'll need it later in this exercise, and ensure it is in the present tense i.e. it is happening now. With that written down in your own words, run through these set of steps:

Step One:

First of all, get yourself into a comfortable position where you'll be undisturbed for the period of this exercise. Then start to think about typical situations whereby you used to feel low, lack positivity and have a dip in mood.

Ideally, pick a single situation, where you have negative conditions that accompany the dip in mood.

Step Two:

With that in mind, with your eyes now closed, picture yourself in that typical situation that you thought of in step one. Truly immerse yourself in it. See what you see, hear what you hear, tune in to the place you are in. As much as possible, imagine as if it's happening right now.

As unusual as this may initially seem, repeat the old, negative cognition to yourself like you really mean it. It is likely that this will bring on some of the old unwanted low mood sensation, and it is ok to tap into that as much as is useful for this technique. Then just carry on repeating those negative thoughts to yourself in your imagination. When you've noticed the negative feeling increasing within you, start to examine your current experience. Tell yourself how that feels, just explain it to yourself in your own head.

Ideally, you will be noticing, that when you believe what goes on in your head, it can make you feel bad and can dip your mood to uncomfortable and unhealthy levels. When you have got a real sense of this, move on to the next step.

Step Three:

The plan from here is to now undermine that old, unwanted thought process and accompanying unpleasant feeling, by gradually removing it from your mind. That is the reason we developed the positive suggestion before we started this. You wrote that down immediately prior to step one, remember?

Keeping your eyes comfortably closed, continue to imagine that you arc immersed in that typical situation. Now though, start to say the new, positive cognition to yourself in your mind. Don't just repeat it in a drab fashion. Really mean it. Put some ooomph into it! Say it in your mind in a way that you find it to be beautifully irresistible, undeniably convincing that this is who and how you choose to be now.

Keep repeating that to yourself in your imagination, over and over with some conviction. When you say it with meaning and conviction, you should start to notice that you feel different as a result. Tell yourself how it feels different. Tell yourself how it feels better. Start to increase the good feelings you notice and continue to repeat the new positive thought process with meaning. Just as before, you should also now be learning and noticing that when you think these kinds of thoughts and allow these cognitions to dominate your mind, you feel better. Additionally, when you say it to yourself in a way that makes you believe it, you feel even better.

This can now be reinforced and built upon. You repeat this process over and over until it becomes a habit. That is, it becomes your instant reaction in real life when you enter those situations – you repeat that cognition and get it lodged firmly inside of your mind.

Step Four:

Now induce hypnosis in whatever way you choose.

Repeat the process of turning the negative thoughts into positive, progressive thoughts. The repetition ensures the learning is getting lodged into your mind and forming a habit that'll influence your feelings more in the future. As you did earlier, picture yourself in that typical situation that you thought of in step one. Really immerse yourself in it. See what you see, hear what you hear, tune in to the place you are in. As much as is possible, imagine it as if it's happening right now.

Repeat the old, negative cognition to yourself like you really mean it. It is likely that this will bring on some of the old unwanted low mood sensation, and do allow yourself to evoke those old accompanying unwanted feelings.

Then just carry on repeating those negative thoughts to yourself in your imagination. When you've noticed the negative feeling increasing within you, start to examine your current experience. Tell yourself how that feels, just explain it to yourself in your own head.

Now you're going to banish those old, negative thoughts and feelings, and replace them with the new, positive ones. As you did earlier, start to say the new, positive cognition to yourself in your mind. Don't just repeat it in a fashion that makes it seem like a chore. Really mean it. Keep repeating that to yourself in your imagination, over and over with some conviction.

When you say it with meaning and conviction, you should start to notice that you start to feel different. Tell yourself how it feels different. Tell yourself how it feels better. Start to increase the good feelings you notice and continue to repeat the new positive thought process with meaning. Just as before, you should also now be learning and noticing that when you think these kinds of thoughts and allow these cognitions to dominate your mind, you feel better. Additionally, when you say it to yourself in a way that makes you believe it, you feel even better.

As much as is possible, repeat it until you believe in it. Really believe in it.

Repeat this step of the process as many times as you can, until you feel that the positive cognition and new thought process is firmly lodged in your mind. If you are unsure, then do it some more to be sure. Repetition is key here.

Step Five:

Once you have run through that enough times, and you feel that you have truly learned the new cognitions and got them installed in your mind, tell yourself that this is going to advance and enhance your mood in a wide variety of situations, and that the good feelings begin to generalise into many other areas of your life.

You may consider running through the process for a number of other typical situations from your life too. You could choose to use this skill and process in a variety of other aspects of your life – for example, for your confidence, self-assuredness, as well as mood enhancement and satisfaction as we have done here in this chapter.

The key learning here is being aware of how to turn that negative thought process automatically into positive thoughts and feelings. It gets easier the more you do it.

Step Six:

Count yourself up and out of hypnosis from one through to five and open your eyes.

Once you have practiced this a few times, go and take some action that is proof to you that you have made this change. Challenge yourself to go and test this, and use it in those real-life situations. Let your cognitions be progressive and powerful and enriched with belief.

Creating A Happiness Filter

My Nana used to tell me that there was a lady in the village who wore rose-tinted spectacles, so whenever we visited them and went into the village or the neighbouring town, I was always looking out for elderly women with glasses that had roses on them. I never saw them, but I did imagine exactly what I thought they'd be like. Later on in life, of course, I got to know what she actually meant. That there are some people out there who perceive the world in a particular way. I got the impression that my Nana and perhaps lots of other people tend to think that at times, this could be a bad thing, or at the very least, it is unrealistic. I get that. Yet I also think it is very useful to reflect on our lives in a progressive and positive way.

When you look at people who are unhappy or down in the dumps, or even depressed, they do tend to perceive the world in a way that reminds them of all they have to be unhappy about. Often people reflect on their life and see only the things they consider to be bad or unpleasant. There is a well documented and much used process of journaling that therapists often recommend; this involves an individual writing in their journal before they go to bed at night, listing 3-5 things in their day that made them happy.

This points the mind towards the things that are considered good and laudable, and allows us to filter our experience in a way that helps make us happier. For some people this is what they need – to take a period of time out each day and don some rose tinted spectacles to look at their day. Then after a couple of weeks of doing this, getting into the habit of doing such, it starts to have a generalising, happiness-inducing effect that I think many people can greatly benefit from.

This next technique has this kind of thing in mind, and is simply doing that process of filtering, but using self-hypnosis to reflect and filter. As a result, we get to amplify the good feelings and focus in a deeper manner.

Step One:

Induce hypnosis using whichever method you prefer.

Step Two:

Imagine that in front of you is the book of your life, and each chapter represents a chapter of your life. Flick through the pages, going deeper and deeper inside your mind as you turn more and more of the pages.

Tell yourself, that as you start from the beginning, turning the front cover over, that each page you turn takes you deeper inside your mind, yet you remain focused and engaged in the process. Take all the time necessary, do this slowly and thoroughly, maybe even exhaling each time you turn the page over. When you get to today's page, move on to the next step.

Step Three:

As you look at the page for today, allow your mind to scan through the page and notice some bits are highlighted, golden and colourful, they really stand out on the page. They might be moments when you laughed or shared some laughter with another person. It might be something that made you smile. It might be a compliment you received, it may be something you felt you did well or that others recognised; it can be absolutely anything from the day gone by that you and your mind consider to be a good moment: a golden highlight from that day.

Go to the first one of these highlights of the day, and recall what happened, who was there, what you saw, what you heard, how you felt. Imagine for a few moments that you are there again, enjoying those feelings. Spend a few moments reminding yourself of that highlight, bask in the feelings of it and when you have noticed those feelings, perhaps even amplified them, spread them through your body, then move on to the next step.

Step Four:

Now go to another highlighted area on today's page of the book of your life. Again, recall what happened, who was there, what you saw, what you heard, how you felt. Imagine for a few moments that you are there again, enjoying those feelings.

Spend a few moments reminding yourself of that highlight, bask in the feelings of it and when you have noticed those feelings, perhaps even amplify them, spread them through your body; maybe picture the feeling as a colour or a sound that resonates with you, or try a certain sensation that you can develop. Once you have really enjoyed reliving and reminding yourself of this highlight, move on to the next step.

Step Five:

Now repeat step 4 two or three times. When you have repeated it and enjoyed a total of 3-5 highlights from your day, and have truly engaged in the happiness and reflected positively on your day, move on to step six.

Step Six:

You know that each and every day has its ups and downs, and you are realistic about life, but today, you had a good day. You have recalled a number of highlights that surely constitute a good day.

Look at the book of your life again and colour the entire page of today gold, to signify that this was indeed a golden, enjoyable and happy day, and that you intend to have more and more of these kind of days. More and more, you start to notice the things that make you readily happier and more capable of happiness. Once the page is entirely golden and you know it was a good day, move on to the final step.

Step Seven:

Knowing what a good day you have had, take a deep energising breath, wiggle your fingers and toes, open your eyes and bring the session to an end.

Decide to practice this every day for a week, maybe just before you go to bed at night, so that you'll look back and think, wow, that was a great week, a golden week. Maybe you can even carve out this time in your life as a halcyon era that stands out for all the right reasons. Choose to make your perception of life contribute to your well-being and help enhance your general mood.

First Aid for a Bad Mood!

Sometimes we just want to give ourselves a lift, especially if we have been in a bad mood for a while, or maybe been subjected to a number of problems in our life that have made it seem difficult to achieve a great mood. Perhaps we've been ignoring good things or felt that there has not been a lot to get excited about. This next process is for giving ourselves a pep up.

The reason I refer to it being 'first aid' for a bad mood is because it deals with the symptoms of a bad mood. I can remember being at an NLP training event and watching Richard Bandler on stage. He suggested that we all force a smile on our faces three times in succession to observe closely what happened within us. All those of us that did it, felt better and got a shot of well-being (though it varied in intensity). It was a great way to alter mood. It actually started me off with a fit of giggles at the time, and just thinking about that experience continues to make me smile.

Likewise, when I think of Frank Spencer or Tommy Cooper and their hilarious facial expressions in their comedy routines, I get a shot of humour and joy in my head that advances my mood for sure. I am also one of those people who laughs at comedy shows where there is some misfortune experienced, so I sometimes laugh at facial expressions of disgust or failure too.

Then there are funny sounds. I think most boys find whoopee cushions hilarious, and therefore farting sounds make them laugh, but there are many sounds that we hear or imagine hearing that are considered hilarious by us all. The classic circus clown music or the Benny Hill theme tune seem to be the kind of sounds that are impossible to maintain feelings of misery while they are playing. If all these things can help you feel better and offer up some first aid for a dip in mood, then why not combine it all?

That is what Assen Alladin *(2008)* suggests to help deal with the initial symptoms of depression, as demonstrated in the ***Handbook of Cognitive Hypnotherapy For Depression***. Of course, as already mentioned at various stages in this book, if you have depression, then you'll need to see a qualified professional and get tailored solutions, and not rely on non-exhaustive snippets and techniques offered up in books. I can't claim that these processes are anywhere near as effective as proper therapeutic solutions offered by a therapist who tailors things for your specific requirements and needs.

Prior to starting this process, make sure you are in a place where you'll be undisturbed for the period of time, and get in a seated, not a lying position. Let your arms and legs be uncrossed and not touching each other. Take a couple of good deep breaths and as you exhale, consider having a good 'sigh' or even letting out a groan as you get plenty of air in your lungs, which is going to help build a foundation of letting go of the old unwanted mood (if you were in a bad one) and help you get into a great mood.

While taking your deep breaths, think about a word which you love or a word that you associate with happiness, or a word that is silly and funny in some shape or form. Something that you do not have to share with anyone, that is personally funny, fills you with cheer or that you consider to be quirky. It is going to be a word that is used in this session today and thereafter to rekindle and generate good feelings. Get that nicely lodged in your mind as you continue with your breaths.

As you get comfortable in your seated position, adjust yourself so that you adopt a strong and purposeful posture, whereby the crown of your head is pointed straight up at the ceiling and your shoulders are broad but not raised or hunched, almost as if you are a guard on sentry duty. You want to adopt a good strong positive posture, so that your body, the vehicle for this mood enhancement, is in a different place than it was previously, and is ready to help advance the mood. With your posture strong and positive, begin with the process of inducing hypnosis.

Step One:

Induce hypnosis using your method of choice.

Step Two:

To deepen the hypnosis and to start our good mood creation and its subsequent advancement, you want to lighten the sensation of the head. People often refer to feeling light-headed, and we want it to be a good light-headed sensation. What's more, negative states of mind are often associated with a heaviness of the head. To do this, imagine that your head is a big, heavy bag of sand and that there is a hole in the back at the bottom where the sand is pouring out slowing and thoroughly. As it pours out, you go deeper into hypnosis and your head feels lighter and more comfortable.

Tell yourself that it feels lighter as you imagine it to enhance the effect. Spend as much time on this step as is necessary for you to develop a notable sensation of lightness in your head, and once you have that, move on to the next step.

Step Three:

With the lightness sensation in place, maintaining your positive strong posture, you now force a smile on your face three times. Even if it feels false or forced, just smile widely and broadly, as if posing for a photograph. Then when you have relaxed the muscles after the smile, repeat it twice.

Imagine seeing your face smiling, imagine watching your lips curling in a big smile and think about smiles in general as you force the smiles onto your face one at a time, three times in succession. Be thorough with this, notice how it makes you feel, even the tiniest of sensations. Notice the sensations somewhere within you. Once you have noticed them, then move on to the next step.

Step Four:

Now think of and imagine a funny face. This could be someone you saw or knew in real life, or someone you have seen on the television or in a film, or even something you just imagined and created in your own mind. Maybe it is someone who made you laugh for some reason. Choose someone that makes you smile when you think about them.

Imagine that face in as much detail as possible: the expression, the colours and even think of any sounds as you remember how much it made you smile or laugh when you saw it (maybe they spoke in a funny manner). Think about what it is that you find so funny and amusing about that face, and really imagine it there in front of you. Once you have that vivid in your mind, notice how it makes you feel to see and watch it again, and when you notice those feelings, move on to the next step.

Step Five:

Now recall a time in your life that was a happy, funny time where you shared uplifting feelings or laughter with others. Remember where you were, who you were with, hear the sounds of laughter or happiness, and see the colours of the place, the shades of light, notice how you feel to be there again in your imagination. Truly go there, in those shoes, seeing through those eyes, hearing those sounds and experiencing those great feelings.

Spend as much time as necessary for you to really feel as if you are there in that place, enjoying those feelings of well-being, happiness and laughter. When you have those great feelings, move on to the next step.

Step Six:

Continue to enjoy the feelings of smiling, of that funny face and then that occasion of happiness, and as you notice the feelings you are enjoying, think of your happy or funny (or silly) word that you chose prior to starting step one. See the word in a bright colour in your mind, imagine saying it and even imagine funny music playing as you look at it – or even a funny sound. Play the word loudly, brightly and in a funny manner to yourself in your mind, and associate this word with all these good feelings you have created.

Once you have spent enough time on this step, and you feel that the word is associated with those great feelings, tell yourself that when you repeat this word it starts to remind you of these great feelings and rekindles them. Then move on to the final step.

Step Seven:

Exit hypnosis by counting yourself up and out from one through to five. Remember to keep all the progressive, good sensations and elevated mood with you, once you have emerged from hypnosis.

As I often say with these techniques, choose to go and take some action that shows that you have changed your mood, or at the very least notice how differently you behave and respond as a result of your mood being a good one. Make it your aim to practice this process. Practice this process and repeat it in its entirety a few times. Then start to practice using and saying your word to yourself as a means of accessing that good mood when you choose; with practice, effort and repetition you'll be able to do it with ease.

Lifting The Fog

When I think of foggy city environments, I tend to think of the gaslight era, which is the scene of many a chilling crime story. Without wanting to get embroiled in terrifying street scenes, I want to mention and talk about fog and clouds (though not of the pink fluffy variety) as I build upon the previous techniques for mood-enhancement.

Sometimes in life, it can seem like there is a fog and we can feel thick-headed if we experience depression or even just have a depressed episode of some kind in our life. Our senses can become numbed, and the world can become dark, gloomy and unpleasant. This is what the gaslight era streets were like. Ideally, we'd like to contrast that with uplifting, happy environments that are not scary, and are colourful and pleasant to be in and around.

That is what this process is all about. It is not the kind of process that is right for everyone all of the time, but if you feel muffled and numb, like you have a foggy head and require some clarity, then this could well be just what you are after. Before you start, have a good think about how you'd like things to be in your life and your perception of your world.

In a place where you are going to be undisturbed for the period of this exercise, get yourself nice and comfortable, sit down with your feet and hands uncrossed and not touching each other. Take a nice deep breath, and as you exhale allow your eyes to close and begin.

Step One:

Induce hypnosis using whichever method you choose.

Step Two:

Imagine what you would be seeing if your mood were lifted. How would life be? Where would you be? Who would you be with? Start to create that kind of environment in front of you. Notice though that it may appear vague, foggy and unclear. You have an idea of sorts of how you imagine things will be, but you are struggling to get it vivid inside your mind. It is all here in front of you, how you imagine things will be when you are feeling upbeat, happy and enjoying your experience of life.

The sounds are muffled, like someone speaking into a folded blanket. The images are unclear, vague, and lack any richness of colour or texture, and you cannot make out any detail. You notice how it makes you feel, lacking the ability to get this clear and enjoyable in your mind. Notice enough of that frustration to be useful for this exercise, and when you sense enough of that frustration, move on to the next step.

Step Three:

Imagine that you have an imaginary pen or crayon with which to draw and edit your thoughts. Use it to draw a line on the ground underneath the scene before you. Right there as you look at the muffled, foggy imagery before you, draw a line underneath it with your mind's eye, using a pen of your mind. Do it with a sense of purpose and in a deliberate fashion. With that line drawn underneath the scene before you, start to think that enough is enough. You are no longer going to put up with this clouded perception, you know that life is full of colour, joy and resonance.

Step over to the line you have drawn and reach down, bend right down and force your fingers under the line and start to lift it up… Start to raise the line and notice what is happening. As unusual as this may sound, start to lift the line up, and as you do so, start to notice that it is almost as if you are lifting a cloudy screen.

Notice that it is as if you are lifting up a cloudy, foggy screen of some sort that was inhibiting the view in front of you. Imagine reaching deep inside your mind and finding all the strength and power you need to powerfully lift this up, higher and higher, and as you lift it higher, you go deeper inside your mind and the line starts to feel lighter and lighter, and it becomes easier and easier to lift. Tell yourself that it is so, and continue to lift it until it is above your head and starts to float up and away.

When it is out of your reach, it floats all by itself, out and away until it is no longer visible at all. You might find yourself squinting slightly, as it gets brighter as you look upward and in front of you. Then move on to the next step.

Step Four:

There before you, you see the world as it is when the fog has lifted, when the cloudiness has gone, when the mufflers have ceased. See your life in full and glorious colour, clear and sparkling. You distinguish colours, textures and sounds, and it feels wonderful to have this level of clarity.

Enjoy the feelings, let them grow. Notice where in your body you feel the sensations of freedom and clarity, and start to get excited at how much more you can now see. Think deeply and contemplate about what was beyond your perception before, what was being obscured, and start to see things anew. Notice how fresh and alive everything seems to be, like a cloud has been lifted. Consider breathing out slowly, and as you exhale giving off a sigh that indicates you have let go, you have opened your senses to the world and everything that seemed stale and old is now fresh, new and enjoyable.

Step Five:

As you gaze upon the colourful scene of your life in all its glory, start to tell yourself that each of the things you see in your life from now on, you will choose to get excited about and be fascinated with. As you look at the people and things in your life, you look upon them with a healthy naivety, almost with a sense of awe, like a child experiencing something for the first time. You sense the detail, colours and textures that maybe have been taken for granted in recent times, and you allow the simple things in your environment to contribute to your well-being and happiness.

It is not just your environment that contributes to your happiness – you get happy about the wonders of being alive, enjoying the sensation of breathing, the sense of your organs working within you and the strength in your muscles. You become aware of how amazing it is to be able to see, hear and feel at all, and you choose to never take that for granted again. With your senses primed and ready for engaging with the world around you, move on to the final step.

Step Six:

Exit hypnosis by counting from one through to five and take a couple of energising breaths. When you open your eyes, start to make a conscious effort to see the light and shade, the contrast and colour; hear the sounds, the tiniest distinctions of sounds and feel the full range of sensation that comes with being human. Then celebrate being alive and having lifted that cloud that was numbing and filtering your senses before.

Practice this self-hypnosis process repeatedly for a few days to make it work even better. Even if you are not having a depressive episode, this is a lovely process, and we could all do with this kind of perspective and intention once in a while to keep the fog at bay.

Tame Your Inner Critic

Sometimes we can be our own worst enemy. This process can be used to alleviate anxiety as well as depression. Back in May 2012, while I was speaking at the change phenomena conference for the first time, I watched fellow hypnotherapist and friend, Gary Turner, presenting. He was quoting a technique he enjoyed using for getting the unwanted internal dialogue in our heads to be quiet. It involved wrapping duct tape around the mouth of the voice of the unwanted internal dialogue. I rather liked it, and what with Gary being a 13-time world champion at various fighting disciplines, I thought it beautifully apt.

There are so many ways to quiet internal dialogue, or to get the internal chatter to shush. Some I have written about before. Here, today, is one simple way for not just disputing thoughts and stopping them, but to tame your thoughts (if they are being critical) and turn them into something effective, useful and beneficial to you. Critical thoughts can cause us to be unhappy.

Before we start with this process, think of someone who always wants the best for you, perhaps someone who loves you and even someone who encourages you and supports you unconditionally. If you are struggling to come up with anyone, then create and imagine what it would be like. Also have a think about a typical situation where you tend to be critical of yourself, or where your internal dialogue tends to talk you out of taking action, or where it affects you detrimentally in some way. This is evocative imagery that we want to use to access feelings.

Then let's begin. Get yourself into a comfortable position where you'll be undisturbed for the period of doing this exercise, and follow these simple steps:

Step One:

Induce hypnosis using the method of your choice.

Step Two:

Scan back through your day, or the past week and think of your activities and actions. As you think, imagine drifting deeper inside your mind as you consider your recent life. As you scan through your recent life, notice anything that might be considered an issue or a problem that you are currently working on, or a challenge you are facing – ideally a circumstance where your internal dialogue hindered, mal-affected, held you back or was unduly critical.

Start to gather the details of what happened on that occasion. Recall where you were and who you were with, recall the sounds, notice the sights of the place and be aware of how that makes you feel. Just notice enough of these feelings as is useful for the exercise.

As you imagine that you are there in that place, also start to recognise what was happening inside of your head. That is, what were you saying to yourself, what ideas went through your mind, what was your internal dialogue saying? Notice any negative elements. Notice the unwanted internal dialogue, become aware of the qualities of how it was said, as well as the words that were spoken in your mind, and with a good sense of that, move on to the next step.

Step Three:

As you notice the old unwanted criticising voice, start to build that voice a body or a character of some kind. Maybe it is an animal or a beast or famous person, or even an object. Start to create in your mind a physical presence of some kind that you think and believe best suits your internal dialogue.

Fashion the voice with a body, a face of some kind and start to create a very particular physical presence and representation inside your head that represents your internal dialogue. You choose, you imagine, you create. Make it detailed and spend all the time necessary to get this in your mind. As that becomes fashioned and created, also now get a sense of what the underlying meaning or hidden benefit of this inner critic might be; start to frame it in a way that could be seen as being progressive or positive in some way.

If you feel that the words or sentiments of the voice, the critical voice were just harmful and had no positive intention at all, then that's fine, there does not have to be. When you have done that, then move on to the next step.

Step Four:

This is the fun part of the process. Start to morph the critic into the person who you thought of prior to step one. The encouraging and supportive person (or the imaginary person). Imagine the change happening in the features, in the details of how they look and the colours updating. Notice the sound of the voice beginning to change, the tonality and pace of what is being said. Notice how it makes you feel to see this person.

Really create the change (I love this part because of my penchant for sci-fi and fantasy films where this happens a great deal). Once you have got the old critic transformed into the new person, then move on to the next step.

Step Five:

If there was some kind of positive intention behind the critic's previous dialogue, then now is the time to refer to it, and let the new voice start to encourage you and support you with the same positive intention. If there was no positive intention that you could decipher, then let the new person start to encourage and support you – let them say the words that are undeniably convincing and well meaning, that you belief unconditionally, and let them be words that make sure you take action, or that change how you respond to that situation, or that empower you, or that really put a smile on your face.

You'll know what is most useful for you in this situation, so let that start to happen. Let that be said.

Start to notice the words of encouragement are dominating your mind, filling your mind with progressive sentiments in that situation, and notice the words beginning to appear in written form, in bright colours and with more pronounced sounds. As you focus on the progressive words repeating in your mind, let them affect your feelings. Notice the good feelings growing and developing, and imagine them spreading through your body in some way.

While the encouraging, positive dialogue persists in your mind, take all the time you need to spread relaxing and enjoyably good feelings throughout your body, then move on to the next step.

Step Six:

Now imagine a time in the future when you'll be in a similar situation. Truly be in that place and in that scenario. Then start to let the positive, progressive internal dialogue start to play inside your mind. Mentally rehearse the new voice dominating your mind in that situation.

Notice how this changes things for you. Notice how you behave as a result of the internal dialogue – how you take action, how you feel good – notice what is different. Tell yourself that this is how you communicate with yourself in the future and that each time you practice this process you become more naturally inclined to let go of the old unwanted critic, and enjoy the new, progressive encouraging internal dialogue. With that completed, move on to the final step.

Step Seven:

Exit hypnosis by counting from one through to five and opening your eyes. Remind yourself of the new, progressive internal dialogue, and think about going and putting yourself in that situation where you can become encouraged by it.

Then that is it. Enjoy it, practice it a few times and then let that voice inspire you, motivate you, drive and support you.

Many people have been told that depression is simply a result of some kind of brain anomaly that can be corrected with medication. These people tend to subsequently believe the issue is simply one of brain chemistry that they are a fairly passive recipient of. Today, we do have significant evidence that shows this to be inaccurate *(Burns, 1980; Yapko, 1997; Healy, 1998)*, and therefore this chapter aims to equip you with some means of actively taking control of your mood.

The very nature of depression is such, that anyone suffering with it is often less inclined to take action or seek help for a wide number of reasons that are written about in specialist books on the subject. You have read this far, and are reading this book, and that kind of action is part of the process that helps you create progressive change in your life with regard to controlling mood. This chapter is not about curing depression, because there is no strong evidence to suggest you can do that all by yourself, equipped with just self-hypnosis. As an adjunct to your other advice, care, treatment and lifestyle choices, as well as a range of techniques featuring in other chapters, the techniques in this chapter can really help make a difference.

Chapter Ten: Sleep Enhancement

"When I woke up this morning, my girlfriend asked me if I had slept well. I said no, I made a few mistakes"
(Steven Wright, Comedian).

This chapter, as the title suggests, is aimed at helping you get to sleep, stay asleep for healthy periods of time, have better quality sleep and get back to sleep if you wake up prematurely, and you are offered structured self-hypnosis techniques to help with each of these. This is a self-hypnosis book and my aim is to mostly offer assistance through self-hypnosis interventions. However, these self-hypnosis techniques will be advanced greatly by following some additional guidelines proven to help enhance sleep, and there are a couple of other considerations to bear in mind too.

If you have sleep problems, it is important for you to decide, or to consult a therapist or your doctor to help you decide if your sleep impairment is actually a symptom of more general problems. If so, the focus of your self-hypnosis sessions may also be to address other problems, such as depression, anxiety or stress, for example. Also, if you are not sleeping and have a drug or alcohol problem, chronic depression, or even if you snore or have sleep apnea, you are advised to seek professional help prior to attempting to use self-hypnosis to enhance your sleep.

Research Into Advancing Sleep

Individuals who complain of insomnia do tend to overestimate the time that it takes them to fall asleep *(Franklin 1981)*. In a study by Stepanski et al. (*1988),* there was not a dramatic difference in the total monitored night-time sleep in patients complaining of insomnia, contrasted with those not complaining of it. Regardless of this, it is possible that the quality of sleep is poorer in complainers of insomnia, who cite greater periods of restlessness. Horne *(1992)* suggests that psychological factors, such as stress, anxiety and tension play a role in as many as 80% of all insomnia cases.

Psychological therapies that emphasise relaxation, cognitive restructuring and 'sleep hygiene' are medically recommended treatments   *National Institutes Of Health, 2005*

What is Meant by 'Sleep Hygiene'?

Sleep hygiene is basically a set of guidelines and general considerations aimed at advancing your overall ability to sleep and stay asleep for healthy periods of time.

Some typical recommendations are as follows:

- Having a bed that you find to be comfortable, which is in a dark, quiet room at a temperature that is neither too cold or warm.

- Prior to sleeping, avoid consumption of stimulants prior to bed, avoiding tea, coffee (and any other caffeinated drink) as well as processed sugar; though you may want to consider giving them up altogether. Alcohol is considered by some to help in getting them off to sleep, but it does result in waking in the night and results in poorer quality sleep. Eating a large meal quite soon before bed is not recommended either.

- Studying before bed is considered to hinder good quality sleep. However, many people find reading or watching a gentle (i.e. probably not high tension or horror films) television programme helps to get you off to sleep *(see Horne 1992, Parkes 1985)*.

- Vigorous exercise prior to going to bed is also not recommended, as your metabolism will be fired up and will make it difficult for your system to be able to relax enough to drift into sleep (that said, regular exercise is considered to help promote good sleep patterns).

- Fixing the times of going to bed and getting up is recommended: a regular routine or sleep pattern promotes the ability to sleep.

While these are not necessarily directly related to self-hypnosis, if you adhere to these types of recommendations, your self-hypnosis is likely to prove more effective. Likewise, you can create hypnotic programmes for better quality sleep that include doing the above mentioned things.

If we look at the research into the use of psychological methods to help improve sleep, in randomised controlled studies, participants treated with CBT showed significant improvement in quality of sleep, and they reported more satisfaction with their treatment than those just prescribed popular sleep medication *(Jacobs, 1993; Edinger et al., 2001).*

Hypnosis has proven useful as an isolated intervention, but the research has been limited. Unfortunately, the effectiveness of hypnosis for treating insomnia has not been thoroughly researched. As with the 1995 Kirsch study previously mentioned, there are numerous case studies and clinical experiences by professionals that suggest CBT interventions could be more effective when combined with hypnosis, but empirical evidence relating specifically to sleep interventions is currently lacking.

Relaxation, Mental Imagery and Self-Hypnosis

Despite the fact that there is not as much evidence as we would like to support the use of self-hypnosis in advancing sleep, hypnosis and relaxation procedures are of proven benefit for insomnia. The simplest approach is for us to build upon what we have learned in an earlier chapter, combining relaxation processes with self-hypnosis, and using that relaxation while in bed or preparing for sleep. Evidence does suggest that the use of relaxation results in individuals rating their sleep as more restful *(Espie et al., 1989, Turner and Ascher, 1979).*

There are a number of strategies coming up that use mental imagery, and you already know how to use the 'safe place' technique that is used by many professionals when teaching their clients how to get to sleep. If you record your self-hypnosis sessions (which many people tend to do with sleep enhancement issues) make sure you do not include and record step E of the protocol, as you don't want to be woken from your slumber!

Stopping Unwanted Thoughts

The majority of people with insomnia or similar sleep issues complain that their overactive mind keeps them awake at night. They may 'churn over' things that occurred during the day, which seem worse when lying in bed, but are often trivial in reality. Of course, problematic thought processes, such as catastrophising while lying awake in bed, contribute to problems with sleeping.

With this in mind, I advise you to revisit the section on controlling and restructuring thoughts that featured in the anxiety chapter, as these skills are very relevant here.

From here onwards, the chapter provides a number of techniques and strategies. As well as focusing on getting to sleep in the first place, we'll also look at how to maintain sleep, and some techniques to use if you wake up during the night and are unable to return to sleep.

Torching Unwanted Thoughts

Early in 2012, at a charity firewalk event I had organised, as we lit the logs I joked that "as a boy, I dreamed of moments like this" and it is true, I really did. I recall during winter watching my Dad build and light the home fires we had, and never being allowed to do any of the lighting or prodding with the poker, and not being allowed to throw stuff on it to burn. I was so deprived by the responsible attitude of my parents!

These days, we have our own open fire at home and we get our annual delivery of logs to get all toasty in our front room during winter. I love it. I love the very subtle aroma of burning wood, the sound of the logs crackling and rolling into embers, the sensation of the sedating heat (some of my early memories are of my grandfather coming in from a day's work on the farm, sitting down in his armchair in front of the open fire and falling asleep – so I think I associate that heat with sleep, and I think we've all felt sedated sat in front of a fireplace) and I also love to watch it, the flames that roar at the beginning and then flicker calmly once the logs become embers, the varying glow and the multitude of colours that exist within the fire.

Of course, I'm not the only person fascinated by fire. For centuries, it was a sign of power and a source of great need for early mankind; it instills fear in people and animals, and of course, needs to be respected because of the damage it can cause.

When something is burned to ashes and dust, there is a sense of finalism, a sense of no return. Some people are cremated to signal the end of their life and body. Yet burning can also be a very fertile thing to do, as some woodlands and scrub areas are burned on purpose to make way for new life and beginnings. The areas that surround volcanoes are often some of the most fertile and mineral rich places on the planet.

This upcoming process uses the notion of burning unwanted

thoughts to still and quiet the mind; it is useful for sleep and other applications too. This can be done in all manner of other ways by using mental imagery to let go of thoughts. You are going to be given a couple of ways to do this, and once you understand them, you'll be able to create your own if you prefer.

This process can be used for helping to let go of non-useful thoughts, beliefs, worries and frustrations. The main inspiration for this process comes from the work of Stanton *(1990)* as cited in Corydon Hammond's (Ed), Handbook of Hypnotic Suggestions and Metaphors, and I have adapted it here for use with self-hypnosis and tweaked the process accordingly. I use this kind of application in a variety of ways within my therapy rooms, and often teach my client the process to practice at home, so it can be developed and altered to suit the requirements of the client or the individual. Likewise, you can use it to get rid of anything that you deem to be non-useful or a hindrance in your day-to-day life.

Prior to starting this session, make sure you have a good think about what it is you are going to focus on letting go of. Make sure you are comfortable about letting go of it, and be prepared to let go of those thoughts. Then proceed with this session.

Step One:

Induce hypnosis using a method of your choosing.

Step Two:

Find yourself on the top floor, perhaps the tenth floor of a building of some kind. It can be a hotel, an apartment block, office building or whatever you prefer to create in your mind for the purpose of this process.

Depending on your preferences, you can take the lift, escalator or the stairs and start to descend to the lower levels of the building, aiming for the basement. Take some time to use this part of the process as a means of deepening your experience and perception, you can tell yourself that you are going deeper into hypnosis as you move lower down into the building. Be sure to engage your imagination throughout this part of the process: see the sights, hear the sounds and enjoy the sensation of moving deeper down inside of the building. When you have taken your time and reached the doors of the basement, proceed to the next step.

Step Three:

Walk into the basement and find it to be an incredibly welcoming and cosy, comfortable room indeed.

At the far side of the room is a large fireplace. Engage your imagination here: become aware of the colour of the room, the lighting and the shades and textures throughout. Then become aware of the sounds all around this room, and how comfortable and at ease you feel to be here.

Then gaze at the fireplace, notice a comfortable armchair of some kind beside it and take a seat at a comfortable and easy distance from the fire. Notice how the chair seems to have been designed especially for you. Notice the way it supports you perfectly, notice how it is incredibly comfortable; maybe you can even imagine it melding to the exact contours of your body. Settle into it and relax further, notice what the chair is made from and enjoy being sat in this chair gazing at the fire before you. Watch the fire for a while. Tell yourself that as you watch it, the movement is soothing your mind and taking you deeper into hypnosis. Enjoy the colours, the movements and sound of the fire. Bask in the heat of it and really enjoy this step. Once you have everything set to your own design, then move on to the next step.

Step Four:

Imagine placing your palm out in front of you and placing your worries, fears, beliefs or concerns (whatever you decided that you need to let go of) on to the palm of your hand, like they are real and actual things.

Then one at a time, start to cast those things into the flames. As each of those items reaches the fireplace, notice the flames increase temporarily; like someone has turned the gas up underneath somewhere, and the flames engulf and burn the item. Watch it burn and blacken, and then turn to ash and nothingness with the last traces of dust flying up the chimney. They are gone, entirely burnt, flamed, torched, and disappear for good.

Take all the time you need to do this thoroughly and at a good, methodical pace to make sure you let go of all the things you no longer need. As each one goes and disappears, start to notice a sense of release within you (maybe imagine that you are feeling sleepier too). Imagine that you feel lighter and more at ease, and notice what it means to you to let go of those unwanted thoughts. Once you have worked your way through all the things you patiently and thoroughly placed into your palm, then move on to the next step.

Step Five:

Now do make sure that you spend plenty of time enjoying the lightness and easiness of letting go of all those things. Notice how you feel different. Tell yourself what you notice to be different and start thinking about the day ahead of tomorrow, thinking about how things are going to be different as a result of you feeling so much better and lighter and at ease.

Maybe you can imagine the new feeling as a colour that spreads through your mind and body, or maybe you can imagine it as a sensation or a sound that spreads and resonates through you. Just build it and enhance it and enjoy it. Once you have spent enough time making sure that you feel different, then complete the process with step six.

Step Six:

If you are doing this at any other time (other than bedtime), exit hypnosis to let go of thoughts, otherwise, just drift off to sleep.

Leaves on a Sleepy Pond

This is another mental imagery technique to be used in conjunction with self-hypnosis. It is a technique that has a variety of applications and could be focused on various outcomes for any individual. This process could be used for letting go of unwanted thoughts and/or feelings, and thus it is useful for lifting mood. It could also be used to quiet the mind prior to a period of required concentration or for helping with drifting off to sleep.

The surface of water is often used as a metaphor within personal development or self-improvement circles. The surface has some kind of relationship with what is going on down below, whether that is obscuring what is going on or accurately depicting what is happening down there. This process is going to use a number of traditional themes: nature, water and natural processes to aid letting go of unwanted thoughts.

Again, before we start, have a good think about what you are going to use this session for. Do you want to let go of something? Are you hoping to clear your mind for a particular purpose, such as going to sleep? Or would you just like some extra peace of mind?

Step One:

Induce hypnosis using a method of your choice.

Step Two:

Imagine yourself in a favourite place in nature. Create this place and let there be a pond there. A pond connected to a gentle river some way away that you can hear in the distance. Beside the pond notice a tree of some kind, with leaves of a shape that you decide upon.

Become aware of the colours, the shades of light, tune in to the sounds of the place and notice how it makes you feel so comfortable and safe to be in this place of your own design. Notice the temperature, the weather, the colour of the sky and feel the breeze if there is any, notice the smell in the air and truly immerse yourself in this place. Use this step to imagine being in this place and deepen your hypnosis at the same time. Let every breath guide you deeper while you relax in this place. Once you have created this place and feel tuned into it, move on to the next step.

Step Three:

Take a seat beside the pond. As you sit, imagine any discomfort drains from your body and is absorbed by the ground, relaxing you. Gaze upon the surface of the calm pond and notice the reflection of the pond. By adjusting yourself, you can see your reflection too. Spend a few moments getting deeply relaxed, enjoying the place and the scene, then move on to the next step.

Step Four:

A firm gust of wind blows through the place for a moment, you breathe in that clean air and listen to the sounds all around as it fills the place with a momentary movement. As it blows through the tree beside the pond, several leaves fall onto the surface of the water in the pond. You watch some of the leaves, spiral deeper and deeper down through the air and into the pond.

The surface of the pond is now obscured by the leaves and you cannot see the reflection on the surface. Some of them move, they roll slowly upon the gently moving surface by a tiny, noticeable current from the attached river that connects a short distance away. Many of the leaves are gathering around the edge of the pond, close to you. Observe them for a while and notice them. You can even reach out and touch them if you wish, get a sense of their texture. When you have noticed them gathering nearby, move on to the next step.

Step Five:

Start to consider yourself and contemplate your goal for this session. Start to think of what it is that you wish to let go of. Or the thoughts you wish to leave you for a while. Or feelings that you would benefit from letting go of. As you think about them, in this wonderful place of your imagination and creation, now start to place them one by one on to the leaves, and as you intend to let go of them, notice the leaves beginning to move slowly and surely away from you and towards the part of the pond that connects with the river.

Watch as you place each worry, or unwanted thought, or distraction or whatever onto the leaves, and the leaves then transport it away. They move away, out of sight, out of mind and leave you feeling clearer, more comfortable and more at ease. Continue to do this deliberately and purposefully until you have let go of everything that you wanted to for this session. Then move on to the next step.

Step Six:

Spend some time watching the pond clear and enjoying the relaxation and peace of mind that brings. Notice the reflection coming back and enjoy basking in the tranquility for a while.

Step Seven:

Once you have enjoyed that experience, then bring this session to an end by counting from one through to five. Alternatively, if you are using it to lull yourself to sleep, just continue to bask in restfulness after step six and drift off comfortably.

Utilise Your Regular Routine to Enhance Sleep

Some people do not sleep well because they associate their bed with activity. Some people use the telephone in bed, do accounts in bed and all manner of other stimulating activities. These people may well be viewing the bed unconsciously, as a place of activity, when it wants to be associated with tranquillity and calmness, and of course sleeping, so that your mind starts to drift off every time you climb into bed.

The next strategy is going to build upon this notion greatly. It is not just going to build an association with your bed as a place to sleep, but it is going to associate your entire bedtime routine with sleeping. This process is not about lulling you to sleep, it is about creating an expectation that you will sleep, so it can be done during the day or at any other time, and not just used at bedtime.

One of the things that Milton Erickson introduced into the world of hypnosis in a much more pronounced manner than his predecessors in the field, was that of 'utilisation'. That is, he would use noises, distractions, routines, feelings and anything else that was presented to him during a hypnotherapy session, and instead of ignoring it or trying to divert away from it, he would use it in some way. If a door was heard closing shut in the background, he might suggest to the client "as one door closes in your mind, so another door of change opens…"

With this self-hypnosis process, we are going to utilise many things that you may well already do, and use them to enhance your ability and expectations of sleep. First you are going to mentally rehearse the process, then you are going to let it affect and influence how you prepare for sleep, in order to advance your ability to sleep.

Before we start, have a good think about the things you do to prepare for sleep: most people brush their teeth, change their clothes, pull the bed clothes over them when they get into bed and so on. It is these things we are going to use within this hypnosis session. Once you have considered and thought about your usual routine, then proceed to get yourself comfortable and in a place where you will be undisturbed for the duration of this session, and we can begin.

Step One:

Induce hypnosis using the method of your choice.

Step Two:

Imagine the routine that you usually go through, take some time and imagine that you are at your home in a favourite room or part of your home. Take a few minutes to engage your imagination. Notice the colours of the place, the shades of light, notice the sounds that are there and how you feel to be in this comfortable part of your home. Take some time on this step and use it to help deepen your experience of hypnosis to drift deeper, while still keeping a good level of focus.

When you are truly tuned in to that place, then move on to the next step.

Step Three:

Now imagine that you are getting changed for bed. Imagine that as you take each item of clothing off, that you are letting go of your routine of the day. As you take each item of clothing off, you are letting go of your connection to the day. As you take each item of clothing off, all the interactions, all the memories, all the communications, along with any concerns or issues, just seem to get dismantled and let go of..

It is as if each item of clothing represents some part of your day, some distraction. Some items you place into the laundry where they will be washed clean, and others go into the wardrobe, where they are kept to deal with another time, but while they are there, they are shut away while you sleep. Whichever it is, the old thoughts, distractions and aspects of your day and busyness of mind are let go of. Once you have imagined that and let go of everything, then move on to the next step.

Step Four:

Now, having let go while taking off your clothes that day, imagine that having changed into your sleep attire, you go to brush your teeth, and as you brush them, you are washing away and brushing away the last remnants of your day. Imagine that each brush stroke also cleanses your mind and helps you to have a mind that is clean, fresh and prepared for sleep. Imagine that you are brushing your teeth and calming your mind, washing your mind and letting go of anything unwanted or distracted. Feel the actual difference happening as you imagine this. When you really notice a difference, then move on to the next step.

Step Five:

Now imagine getting into bed and as you pull the covers over you, they protect you from disturbances and distractions. Imagine that the bed clothes are like a protective shield that prevents any unwanted thoughts reaching you. They protect you from noise, sights, feelings that you do not want to reach you while you sleep. You might like to imagine a colour or a glow of some kind as the bed clothes cover you. When you feel secure, protected and at ease, then move on to the next step.

Step Six:

Now you turn the lights off in your bedroom. Imagine that as the lights are turned off, so you switch off totally from the day you have had, you switch off from old issues, you switch off from any problems, knowing that you can deal with them another time. As you flick the switch off, you notice a switch getting flicked off in your brain that lets go of anything and everything unwanted, and lets you drift to sleep. Do all you can to imagine that switch being flicked inside your mind, and once you have done that, move on to the next step.

Step Seven:

Now imagine watching yourself, lying peacefully in bed, sleeping happily and deeply, and maybe even dreaming of wonderful things before drifting into a deep, non-dreaming sleep. Just watch yourself sleeping profoundly and deeply and beautifully, and as you watch that, think to yourself, I just know that is going to happen, and truly get a sure sense of knowing that you'll be sleeping that way very soon. Spend a little bit of time just observing yourself sleeping blissfully and then move on to the final step.

Step Eight:

Bring yourself up and out of hypnosis by wiggling your fingers and toes, take a deep breath and open your eyes.

Make a decision to practice this session and repeat it over and over for a week. Then after you have practiced it in your self-hypnosis sessions, start to then incorporate supporting thoughts into your real-life routine. For example, when you brush your teeth, imagine your thoughts being cleansed too, when you switch the light off, imagine the switch going off in your brain too. Practice that persistently and as often as you can, and it'll start to have a really wonderful effect.

Using Boredom as a Cure for Insomnia

In July of 2013, I was presenting a seminar to a group of students. In the afternoon of the Saturday, prior to an evening event my school was hosting, I gave a lecture about using hypnotherapy to treat insomnia. The irony of this lecture being that it was an incredibly hot day to be in a room with no air conditioning, and many of those in the audience were struggling to keep their eyes open. I blamed it on the heat and lack of breeze coming in through the open windows, and not my presenting style! Even more ironic is that while experiencing unusually warm weather conditions, so many people complain of an inability to sleep in the evenings, and I have had lots of messages from people, and seen many people saying as much on various social networking sites.

While discussing it with some attendees in the bar after the lecture, we recalled what it was like at University or at school when fighting fatigue or an incredibly boring subject matter. While reading a section of a 1980s book by Arnold Lazarus (originally written in the 70s, reprinted in 1984, named In The Mind's Eye) about mental imagery in preparation for this lecture, I noticed that Lazarus described using scenarios which were incredibly boring to help lull himself[?] back to sleep. Lazarus explained that he used similar scenarios with his clients to teach them how to get to sleep.

A place of complete and utter boredom provides us with a brilliant way of overcoming insomnia. I am going to use a lecture scenario here, but you can adapt it to any environment where you are doing something that you find to be totally boring. Maybe you could imagine doing something you dislike, or something boring at work, in a classroom, or any other circumstance; then apply similar steps to those I am presenting here.

Who'd have thought that being bored would ever come in so useful? Follow these simple steps while lying in bed.

Step One:

Induce hypnosis using whichever method you choose. Once you have induced hypnosis, move on to step two.

Step Two:

Imagine being sat in a reclining armchair. Let it be made of your favourite material, upholstered in a way that you like, and although it is in an upright position, it is comfortable and relaxing to sit in. The comfortable chair is in the centre of a lecture hall or lecture theatre of some kind.

Notice the sights around you: the colours, the shade of light, the people around you and the décor of this place. Notice the sounds: the sounds of people moving and breathing, the sounds that are distant and those that are closer; most importantly, notice the sound of the droning voice of the lecturer. Notice the feeling of boredom, how do you know you are bored? What are the signs? Truly notice how you know that you are so bored. All the sights, all the sounds and all the feelings take you deeper into hypnosis, deeper into the boredom and you physically relax more and more. Once you have truly got this boring scene in your mind, move on to the next step.

Step Three:

Try to focus on the lecturer and the lecture being given. As you listen to the lecture, the voice becomes a monotonous drone. It just goes on and on. It becomes harder and harder to make out the words, it just blends into a moving set of tones, a noise that makes you feel even more bored.

The sound seems to make you feel sleepier and sleepier. Convince yourself that you are there. Believe in the scene. Notice how you fight and struggle to stay awake, maybe even attempt to shake off the weariness. The boredom grows and it starts to affect you physically. Heavy feelings spread through you, weighing you down. You imagine your eyelids getting heavier, and that heaviness seems to be in your limbs and your head and neck ,and your head droops from time to time, and you struggle to lift it up. All the time, the sights, sounds and feelings take you deeper and deeper in to hypnosis, making you more physically relaxed, and bored... Move on to step four.

Step Four:

As you gaze vacantly around the place, feeling restless, trying to fight the boredom and fatigue you feel, you notice the other attendees in the lecture have their eyes closed or their eyes are closing slowly. You notice that most have their chairs in the full recline position.

You recline your own chair and hold your head so that you can vaguely make out the lecturer, then you continue to struggle to listen to the droning as it starts to fade. The droning starts to fade. It fades more and more into the background. The sights in front of you are fading, they are getting darker and dimmer and you can see less and less detail. You notice your eyes are closing gradually and surely. You fight it, you try to fight it and not give in. The heaviness in your body is spreading and deepening. All the energy seems to be draining from you.

You continue to struggle, you struggle to keep focused, you notice the deeper feelings spreading through your body as your senses drift and drift.

Whenever you are ready, you surrender to it....

Step Five:

Sleep.

I struggled to stay awake just writing that process.

Quiet The Mind and Drift to Sleep

This next process is a means of lulling yourself to sleep when your mind is busy. It does not aim to stop unwanted thoughts or let go of them in the same way that some of our previous techniques do. Instead, it generally lulls you to sleep as you'll see. We often have busy minds, especially if we have a busy life or are encountering a lot of issues. Therefore having a strategy to deal with that is incredibly useful. If your restlessness is caused by your mind's activity alone (i.e. you are not trying to sleep with stimulants in your system or having just exercised rigorously), then this is going to work a treat.

Step One:

Induce hypnosis using any method of your choice. Then move on to step two when you are hypnotised.

Step Two:

Engage your imagination to picture that you are on the highest floor of a big, bustling and busy office block in a city centre. Notice the view outside of the window, of all the other office buildings, and you can see traffic everywhere and people bustling here and there. Here in the office, things are also bustling. There is a deadline of some kind looming, and as a result, there are many office workers milling around at speed, others rushing at their desks. People are shouting into phones, making speedy photocopies, and the phones are ringing constantly. It is tough to try and keep up with all the movement, noise and activity in the office.

Many people look flustered. Many have looks of anguish and uneasiness on their faces. No-one is smiling. Some people argue and exhale loudly. Some are pushing past others as they move around the open plan area that does not seem big enough for all these people. More people seem to arrive and add to the busyness and noise, and it is hard to focus or concentrate at all. You notice that it feels hot and humid up here too.

Engage in this scene, see the sights, colours, shades of light and hear the incessant sounds, noises and distractions happening everywhere, perhaps making you feel agitated. As soon as you notice a slight sense of discomfort with the scene, then move on to the next step.

Step Three:

Noting that you feel a slight discomfort at the scene before you, you choose to head for the staircase and get out of here. As you open the doors to the staircase, you notice that there are people rushing up and down these stairs, looking pained and frustrated. The levels of frustration appear to have spilled out and the people walking around here are doing so quickly and without consideration. You choose to take the stairs downwards to the next floor. Each step that you make, takes you deeper into hypnosis.

As you arrive at the next floor of the office building, it is with a sense of relief, as you notice that the office space here seems to be 50% as congested. There are less people and as a result, there is less of a sense of anguish. A few people from upstairs still move at pace and exit again, but it is far more comfortable than where you were previously.

Maybe it is because this is a different department, maybe they are not on the same deadline as the people upstairs, but you notice the distinct difference of pace and volume of people, but there is still some overlap from the frantic atmosphere above (the offices are related after all). Once you have engaged and noticed all around you on this floor, once you have spotted the notable differences between here and upstairs, you move on to the next step.

Step Four:

You decide to head for the stairs again, leaving this still busy place and its ill-feeling behind you. As you step out of the doors, you notice that this staircase downwards is not nearly as congested or as busy as the previous one. Each step you take down the stairs takes you deeper inside your mind, all the time going deeper down inside the building and deeper into your mind.

As you arrive in the next open plan office, you notice that this one is distinctly calmer. There are leather seats and waiting areas, less work spaces and many of the fewer workers here are relaxed back in their chairs and you can only see a few workers around the place. They all seem to smiling and there is a noticeable lack of noise. There are pictures on the wall and plants that are healthy and thriving here.

This makes you smile and breathe a lot easier, it is refreshing and enjoyable to be here. There are fewer windows and these ones look out across quieter areas. The temperature here is cooler and more soothing. Enjoy this place, engage with it, notice all you can see, hear and feel and then when you notice how different it is, move on to the next step.

Step Five:

Yearning for some solitude and a deeper, more peaceful place, again you take the stairs to the next floor down, going deeper. Each step takes you deeper inside your mind as you drift further down the building and deeper into relaxing hypnosis.

It is wonderful to notice that there is virtually no-one else using these stairs; there is room for you to use them comfortably, and from time to time, you stop concentrating on the stairs and drift away while you go deeper down each step. You reach a level, you think it is the next level, but it feels as if you have gone further and deeper than that. You notice that this is some sort of executive level. There is a gentle soothing sound playing in the background. There is hardly a soul around. The air is clean and cool and smells like fresh mountain air.

Anyone that you do see moving around, does so deliberately, slowly, and with a sense of flow and balance and poise, with a smiling face and sense of serenity. They clearly enjoy being here. It is tranquil and optimum, and you take a few moments to absorb the surroundings of this level. You enjoy feeling deeply calm and peaceful with a notable physical relaxation working through you. Once you have noticed that sense within you, move on to the next step.

Step Six:

You step out of the doors again, and head down the stairs. You are now so relaxed that the non-populated staircase seems to be moving beneath your feet. You keep moving down a number of flights of stairs, enjoying the serenity and calmness. You lose track of how many flights and seem to float effortlessly down. With every step you take, you drift deeper down inside your mind.

Until you reach the bottom floor. The stairs end and you can barely believe you travelled so deep to this seemingly silent part of the building. There is no-one else around at all. You open the doors to see a number of quiet, dark, sumptuous sleeping pods that you have heard so many modern office blocks have these days. Clearly, no-one else is using any of them at the moment.

You lazily and casually stroll to whatever booth you find to be the most inviting and look in. It is lit in the perfect fashion. It has the colours, aroma, feel and sound of the perfect place for you to relax. Let your mind create the single most relaxing enjoyable space for you to relax and let go. As you look upon that relaxing space, when you have it perfectly in your mind, move on to the next step.

Step Seven:

You step inside this relaxing area and just fall onto the bed, languishing and surrendering yourself to it. The door locks quietly behind you. You lay on the bed. You loosen your clothing and kick off your shoes and put your feet up. You stretch out on the bed, it is the most comfortable bed, it supports you and your body in the ways that you enjoy the most. It is made of the material you like and has clean, fresh sheets and covers on it. You tuck yourself in and snuggle up as the lights soften further, almost as if they respond to your eyelids closing….

As you lie on the bed, a deep comfort seems to fill every pore of your entire body, relaxing you, calming you, lulling you into a deep and relaxing sleep. A deep, sound, beautiful sleep. The bed seems to mold itself to the exact contours of your body, and you feel as if you are settling a little deeper into it. As you sleep, your mind dreams about the most enjoyable times in your life, happy times, and you are filled with a deep satisfaction as the dreams gently dissipate and you drift into a deep, non-dreaming sleep.

You start to feel parts of your body relaxing even more, and the bed begins to gently sway subtly in time with your breathing. Sensations of relaxation start to spread through your body, relaxing and softening each muscle of your body. The relaxation is warming, softening, loosening, so that as long as you hold on to this quality of relaxation, every muscle of your body becomes loose, limp and dormant.... It almost feels as if your muscles are melting into the bed, and it is only gravity that you feel keeping you on the bed.

Step Eight:

Now you simply drift off and away... (there is no step to exit hypnosis, as you now drift off to sleep) Consider yourself lulled!

Getting Back to Sleep With Mindfulness, Self-hypnosis and Dissociation

One of the big issues I have found with people who have trouble with their sleep patterns and habits, is that if they wake in the night, their thoughts prevent them from getting back to sleep. There are a number of techniques and strategies that can help deal with such, including those already explained. This process shows you how to dissociate from the constant flow of unwanted thoughts and thereby stop those thoughts from having a physiological effect upon you. You can then relax and get back to sleep much more easily.

You see, often there is a degree of resistance that creates more of a problem. For example, when someone panics, they are medically safe to all intents and purposes (though the behaviour that accompanies panic can cause a potential problem) if they were to step back and let the panic happen, but without resistance, it would subside. What fuels it, are the combined thoughts, fears, worries and realistic imagery inside the head.

With this process, we learn to step back, let the thoughts just happen without resisting them, without fighting them. We also dissociate from the thoughts to leave a relaxed body behind. We start with some mindfulness, then move on to use the unwanted thoughts that we dissociate from. We then actually utilise those thoughts to help us relax and lull ourselves back to sleep. Here is the process to use as and when you require it:

Step One:

Induce hypnosis using any chosen method.

Step Two:

Begin by being aware of your entire body as one. From the top of your head, all the way down into your fingers and finger tips, and down into the tips of your toes. Be aware of your entire body as one. Just be aware of it and watch it.

Don't try to change anything; don't try to stop anything from changing. Sometimes things change all by themselves when you watch them. Embrace what is happening within you instead of fighting or resisting it. Be passive, a detached observer, be contented to notice what you notice, feel what you feel. Once you feel really tuned in and aware of your body, move on to the next step.

Step Three:

Tune in to your breathing next. Notice the sensations of your breathing, notice your tummy rise as you inhale and fall as you exhale. Notice your chest expand and relax. Notice even the faintest of sensations; even the tiniest feelings caused by the breath anywhere and everywhere in the body.

Don't try to change the breathing and don't try to stop it from changing, just be a passive observer. Let the body do the breathing. Observe it, as if you were watching a bird on a tree breathing, or as if you were watching someone else breathing, or as if you were watching a well-maintained machine. When you are truly tuned in to your breathing, very aware of it in its entirety, then move on to the next step.

Step Four:

Be more and more comfortably absorbed in the feelings of the body in this moment. One by one, turn your attention to the sensations in your arms, legs, chest, tummy, head and everywhere else.

As you focus on each area, let your awareness spread over the surface of your skin, deep into the muscles and even into the bones and joints. Let the breath guide your awareness deeper and deeper into the body. Let your mind be more patiently absorbed in even the smallest feelings. Once you have been through the entire body, let your awareness rest on your entire body as one. Let your body continue to do the breathing. Once you have this deep sense of awareness of yourself physically, then move on to the next step.

Step Five:

Now turn your attention even deeper toward your mind. Turn your attention to your thoughts. Become more aware of your thoughts and of anything you say to yourself in your mind. Notice the imagery that is there and the speed at which it is all moving. Become mindful even of unspoken thoughts at the back of your mind. Notice deliberate thoughts, or one's that just happen to cross your mind. Don't judge them, just accept the fact that they are happening, and allow yourself to become a detached observer of your own stream of consciousness.

Notice in particular, how you respond to your thoughts, as they occur, moment by moment, and how you feel about them as they happen. Just watch them happening, then move on to the next step.

Step Six:

Imagine that out there in front of you is a huge screen of some kind. Maybe it is a television screen, maybe it is a cinema screen, maybe it is just a vast frame of some kind. Create it in your mind in detail.

Simply let your entire stream of consciousness move into and upon the screen. Let it all be up there on that screen or in that frame, dissociated from you and out there. Now just watch it all happening over there and start to notice the difference that you feel in your body as you lighten up, relax deeper and drift comfortably back to sleep. Imagine your body relaxing more with each image that you watch on the screen before you. Just keep on suggesting to yourself that you relax further with each thing you watch and see on the screen, keep dissociated from it all, observe it and enjoy relaxing more. Let yourself drift away from there.

There it is, there you have it. You just drift to sleep from there.

Though many other sections of this book have techniques that can be applied to helping you sleep, this chapter has offered up a range of ways to use relaxation, mental imagery and other general guidelines in addition to self-hypnosis for enhancing your sleep. Now for something completely different...

Chapter Eleven: Reducing Pain

"For all the happiness mankind can gain
Is not in pleasure, but in rest from pain."
– John Dryden

"And the Lord God caused a deep sleep to fall upon Adam,
and he slept: and he took one of his ribs."
– Genesis, The Bible

I am not sure that the book of Genesis is referring to hypnosis, but myself and many other hypnosis professionals like to assume so.

When using self-hypnosis to lessen, control or overcome pain, it is important to distinguish pain from sensation. Pain is basically your reaction to sensations that you believe are hurting you, or are intolerable, unbearable or overwhelming. Your body deals with those perceptions biochemically by very cleverly manufacturing its own narcotic-like substances; namely endorphins. These endorphins block or reduce pain-triggering signals from reaching your brain.

The research evidence that I am going to present to you in the early part of this chapter tends to suggest that hypnosis works at a different level. Pain control by suggestion involves asserting your hypnotic mindset so that you do not respond in a mechanical fashion to such stimuli, and you refuse to be a victim to those sensations. With the mental imagery techniques and cognitive strategies in this chapter, you will also learn to alter your perception of potentially painful sensations so they don't bother you. You can also distract yourself, and distraction is made easier with self-hypnosis to help you keep your attention away from the source of pain, ignore the sensations, or redefine them to mean something other than pain.

Firstly, I am going to give you some examples of this happening in daily life, but also in some very impressive media demonstrations. In April 2006, on a live television broadcast, a show entitled Hypno-Surgery on More4 channel, showed Dr John Butler helping a man to experience anaesthesia using only hypnosis (i.e. no drugs), so that he could have a hernia removed from his stomach. It was a successful operation and once stitched back up, the man got up off the operating table and walked away. You can watch the full footage of this programme on YouTube. I think it is impressive viewing and shows what can be done with hypnosis. The same show also broadcasted a number of clips of dental surgery taking place with only the use of hypnotic anesthesia.

Speaking of which, in 2011, a friend of mine and graduate of my hypnotherapy training school, Gareth Lee Morgan, had 3 teeth removed using only self-hypnosis. If you google his name and mine together, you'll be able to read the full account that I wrote on my blog about his experience, including his comment that when his teeth were removed by the dentist, it felt as if his teeth were being scooped out of his mouth with a spoon.

Back in 1980, a dentist named Victor Rausch had his gall bladder removed while he helped instruct surgeons. He used self-hypnosis to undergo the surgical removal of his gall bladder. That is major surgery and he had no pharmacological anaesthesia or analgesia.

There are many other darlings of the media who have championed the use of hypnosis in surgery, including Alex Lenkei in 2008 who had a walnut size chunk of bone and tendon removed from hand could hear sawing and cracking bones but felt nothing (he is a hypnotist himself and has had 6 surgical operations using only hypnosis for anaesthesia, including ankle replacement surgery in 2013) and an Iranian cesarean section conducted using only hypnosis without anaesthesia (there are two such reports that can be found on YouTube).

When I was younger and was skiing, my dad (who at the time had metal pins holding his hip together from a schoolboy rugby injury) while he was skiing fell awkwardly and snapped his femur: the long bone in the thigh. If I just fall over in the soft cushioned snow I used to scream my head off, whereas my dad with his tolerance and way of responding to pain just carried on walking around with a limp and struggling about for 3 days with a snapped femur. The x-rays showed that it was actually snapped fully. Amazing. Now we cannot allow all the credit to be taken by a couple of extra mugs of gluwein in the bar over those three days. When he went to give blood in the years that followed prior to a full hip replacement, because I had helped him prepare for surgery giving him hypnotic suggestions for bleeding control, we found that it became difficult for him to give blood to use during his own operation! I am sure you have many examples of this of your own or from people you know and have encountered.

This is what can be done with hypnosis and self-hypnosis when it comes to pain. Using your self-hypnosis skills, you can put this ability within your conscious control.

The Evidence For Using Hypnosis to Deal With Pain

In addition to the experiences of those mentioned in the introduction to this chapter, I want to give you a brief overview of the main findings from the research. There has been a lot of research conducted exploring the effects of hypnosis on pain. While there are some specific studies examining self-hypnosis, a number of the studies include self-hypnosis as part of the treatment, and some of them are really only based upon hetero-hypnosis. However, since this is a book claiming to use evidence, I want to give a rounded perspective about the evidence. Furthermore, for those new to the field, this application of self-hypnosis can seem the most impressive, but also the most challenging. I want to encourage you.

The evidence indicates that hypnotic suggestions can influence physiological processes at the site of an injury. For example, in a classic study (that would probably not pass research ethics committees of today!) Chapman, Goodell, and Wolff *(1959)* contrasted the responses between right and left arm. Hypnotic suggestions had been given for one arm to be 'normal' and the other to be 'vulnerable' (or 'painful,' 'burning' etc.), and then harmful heat sources were applied to each arm. In 75% of the time, this resulted in greater inflammatory reactions and more tissue damage to the skin of the 'vulnerable' arm.. This study has been replicated with similar results.

I hope you got a sense of being able to influence vascular activity when practicing your hypnotic skills in the earlier psychosomatic section of the book (with the heating of the arm?). I'll be mentioning the phenomena of vascular activity again in this chapter, but for now I want to mention that evidence also supports the notion that we can influence vascular activity using hypnotic suggestions *(Casiglia et al., 1997; Klapow et al., 1996)*, which means that if the pain itself is influenced by inflammatory or vascular responses, hypnotic suggestion can help. My experience over the years of carrying out a great many live demonstrations at lectures, in classrooms and to some big audiences has been that the arm I was helping the individual to anaesthetise, often changed colour, due to blood moving out of the area (and often felt notably cooler to the touch). I continue to be amazed each time I see this happening.

With the advancements in the use of fMRI (functional magnetic resonance imagining) and PET scan (positron emission tomography) technology, researchers have been able to examine the effects of hypnosis upon the brain in relation to using hypnosis for anaesthesia and analgesia. Studies have shown how different parts of the brain have decreased levels of activity when suggestions have been given for pain decrease *(Faymonville et al., 2000; Hofbauer et al., 2001; Rainville et al., 1997; Wik et al., 1999)*. Similarly, studies showed that hypnosis can also alter the process of brain activity *(Faymonville et al., 2003; Fingelkurts et al., 2007)*. An important conclusion that gets drawn from neurophysiological research is that hypnotic suggestions do not just affect one particular mechanism in the brain, rather, they affect a number of them. As a result, there are many variations of hypnotic suggestions that can affect and influence different responses. Therefore, as a self-hypnotist, you are recommended to be persistent and to examine the effects of your own suggestions upon your pain responses to fine-tune the best hypnotic suggestions for you and the type of pain you are working on (because different suggestions may be influencing different parts of the brain, and it would be another book entirely to attempt to list each and every trend that would still not necessarily guarantee you the same results).

What is incredibly encouraging from the studies and reviews is that hypnosis consistently proves more effective in controlled trials [?], and continues to do so for as long as the research follow-up goes on for; even when the participants have been followed up a year later (Jensen et al., 2008). As many studies have demonstrated, hypnosis has also proven to be as effective, and often more effective than other treatments when it comes to reducing pain *(Andreychuk and Skriver, 1975; Anderson et al., 1975; Edelson and Fitzpatrick, 1989; Friedman and Taub, 1984; Gay et al., 2002; Haanen et al., 1991; Winocour et al., 2002).*

Importantly for us self-hypnotists though, research shows that benefits of hypnosis treatment would actually increase over time as patients practiced self-hypnosis *(Jensen et al., 2005).*

Sellick and Zaza *(1998)* examined 6 studies using hypnotic analgesia for cancer pain. Three of those studies were on adult patients *(Spiegel and Bloom, 1983; Syralja et al., 1992, 1995)* and three were working with children *(Zeltzer and Lebaron, 1982; Katz et al., 1987; Wall and Womack, 1989).* Sellick and Zaza concluded that there was *"much support for the specific use of hypnosis in managing pain associated with medical procedures and some support for its use in managing chronic cancer pain"*(p. 13).

Smith et al. *(2006)* completed a review of complementary and alternative therapies for pain management in labour, which included five studies on the use of hypnosis for reducing pain *(Rock et al., 1969; Freeman et al., 1986; Harmon et al., 1990; Martin et al., 2001; Mehl-Madrona, 2004)*. Smith et al., concluded that *"the data available suggest hypnosis reduces the need for pharmacological pain relief in labour"* (p. 10).

It is worth adding that a study has also indicated that using hypnosis in conjunction with cognitive therapy can advance the reduction in pain *(Jensen et al., 2011)*, when the pain-related cognitions are dealt with. Therefore, it would make sense that I include some techniques that utilise cognitive strategies, but also suggest that you address how you use your cognitions when you relate to your pain. You can do this using principles of progressive language described earlier in the book, using the cognitive disputation methods detailed in the anxiety chapter, and by considering some of the other relevant content coming up in this chapter.

There is also evidence that shows a range of mental imagery protocols will help decrease pain, even those as simple as spending time hypnotised imagining being in a 'special place' *(Jensen, Barber, Romano, Hanley, et al., 2009; Jensen, Barber, Romano, Molton et al., 2009)*. Most of the processes that follow in this chapter are cognitive strategies or mental imagery techniques; you have enough information on just using suggestion following the earlier section of the book. Not all of the techniques shared in this chapter have randomised controlled trials supporting them, and[?] the underlying principles of all the processes are in line with research findings.

Before I launch into what I consider to be amazing stuff, I need to make something clear: before altering your perception of pain with hypnosis and the other techniques and strategies we use here, be sure to get in touch with your doctor or physician about your pain. Pain is often there for a reason, and pain is often the body's way of advising us that we need to take care of, or pay more attention to ourselves.

Of course you undoubtedly know that each and every one of us experiences pain in some shape or form in our lives, regardless of who we are, where we are, how old we are, or our background or whatever. However, we all perceive pain in our own unique and highly individual way. Two people with the same injury or the same source of pain, may well be having two very different responses to that same injury or that same complaint. Some people have what is often referred to as a higher pain threshold, and can seem to cope with more than other people. It is this varying and extremely subjective, personalised response to pain that we all possess that gets the medical world baffled at times.

There are some important aspects to using self-hypnosis for the purpose of pain relief. Firstly, it is particularly important with pain relief that you practice your skills repeatedly and persistently. Simply conducting a single hypnosis session and then leaving it there is unlikely to yield lifelong self-efficacy, or the benefits you are looking for.

You really do need to continue to practice and experiment with the various techniques and strategies that are described in this chapter. To enhance the length of time and the effectiveness and quality of the pain relief, requires practice combined with the attitudes inherent within the hypnotic mindset. If the pain has been a persistent pain that has been put up with for a long period of time, the pain may well be more difficult to initially alter, and it may well be firmly installed within your belief system; so it is likely to need plenty of persistence.

Our belief system with regards to pain is where the root to success lies. We have had a certain belief system installed within us throughout our lifetime. With the emergence of modern medicine in the last few generations, we have learned to expect pain relief from an external source: through medicine or from someone else that would help us to overcome it, such as a parent or a doctor, and add to that the persistent media coverage and advertising from pharmaceutical companies, which further develops the belief that pain comes from outside our bodies, not from the inside.

Pain, of course, does have its purposes and values. Some very important purposes at that: we need pain to tell us to move our hand away from the hot iron or the recently used hot kettle, or to take it out of the freezing cold water. Our experience of pain can therefore save us from all kinds of life threatening disorders or circumstances. It alerts us. However, the more common experience of pain is quite different and often has less value, and therefore we may want to heighten our understanding of it and learn how to be in control of it. Pain perception differs from person to person and from culture to culture, reflecting cultural expectations as well *(Hardy, Wolff, and Goodell, 1952; Sternbach and Tursky, 1965).* Pain that seems unbearable in one person may be put up with in silence by someone else. Some people even revel in pain; for example, a masochist enjoys it.

Pain is experienced by most as an unpleasant sensory and emotional experience, as well as a physiological experience. It is commonly associated with strenuous activity, disease and injury, and it can also be caused by toxins within the body's system. Pain is there for a reason as I have said; it is a warning system that requires professional consultation. There are times when the pain signal is of little or no value; if it is providing misleading information, such as in the case of phantom limb pain. First and foremost, however, this book recommends strongly that anyone experiencing pain makes a visit to a medical professional, such as a doctor or physician.

Many ways have been used to alleviate pain over the years. I have experienced many and found hypnosis accompanied with a range of mental imagery techniques and cognitive skills to be one of the best ways of overcoming and altering my response to it. That is my subjective experience only, which does not count for much in an evidence-based approach. It is also recommended that you use self-hypnosis as an adjunct to your medical advice and medication (i.e. not as a complete alternative), especially in the first instance.

Pain reduction requires alteration of both the effect (the actual suffering) and cognition (ways of thinking about pain). The self-hypnotist learns to take control of body perception by altering the cognitions and feelings that tend to dominate, or at least flavour our awareness.

Pain is both an intrinsic biological signal that something is wrong in our body and an adaptive response. In this respect, the perception of pain arises as a simple, urgent and primitive message *(Melzack, 1973)*. However, pain is not always perceived after injury, especially when we are engaged in a fully competitive activity. Take the famous example of Berhard "Bert" Trautmann, the German professional goalkeeper, who played for Manchester City in the 1956 FA cup final in England. Trautmann dived at the feet of an opponent, resulting in an injury to his neck. He carried on playing with a noticeably crooked neck and is even seen rubbing his neck as he collects his medal. However, an x-ray later that day, revealed his neck was broken!

How Do We Use Self-Hypnosis to Control Pain?

When working with pain, it pays to have practiced hypnotic skills and in particular, developed a degree of self-efficacy with the psychosomatic notions inherent within those skills. One key point to bear in mind before we start is that whatever your past experiences with pain have been like, by practicing these self-hypnosis techniques and skills, you will get better at them.

Traditionally, there are three main strategies considered to be of most use for self-hypnotists overcoming pain: relaxation, distraction and goal-directed imagining. These can be used in isolation or in combination with each other, and ideally if you punctuate them with the progressive language you have learned in the early sections of this book, your cognitions will advance these approaches.

The Use of Relaxation

As with our chapter dedicated to this subject, relaxation can be your first line of defence against pain. As demonstrated within the chapter for overcoming anxiety, a number of researchers have shown that pain and relaxation struggle to live with each other simultaneously. The tenser you are, the more you hurt; the more relaxed you are, the less the same things pain you. This is why relaxation can be so important in controlling your perception of pain.

Relaxation is used a great deal in helping to reduce or overcome natural childbirth pain. Childbirth places a woman under a large amount of stress with more intense sensations than virtually anything else she could expect to experience in life. Childbirth does not have to be an agonisingly painful experience though.

The British obstetrician, Dr. Grantley Dick-Reade, discovered that by simply reducing fear and anxiety, through educating the prospective parent in the facts of the birthing process, this eliminated most of the pain associated with having babies.

Since then, there have been Lamaze techniques that include progressive relaxation, the Bradley Method that involves nothing more strenuous than deep relaxation practiced throughout the labour, and a number of hypnobirthing techniques that all include relaxation as a way of alleviating pain and discomfort. These methods also tend to show how progressive mental imagery can advance and enhance the relaxation (e.g. with the Bradley method, contractions are viewed as ocean waves rippling through the body). You can therefore use the relaxation techniques already described in this book, as well as all manner of combined mental imagery techniques given in this chapter for great effect.

The Use of Distraction

When I am conducting a glove anaesthesia demonstration at lectures, I often ask the individual to focus all of their attention upon their toes or the other arm (i.e. not the one we want anaesthetized). This way, they create the anaesthesia by being distracted from the site of the pain altogether. With this approach, you concentrate elsewhere or upon something else, so that you aren't focusing on anything in the here and now that may contribute to your pain. The most common way of doing this is to think about something else, such as tuning into your toes when you want anaesthesia in your arm. The other common way is to imagine yourself being elsewhere in a completely different place and scenario, and to engage in it as much as you possibly can.

The use of evocative imagery can also be used to distract. You may imagine going to a place or time when you did not have the pain, and felt comfortable and well. One patient in a study imagined himself at a baseball game when his team won *(Toomey and Sanders, 1983)*. He felt jubilant as a result and experienced comfort while imagining being there.

The Use of Goal-directed Imagining

Goal-directed imagining is whereby the imagination is engaged with the aim of reducing the pain response, such as imagining using ice for inducing anaesthesia, as we'll be looking at shortly. Most of the techniques in this chapter use this kind of process, so I shall not explain them in any more detail just yet.

Self-hypnosis is useful when looking to control pain, partly because of some of the general effects of self-hypnosis: a reduction of the generalized reality orientation and absorption in the inner experience *(Fromm et al., 1981)*. Through the use of mental imagery techniques, the self-hypnotist transforms perceptions, meanings and sensations. When it comes to pain management, the previously discussed hypnotic mindset with all of its structural variables, attitudes and expectancies, all contribute to what can be a truly remarkable experience of self-hypnosis.

Specific Pain Reduction Self-Hypnosis Techniques

Before I start to explain some step-by-step techniques, there are many techniques from other chapters that could be used with pain management too, such as creating a pain dial or gauge, using a balloon (as used with cravings in the habit chapter, but pain gets put inside of it instead) or even using the clenched fist technique that we use in the anger chapter. You can also use the massage/mud bath type of relaxation techniques offered in the relaxation chapter for more of a restorative, pain-relieving result. These upcoming techniques can also be adapted to your specifications, and remember to use your own progressive language and attitude throughout.

Create Numbness and Anaesthesia

One of the classic ways to help deal with pain is to learn to create analgesia and anaesthesia. A method that is commonly used by hypnotherapists for this is called a 'glove anaesthesia' technique, whereby you are hypnotised and imagine placing your hand into icy water and/or ice, which develops numbness and can then be spread elsewhere in the body by touch. Rather than just that single method, I thought I'd offer up a variety of ways to create a really good level of numbness, anaesthesia and analgesia in the arm or other body part.

This is one of those processes that can absolutely create impressive results very quickly. However, I recommend that it is something that is developed and built up over a prolonged period of time – that you practice, utilise repetition and persistence in order to build up your skill level. With a good level of practice, you'll also find that you'll be capable of moving the anaesthesia to other parts of the body if required.

This is a step-by-step process, however, that has a number of options within the guide; so give a thorough read on a couple of occasions prior to practicing. If you want to chart your own progress and development with this skill, you may want to pinch your chosen arm or hand at the start, be aware of how much force you used and gauge the amount of discomfort or pain that is felt. Then later on, when you have induced the anaesthesia and numbness, you can start to test it and compare the measurement made beforehand. I have a friend who practices this by attaching a crocodile clip to the skin on his arm, but that is for more advanced self-hypnotists who have developed this skill. Be safe and apply common sense with this, use it as a convincer, use it with safety and not in a way that is going to cause you harm.

Step One:

Induce hypnosis using any of the processes described in this book. Once you have induced hypnosis, move on to step two.

Step Two:

Tell yourself that every thought you think takes you deeper into hypnosis, and then do one or all of the following strategies to start developing the numbness and anaesthesia:

a)   **Use cognitions and internal dialogue:** Affirm to yourself that the area of your arm that you are focusing on is going numb. This needs to be done in a way that convinces you that it is the truth; that is, say it to yourself in a way that you believe it 100% at an emotional level.

Do not say it with stress, and do not 'try' to will it to happen, just convince yourself with a good level of assuredness. Focus your attention on a particular spot on your hand or your arm and begin to imagine and notice that it is growing numb. Then tell yourself it is going numb. Convince yourself using your internal dialogue that it is so. Utilise any accompanying twitches, or slight sensations by telling yourself that they are proof of it taking effect and working for you.

Tell yourself that "my arm is more and more numb. Feeling is fading, disappearing... More and more numb", or use whatever kind of other cognitions really convince you.

b) **Use of cold and ice:** This is typically my first choice when doing this using hetero-hypnosis with someone.

Imagine that you are putting your hand, finger tips first, and then slowly the rest of the hand and arm into a bucket of icy water. Imagine the coldness and numbness spreads, and then imagine it getting colder until the water turns to ice and the arm is encased. Again, add belief and convince yourself of it.

You can tell yourself that the arm is getting colder and colder, but ensure it is not an uncomfortable coldness that would harm us in real-life terms. No self-induced frostbite here please! Some of my students have imagined pure white snow falling on the arm, building up and getting colder. You may use icy, barren arctic conditions as a stimulus to dominate the mind and accompany what you do with the arm directly, thus creating an internal environment for your thoughts that supports and encourages the coldness in the arm.

c) **Numb colouring:** With either of the previous options and with those that follow, you may choose to use your imagination to colour the area in a way that leads to numbness. Ideally, white and blue tend to get associated with cold and that may prove useful.

However, when I do this with clients or students with hetero-hypnosis, I have often noticed the actual change in colour in the arm as blood is mobilized. Often the arm loses some of its usual colour and turns a more yellow or pale colour. You might consider suggesting the same thing to yourself using colour, imagining that the arm is becoming paler. This use of colour can advance and enhance any of the other options given here.

d)   **A numbing injection:** This is particularly good and effective if you have had an experience of a numbing, analgesic injection in the past, at a hospital, doctor surgery or dentist.

You might notice or imagine being in a doctor's surgery or a surgical environment if that helps create the right feel for you. Then imagine the injection and focus on the cooling, numbing sensation that occurs; focus on it and even add the use of your internal dialogue, colouring and coolness imagery to advance the sensation.

e)   **Turn the arm into something else:** This is the kind of process used by Derren Brown in his recent stage show. This is whereby you use your imagination to picture that your arm and hand are actually made of a different substance. You imagine that the arm takes on the qualities of that substance.

You imagine that the arm and hand are beginning to change gradually into a piece of wood, plastic, or the same as an arm of a clothing shop mannequin. You imagine the arm becoming inert, like painted wood or soft plastic. You tell yourself that it is becoming more and number as it takes on those qualities.

f) **Distraction:** This is working upon dissociation principles. While inducing the numbness, you shift your awareness and focus to another completely different part of your body, you become so aware and tuned in to your toes or foot, for example, that you lose any awareness of the arm and it becomes numb by default.

I recommend that a combination of these techniques and processes be used to develop the desired outcome. Remember to convince yourself and add as much belief as possible without unnecessary stress being placed upon yourself. When you have built up and developed the numbness, move on to the next step.

Step Three:

Now test your anaesthesia if you wish to. Test it with the same pinch you used earlier and see how much of a difference you have created. Congratulate yourself before moving on.

Step Four:

Tell yourself that each time you practice this, your responses become more and more noticeable and developed, becoming better and better. Each time you practice, it is easier and more profound. Tell yourself that the numbness occurs more readily. Tell yourself that you are making fabulous progress. Then move on to the next step.

Step Five:

Start to put the feeling and sensation back into your arm. Imagine it warming, imagine the correct colour of it, give yourself suggestions and instructions that it returns to its usual way of being, and that it is healthy and at ease, functioning well.

You might flex it or wave it and put it all back into place, associating with all the normal feelings of the arm. Tell yourself that this continues to develop and occur after the session is completed. For people wishing to use anaesthesia for actual surgery, dentistry or for some other reason, then you may want to give yourself a time limit for the anaesthesia to continue occurring. Let it be effective for the duration of the procedure.

You may then also give yourself suggestions for improved, enhanced healing and development after the procedure. However, if you are planning on using it for surgery or in a medical capacity, I would not advise using this process without some professional guidance and tuition. A simplified article is not the best preparation for such.

Step Six:

Bring yourself out of hypnosis, counting and opening your eyes if they were closed.

I think you'll be surprised by how much you can achieve with this technique and the ways you can develop it. I hope you enjoy it and get to marvel at what you can do, and that you also do this safely and carefully. We'll build upon this with some other strategies too.

Blocking Pain Messages to The Brain

This technique is showing you how to use self-hypnosis to alleviate pain. However, the technique can be used for a number of other types of applications, as you see fit or applicable yourself. A point that I make to anyone and everyone regarding using self-hypnosis to alleviate pain, is that you must not attempt to alleviate the pain for any longer than a typical pain killing tablet would last for. Do not simply use self-hypnosis techniques to block out pain and ignore it forever.

Step One:
Induce hypnosis using any method you choose. Then, once you have induced hypnosis, move on to step two.

Step Two:
Tune into yourself. Be mindful. Spend some time just observing your breathing rate, noticing the thoughts that are going through your mind and noticing your feelings. Become aware of the pain you are experiencing, while also becoming aware of the details of that pain. Just watch it, observe it without interfering with it for the time being.

Relax your body as much as you possibly can with your thoughts. Methodically relax your body with your intention and focus, and tell yourself that being mindful and relaxing is taking you deeper into hypnosis. Then move on to step three.

Step Three:

Imagine you have two wires/cables carrying all the information from your body to your brain. From the area where the pain was in your body, imagine two thick, coloured wires going from that area of your body to the brain.

The first one carries all the nerve messages regarding pain from the area to the brain. This cable is a particular colour. The second wire/cable is a different colour, and it carries all other impulses between that area and your brain. However, it cannot carry pain signals at all. It is incapable of carrying pain signals, they are all carried exclusively by the other wire.

Notice the details of the wire, notice if you can sense the messages moving within them and really tune in to them. Just know that the more you believe in these wires, the more effective this process is going to be for you. As you look at them, trust that you can use them to change the way you experience the old pain response. Once you have convinced yourself of this, move on to the next step.

Step Four:

Using your imagination, follow the first wire with your awareness all the way to where it plugs into your brain. Follow it and go to the end of the wire, then pull out the wire that used to carry the pain messages. Unplug it. For a while, just pull it out, the same way you'd pull out a telephone cable.

As you do that, notice how the pain signals can no longer reach your brain; it is as if the pain has been switched off. Perhaps you notice the responses happening immediately, or it might take a small amount of time for the response to fully drain away and not be recognized by your brain. Trust that over the course of the next 4 hours, it will gradually find its way back to the socket, but you remain pain-free while it is unplugged, as none of the pain messages can reach your brain.

Step Five:

With the wire unplugged focus exclusively on a completely different part of your body, and spend some time relaxing your body once again. Take your time in doing this. Engage in some progressive relaxation while you have the wire unplugged. You can do this using any of the ways described in the relaxation chapter. Once you have done that for a good period of time, move on to the next step.

Step Six:

If you wish, in addition, you can also spend some time developing and building some numbness and anaesthesia in the area. You can do so by following the steps in the previous technique on numbness and anaesthesia.

Step Seven:

Once you have spent enough time developing and building the anaesthesia, now convince yourself that you have switched off the old pain messages; gently assure yourself and convince yourself using your imagination. Use your cognitions and affirm it to yourself. Say it to yourself, let yourself gently believe in it.

Step Seven:

Exit hypnosis. Take a couple of deep breaths, count yourself up and out of hypnosis. Remember that when you exit hypnosis and have been developing pain relief, you want the pain relief to remain, so do not suggest that all sensations return as they were prior to the session. Be thoughtful about how the effects of your exit procedure will influence what you have done in the session. Bring the changes and the pain relief with you into your real life. As with so many self-hypnosis techniques, this one requires practice and repetition.

Communicating With and Transforming Pain Feelings

Just before marrying Katie, we went on holiday to the Caribbean. I did the classic things of sipping my pina colada, small talking with my beautiful fiancé and soaking up the sunshine, eating well and reading lots and lots.

It was also my birthday while we were there. I love birthdays. I love celebrations of any kind. They give me a nice feeling – I love the feeling of anticipation, I love the excitement and the attention during the day, and the way everyone seems to be. It's as if we filter everything during that day in a way that allows us to focus on good feelings. A birthday on holiday was even more wonderful, I have to say.

In my therapeutic work over the years, I have noticed that it is a rare individual who focuses on feelings at all, let alone focuses on good ones. Often we tend to roll around in our feelings without realising what they mean or what they are actually telling us. What

I want to suggest next is that we actually turn our feelings into 'things'; that is, we objectify them in order to transform them in our mind.

A while back I attended a large Buddhist meditation event. I am not Buddhist, however, I thoroughly enjoy the meditations, and I love many Zen philosophies and ideas, and so I enjoyed this particular event.

One of the things that we were instructed on during a guided meditation was to focus on a feeling and become more aware of it, and then communicate with the feeling. I found it to be incredibly enjoyable and useful, and though meditation has a fairly good evidence base with regards to pain management in and of itself, this process is going to harness it with self-hypnosis. This technique allows you to be acutely aware of the feelings you have in your physical body, and to turn the feeling into an object that can be changed.

I love the idea of communicating with our feelings. I mean if you think about it, the simple process of making them separate things that we can communicate with, is disassociating us from them and helping us distinguish them more accurately. Next up then, is a simple process for turning your painful feelings into objects.

Many of my clients that I work with in my therapy rooms often 'objectify' thoughts, feelings and emotions - that is, they turn a process into a thing. Instead of 'feeling the experience of being depressed', or understanding the process of what they do when they are depressed, they often refer to 'having this depression.' I half expect them to pull it out of their pocket to show me. Pain is the same. Many clients tell me that they have this 'sharp pain' and it can sound like they have a pointy object attached to their head.

In therapy, we conceptualise the client's issue in such a way that they become aware of the process of what they do, so that they can stop doing it, interrupt it and eventually stop it. When we are dealing with things in our own mind and looking at self-improvement, rather than actually receiving therapy, it can be useful on many levels to deal with a 'thing' rather than a mass of intangible feelings or emotions. That 'thing' can be accessed and communicated with if need be. And that is what this pain relieving technique is all about.

Step One:

Induce hypnosis using any process you choose. Then deepen sufficiently and ideally, be very mindful of yourself throughout. This will aid the remainder of the technique. Once you have induced hypnosis and deepened in a mindful fashion, then move on to step two.

Step Two:

While acknowledging that many of us experience sensations that we regard as unpleasant and undesirable, without focusing on it too much, just notice any symptoms of any unwanted pain you may have currently or had recently.

Our aim here is to dissolve and remove all those symptoms. It is sometimes difficult to consciously modify our feelings. It is much easier for some to modify an object in our imagination. So right now, we are going to change any unwanted painful sensation into an object.

Notice whatever the painful sensations are and give the feeling a shape. Whenever you feel those sensations in the future, you can always give them a shape. Just imagine a shape, allow yourself to visualise or imagine that shape. It can be any kind of shape: abstract or concrete. It can be an object or a geometric design, soft or hard. Also give it a colour. Take all the time you feel is necessary to get the right shape, colour and characteristics established in your mind. Then move on to the next step.

Step Three:

As you picture and imagine the size and colour of that shape. You can give it a size by knowing the size or picturing it next to something you know the size of. Recognise and realise that the shape is the symbol of your discomfort or unwanted pain. Perhaps the larger the shape is, the more severe the discomfort it represents. Just assess it from this dissociated stance for a few moments.

Step Four:

Here comes the fun part. Practice making that shape larger and larger. Make it as large as you possibly can without becoming too uncomfortable. Then, just let it grow smaller and smaller and smaller still, and so small you can't even recognise it anymore. When you first make the shape bigger, it is easier to make it smaller.

If you have difficulty making it smaller then use your imagination. If the shape is a balloon you can stick a pin in it or untie the end, letting it get smaller and smaller. You can tie it to the back of a car and let it drive away, or you can pretend it is filled with helium, release it and watch it float away until it is smaller and smaller and so small, you can't even see it anymore. Use your imagination in whatever way is best for you and ensure you diminish it as best as you can. Again, take the time necessary to do that.

Step Five:

As you watch that symbol become smaller, the feelings associated with it are becoming less and less intense, and you can make them smaller. Imagine the old unwanted feelings and sensations get as small and comfortable as you want to make them, and you achieve this by practicing making them smaller and bigger, then smaller again. Turning the feeling on and then off, as much as you possibly can.

Step Six:

Once you feel that you have practiced this enough for this session, knowing that you can give the shape a size and colour, and then instantly and easily make the shape smaller and the colour fade away, then let the shape disappear. Imagine that you are finding it difficult to even find the shape as it shrinks and fades. Then exit by counting from one through to five and opening your eyes.

This process is one that once you have practiced it in hypnosis a number of times, you should be able to employ it in real-life situations and scenarios without formal self-hypnosis.

The Hypnotic Tablet

At the time of writing this, the weekend was a victorious one indeed. I went for my first run following my broken foot 8 weeks previously – I felt out of my usual shape, though I was so happy to have the wind in my hair, the sea air in my lungs and the sun shining on my face.

For many different reasons, the weekend I had was a truly successful one. I predicted fun. I ordered fun. I anticipated fun. I planned fun. I behaved in a way that ensured I had a lot of fun and boy oh boy did we have some laughs this weekend. On Saturday night, upon arriving at our restaurant destination in the far reaches of Dorset, having warmed up with some fizzy drinks, because I was with my favourite people in the world, I was excited and hyperactive, and when joking around with one of the waitresses, she asked my friends: "Is he always like this… He must need a chill pill from time to time…"

The comment is an interesting one that so many of us use in varying ways. It represents that notion that is so prevalent in conventional health care – that well-being is just a tablet away.

One of my favourite bands is a group called The Jam, who were big in the 70s and early 80s – they sang about 'The Bitterest Pill' they had to take. It's a funny expression that alludes to the idea of having to swallow something that is for your good, yet it tastes bitter and is not palatable. Yet, we find it so very, very easy to take a tablet, don't we?

We have a tablet taking culture for when we have a headache, when we are depressed (I know people who have been taking tablets for years to feel happy!), have indigestion, a cold, or pretty much anything else. There are scam-artists and con-men out there who make a living telling us that they have a miracle tablet that will make you thin! It is not proven to work by any credible authority, yet we cling to the notion because it might just work for us.

Yet it would be far more effective to get your mind and body in shape with proven methods that require more concerted effort than taking a tablet, and thus may seem less attractive as a result.

A vast amount of research about the Placebo effect has shown how much faith we truly have in tablets *(Kirsch, 2009)*. Placebo research shows some minor change as a result of placebo medicines. This next self-hypnosis technique, shows you how to create your own hypnotic tablet that you can take and allow your body to respond accordingly. You may be amazed at just how your mind and body respond to taking a hypnotic tablet. We are using it for pain alleviation here, but it can be used instead of[?] taking performance enhancing drugs, recreational drugs or even as a hypnotic Viagra tablet.

Before you start with this process, you may want to have a grape, orange segment, sugar lump or any other thing that could take on the role of your hypnotic tablet (or you may simply choose to imagine taking one in your mind later on). Whether you opt for imagining consuming it later, or if you need a bit more reality in your mind, then prepare accordingly at this stage. As you get settled, have a good think about the pain-relieving effect that you'd like your hypnotic tablet to have on you.

Step One:

Induce hypnosis using a method of your choice. Once you have induced hypnosis move on to step two.

Step Two:

Have some sort of outcome in your mind. Have a think about the affects you wish your special hypnotic tablet to give you. To help with this, using your imagination, think about if you had a miracle cure of some kind, then what would it be for? What would it do? What is the effect that you wish?

Once you have the effect in mind, also think and ask yourself – what would that be like if it could create that outcome? Then have a very good think about what is going to tell you that you have achieved that outcome. What are the signs that are undeniably convincing of the success of your hypnotic tablet? With this in mind move on to step three.

Step Three:

Tune into your body. By that I mean, get a real sense for how you are feeling physically throughout this technique; this is important because you want to benefit physiologically and psychologically from this process.

Now is the time to imagine that tablet. Create it in your mind. Imagine that you have it in front of you or actually hold your grape, sugar lump or whatever you may be using for a real life object to use in the session – charge it – insert all your hypnotic abilities into it.

By that, I mean, imagine that you are enchanting it with all the desired effects. Maybe you imagine the effects that you have had before, and empty them into the tablet. Maybe you imagine it changing in colour as it becomes enchanted. Maybe you imagine it vibrating or pulsing as you add all the specialist elements that you wish.

Imagine the effects pouring out from you and from all nature around you. Filling it with magic, health, well-being, joy and more and more of the things that are going to make this so wonderful for you. If you do not like the idea of magical enchantment, you can simply imagine that the tablet is a painkiller with very strong painkilling ingredients within it.

Once you have completed creating it in your mind, ensure you perceive it correctly.

Firstly, as you look at your completed hypnotic tablet, just think to yourself – 'I know that is going to work.' Trust that it is going to have all the desired effects that you created.

Secondly, recall a time that you have taken a tablet for a similar type of effect, and imagine an enhanced version of that experience. An experience that is even better.

Connect with your body all the time. Tune into your own physiology throughout each step of this process. Allow your body and mind to feel a sense of togetherness with this, as you really want your hypnotic tablet to communicate its effects physically and mentally. Then move on to the next step.

Step Four:

Take the tablet. Pop your pill. Gulp it down, swallow it, consume it in whatever way is right for you. Imagine the tablet's journey. Imagine it dispersing its effects as it enters your body. You may want to spend some time just imagining it spreading through your system. You can use this as a deepener too; as the tablet goes deeper into your system, so you go deeper into hypnosis.

Imagine connecting with all the cells in your being and the tablet having the desired effect. Maybe you can imagine the tablet spreading a healing colour throughout your system. Or an energy or vibration, or just a renewed sensation of well-being.

Bask in the healing sensations and enjoy the effects spreading and multiplying. Trust this tablet to have the full desired effect upon you. Tell yourself what you want to happen and what to expect, use your cognitions and add some suggestion to your hypnotic tablet as it works through your body.

Whenever you feel that you have truly absorbed all that you need to, and are ready for the tablet to do its own thing from here onwards, then move on to the final step.

Step Five:

Exit hypnosis by counting from one through to five. Remembering to keep the beneficial effects of the tablet with you once you are out of hypnosis. All the techniques in this chapter are prime examples of practice advancing your results.

Letting Go of Emotional Pain

In addition to actual physical pain, I also wanted to include a process that addresses emotional pain, or 'suffering' as it is often referred to. This next process is more of a coping skill developer. It is used and applied in a similar fashion to learning relaxation skills and breathing techniques to deal with the symptoms of anxiety, worry or fear.

When we experience loss or grief, or have been emotionally troubled in some way, then it can be of great, great value to be able to dissipate the symptoms in order that we can have space to deal with anything the symptoms may obscure. I know that when I have discussed with my clients the physical symptoms of grief, or separation or jealousy, for example, they often describe it as a tightening of the chest or a knot in the stomach, This process is going to help with that type of pain. We are going to deal with the heart in this session, metaphorically speaking, of course.

Step One:
Induce hypnosis using the method of your choice.

Step Two:
Imagine being in a safe place for a few moments. You can create this place and design it in your mind. You can be in a familiar place. Just choose somewhere and be somewhere that you can relax and feel safe, secure and at ease.

Let the sensations of safety spread through you and engage in the place you are in. See the sights and notice colours, shades of light and detail. Hear the sounds, those that are near and obvious, as well as those that are subtle or distant. Notice how you experience feeling safe. Tell yourself that you drift deeper as you engage with and imagine this safe place, and when you have created it and feel as though you have deepened your experience, then move on to the next step.

Step Three:

Now move your awareness inside of yourself. That is, stop engaging with the surroundings and move your awareness to you and your body. Become aware of your breathing and get a sense of the rhythm of your body, your pulse rate and your feelings. Notice your heart, become aware of your heart beating and allow each beat of your heart to take you deeper inside your mind.

While you focus on your heart, remaining safe and comfortable, also notice that there are bands of some kind wrapped around your heart. They are like ties of some kind that weight and tighten the sensation of your heart. You and your mind know what these ties around your heart represent.

These ties represent the emotional pain that you have experienced recently in your life. Get a sense of what they represent for you, and notice how you experience them being there. It is almost as if the bands are holding the pain in, and from time to time, the bands get tighter and seem to keep the pain there in your heart. Be aware of this sensation as much as is useful for you, then move on to the next step.

Step Four:

Focus on your mind and in your mind create a spark of light of some kind. Perhaps it is like a distant light, of a particular colour, but as you think about it, it becomes brighter and stronger and more radiant inside your mind. Notice the colour, the temperature of it, and let it get bright inside your mind. Add any strength, resources or sense of joy and release to the light and let it signify a deep healing.

Then send it strongly and powerfully to your heart. You might imagine it flying out of you and back to your heart, or that it moves through your body to your heart, or you may make it arrive as if teleported to your heart – do what is right for you to get the light to your heart and watch what happens… Notice the light seems to loosen, lighten and melt the bands. Notice how the ties ease their grip and eventually disappear and dissipate. The light soothes and eases the sensation within the heart, and it spreads to the tummy, shoulders and any other affected areas.

Take time to let each tie disappear and be melted thoroughly as you imagine all that emotional pain is released. At this point, signal to yourself the pain ebbing away; you might sigh out loud, or just exhale deeply. Perhaps you feel sensations let go, or imagine a colour change. Do whatever is right to signify that release and letting go, along with a dissipation of the old, unwanted feelings that are replaced by warmth and soothing feelings, growing and building within you. Spend some time letting that good feeling grow and develop, then move on to the next step.

Step Five:

Pick a typical time or place in your life that has been difficult for you to deal with, that triggers the old pain that you used to have. Put yourself in that place in a future moment and watch how you breathe, create the light in your mind that soothes and dissipates the old pain: loosen those ties, those bands that used to tighten. Spread the good feelings through your body and in detail, watch how well you cope in that situation now. Repeat the process as many times as you like before you move on to the final step.

Step Six:

When you feel more confident that you can (or will soon be able to) use this process in your real life, then take a couple of nice, deep energising breaths, count from one through to five and open your eyes.

Practice this process a few times before you then go on to practice dealing with those tough situations. Notice how marvelously you can let go of old unwanted feelings and symptoms, helping you to progress in the way you'd like to.

Chapter Twelve:
Overcoming Unwanted Habits

The evidence is wide and varied when it comes to using hypnosis to overcome and let go of habits. Specific applications of self-hypnosis for this purpose has even less evidence to refer to. There are a great many habits that people wish to let go of, and it would be impossible to completely exhaust each and every habit.

Most of the research for the application of hypnosis in alleviating unwanted habits is based upon suggestion delivered when hypnotised, so you can construct and create hypnotic suggestions that incorporate the use of the imagination, adhering to the earlier chapters of this book to help you overcome them.

In addition to that, this chapter offers a range of processes for helping you to overcome unwanted habits. You'll then be able to apply these strategies in the way you deem most pertinent to help overcome unwanted habits, such as nail biting, certain eating habits, smoking and more besides. Though there are a few points I wish to make concerning using hypnosis to stop smoking and reduce weight.

Stopping Smoking and Weight Reduction

The vast majority of people that I encounter tend to think that hypnotherapy is first and foremost a great way to stop smoking. It seems to be best known as a stop smoking remedy to many people. My exploration of the evidence available, combined with my own clinical experience leads me, (and many of my colleagues) to believe that hypnotherapy is brilliant for dealing with pain, overcoming anxiety, enhancing sleep and many other applications, but stopping smoking and weight reduction are more advanced and tougher altogether.

In my clinical practice of working with many clients since 1997, I have found stopping smoking and weight reduction to be far more challenging to work with than other issues that many people might consider more complex. I wondered if it was just me and my own approach, but having examined a wide array of processes and looked at a number of evidence-based techniques and strategies to find an effective method,(for my therapy clients), I am certain that it is not just me.

Despite this, I read claims of many hypnosis professionals stating that their single-session stop smoking processes have massively high success rates, and the media often has articles showing before and after photos of svelte looking people for whom new applications of hypnosis for weight loss has been incredibly successful.

Johnston and Donoghue *(1971)* offered up one of the earliest large-scale reviews of hypnosis literature in relation to stopping smoking. Within that, they cited some research claims that were boasting success rates using hypnosis that were as high as 94%. Impressive results. There are also hypnotherapists who market single-session stop smoking programmes who actually refer to that 1964 study by Von Dedenroth (conducted in 1964, published in ***American Journal of Clinical Hypnosis*** in 1968). The study has since been shown to be flawed.

Later on in 1974, Hunt and Bespalec put together a study comparing half a dozen methods for stopping smoking. They investigated aversive conditioning, drug therapy, education and group support, hypnosis, behaviour modification and miscellaneous approaches, including self-control, role- playing and combination treatments. It was their conclusion that hypnosis *"perhaps gives us our best results"* (p. 435), which is marvellous news for us in the hypnotherapy field. Though they did record success rates that varied between 15% and 88%.

Then more recently in 1980, a review by Holroyd of 17 mostly clinical reports concluded that more sessions of hypnotherapy were reported as being better than fewer sessions, which flies in the face of the single session type approach offered by so many hypnosis professionals. The Holroyd *(1980)* study also suggested that individual tailoring of a stop smoking treatment for a client was better than treating every client the same. For a self-hypnotist, this is encouraging because we can create our own tailored approach using our self-hypnosis skills.

At a similar time as the Holroyd review though, there were actual studies involving proper control groups and more rigorous testing *(Barkley, Hastings, and Jackson, 1977; MacHovec and Man, 1978; Pedersen, Scrimgeour, Lefcoe, 1975)* that only tended to demonstrate success rates of 0% to 50%, which was slightly lower than Holroyd had produced. Racing to our rescue in the early 1990s, as featured in the *New Scientist* and referred to by many professionals in the field, was a published study by Viswesvaran and Schmidt *(1992)*, who had conducted a meta-analysis on 633 studies of smoking cessation, which included a whopping 48 studies in the hypnosis category that they investigated. This also had a total number of 6,020 participants, which is impressive. Hypnosis did prove to be better and more effective than just about every other treatment it was compared to, including nicotine replacement therapy and aversion techniques; yet still only really offering up a success rate far inferior to that of the Von Dedenroth *(1968)* study.

There have been other studies, but the most impressive and seemingly thorough review in existence today appears to be the study (in 2000) conducted by Green and Lynn. In it, they examined 59 stop smoking studies and drew the conclusion that when measured against Chambless and Hollon's *(1998)* criteria of evaluation for the empirical support of diverse psychotherapies, hypnosis was a *"possibly efficacious"* treatment. They added that hypnotic interventions appeared to be more effective than no treatment or waiting-list control conditions.

The vast majority of stop smoking programmes given by hypnotherapists include self-hypnosis *(Holroyd, 1980)*. The key points for us here, are that when we examine the evidence, the results are not as impressive as people might like to think. However, hypnosis is considered a better option than many other ways of stopping smoking; and if you tailor your own programme, keep motivated and elicit social support, you'll enhance your chances of stopping smoking using self-hypnosis.

When it comes to eating habits, the challenge is that while we can aim to stop smoking (and alcohol consumption, for example) altogether, we still need to eat. Today, there is little agreement on the best way for people to reduce weight, and it is a major task to unravel all the evidence that exists for such a wide range of approaches. Of interest and use for a self-hypnotist, it is suggested that certain cognitive elements are effective for helping deal with eating habits, such as altering cognitions as discussed in earlier chapters: cognitive restructuring and modifying beliefs *(Gilliland and James, 1983)*. Your level of motivation is important too; it aids the process if you maintain motivation, keep mood progressive and look at ways of advancing self-esteem *(Logue et al., 2004)*.

In general though, there is not a great deal of empirical evidence to support the use of hypnosis for weight reduction *(Stewart, 2005)*. However, there is relatively little evidence for the use of any single treatment in this regard *(Wadden and VanItallie, 1992; Foreyt and Goodrick, 1993; Kirschembaum, 1994)*. This is a chapter about overcoming unwanted habits, and this book is not offering up instruction on weight reduction because there is so much to consider and so many variables. Though hypnosis is commonly associated with weight reduction and stopping smoking, there is not huge evidence to support the use of self-hypnosis. However, there are many techniques used for habit control that can be used to help stopping smoking and unwanted eating habits. Let's move on to those.

Using Self-Hypnosis to Reverse an Unwanted Habit

We are now going to look at a couple of techniques and processes for overcoming unwanted habits. The sort of habits we are going to be able to deal with are habits such as biting fingernails, pulling hair, picking at yourself and so on; though they can be used for help in stopping smoking and certain eating habits too.

We start with a look at the classic habit reversal process, which focuses upon installing a 'counter-habit' or 'competing response' whereby a new habit is installed that makes it impossible to do the old, unwanted habit. Classic habit reversal is a wonderful process from the field of behaviour therapy that I have found to be a very important part of my therapeutic work with clients. There is an impressive body of evidence to support this process.

Nathan Azrin and Gregory Nunn developed the behaviour therapy technique of Habit Reversal in the early 1970s; though the underlying notion had been around in therapy for much longer, arguably as far back as the writings of Braid who recommended inducing opposing muscular contraction to counter-act spasms. Following publication of their research, Azrin and Nunn brought out a simple self-help manual called Habit Control in a Day *(1977)* which outlined the method in very user-friendly terms.

On the basis of treatment with over 300 subjects, Nunn and Azrin found an average 90% reduction in the frequency of the habit. These results followed a single 2-hour session of habit-reversal treatment, improving with practice, to approximately 97% on average after one month *(1977: 28-29)*. Chambless et al. *(1998)* lists two studies on Habit Reversal by Azrin and Nunn (from the 1980s) as meeting the criteria for "probably efficacious" treatment set for Empirically Supported Treatments (ESTs). In other words, their method is still regarded by researchers as one of the most evidence-based approaches to habit breaking in the field of psychotherapy.

In order for habit reversal to be effective, there is some preparatory work for you to complete to enhance the effectiveness of the process. You want to have an awareness of what you do, how you do it, the conditions under which you do the habit and so on. Before we begin with the self-hypnosis, firstly, sit down somewhere that you'll be undisturbed. I recommend that you write down the answers to this exploration in order that you get an accurate account, and it'll help you when it comes to repeating this process. It is a process that requires plenty of repetition.

Firstly, just become aware of the habit itself. Write down and describe what it is that you actually do – what is your unwanted habit? With that written down, now heighten your awareness of the habit even more by making a note of how you do it – by that I mean the actual physical process of doing the habit – how is it done? Think about how often it happens – you might guess or even count how many times you do it in an hour or a day.

With that awareness of the actual habit enhanced, now we want to establish what sorts of situations the habit occurs in. So secondly, write down and describe the circumstances when the habit typically occurs. Note down any common element of the habit, such as whether there are other people with you, or if you are engaged in a particular activity, or if it happens at certain events. What situation does the habit typically occur in?

Now we are going to go a little bit deeper into you: the vehicle of the habit. Thirdly then, when the habit happens, how do you feel? What is the actual physical sensation you have when you do the habit? Whereabouts in your body are those feelings? Do you have an emotional feeling? Are there any accompanying emotions that go with the habit?

Write this stuff down and then we will look at your cognitions. When you engage in the habit, what happens inside your head? What thoughts, ideas or beliefs happen? What is your internal dialogue before, during and after the habit? With all of that information noted down, we are now going to write a couple of things down to use with our self-hypnosis habit reversal process later on.

Firstly, when you are in those typical situations where the habit occurs, think of a positive statement that you can say to yourself in the future. What is a positive, powerful and helpful statement that you can say to yourself? Write down a new cognition, word it in the present tense, from your own personal, first person perspective. For example, I am strong, I can do this, I have beautiful fingernails etc. Word it in your own way, but be sure it is something that is really going to help you deal with the problematic situations in the future.

Then we have the most important part of the entire process. What counter-habit action could you do that will physically prevent you from doing the old unwanted habit? For example, if you had a clenched fist, you'd be unable to bite your fingernails, wouldn't you? If you relaxed your facial muscles, you'd be unable to clench your jaw? Think of some physical action that you can do to replace and counteract the habit, to make it impossible for you to do the old habit. Now you have all that written down, you are ready to begin.

Step One:

Induce hypnosis using your method of choice.

Step Two:

Next, really engage your imagination and picture a typical situation where the old habit used to typically happen. Notice the colours, the shades of light, be aware of sounds and feelings, and all the details of the place. You may even use this time to deepen your hypnosis as you engage your imagination to be in the place where the habit used to typically occur. Truly imagine that you are there and in the scene.

As soon as you feel as if you are really there and have the environment in as much detail as possible, then move on to the next step.

Step Three:

Now start to tell yourself in your own words what you are experiencing. Start to describe what feelings you have and how you are thinking now that you are in this situation.

Tell yourself and talk yourself through the process of those feelings and thoughts (that you previously wrote down and explored in preparation) that are occurring, that used to accompany the old habit happening. Notice the actions you are taking in this environment, truly engage with your thoughts and feelings, and talk yourself through the scenario all the way up to the point whereby the old habit would have happened. When you have worked your way through the situation and get to the point where the habit would usually happen, move on to the next step.

Step Four:

Now instead of the habit happening inside your imagination, now imagine that you do your competing action: the new action, the new behavior that you chose to do before you began this session. Imagine yourself doing that thing forcefully and with enthusiasm.

Imagine that you are blocking the old unwanted behaviour before it actually happens. As you imagine doing that competing, new behaviour, now repeat your positive coping statement to yourself. Say it with real meaning and in a way that is undeniably convincing you that you are in control and capable of doing something new and different.

You can do this thoroughly but it doesn't have to take too long. Imagine that you do the new behaviour and state the positive thought to yourself, truly affirming it inside your mind. Then when you are sure you have mentally rehearsed this new response to the old situation, move on to the next step.

Step Five:

Having run through the new response thoroughly, now just relax. Keep thinking about being in that scenario, in that same situation, but as you imagine being there, now also imagine being more and more relaxed. Imagine scanning through the body and relaxing away any tension you can find; imagine spreading a colour of relaxation through yourself, imagine the muscles softening and loosening and continue to get deeply and comfortably relaxed.

This relaxation is going to become associated with the situation and also help you feel a sense of assuredness with the new process that you previously practiced. Once you have relaxed yourself and you feel notably more at ease, move on to the next step.

Step Six:

Now repeat steps 2-5 of this process a couple more times. You really want to get this new response lodged in your mind. Be sure to do it with as much enthusiasm and vigour each time you do it. With each repetition, be sure that you do it with enough force and be sure you mean what you imagine you are doing. Once you have repeated it diligently a couple more times, then move on to the final step.

Step Seven:

Exit hypnosis by counting from one through to five.

As I have already said, repetition is really important with this process. You are encouraged to practice this repeatedly as often as possible, and at least once a day for the first week. Once you have practiced this daily for a week or so, start to put yourself in those habit-prone situations and scenarios to test your skills. Start to practice your new habit in those old situations and notice how much better you deal with them. This is a simple take on classic habit reversal to be achieved using self-hypnosis.

Installing Aversive Sensitivity to Your Habit

When we were starting secondary school, I recall one of my friends at school still sucked his thumb at the age of 11. He told me that his Dad was going to put mustard on his thumb every night before bed to get him to stop doing it. I am not sure if he actually did it, but remember feeling very sorry for him. We now turn to the often-maligned notion of aversion.

Aversion therapy is whereby the individual is conditioned to associate the habit stimulus with unpleasant sensations in order to stop the unwanted behaviour. For example, old school hypnotherapists might sometimes suggest to a hypnotised client that smoking tasted like burning rubber. You may or may not have seen the episode of the Simpsons where the family got to use electric shocks on each other as an attempt to get them to be kinder to one another, resulting in disaster. I once went to a seminar where the trainer suggested pinging a rubber band sharply on your wrist every time you had a negative thought. They used this in a similar way to the Simpsons' scenario to create aversion to those thoughts by associating the pain with the negative thoughts, encouraging us to make an effort to think progressively and positively instead.

This process uses that notion, albeit in an imagined fashion and not in real-life terms. Prior to starting this process, you need to have a good awareness of the exact procedure of the habit that you go through. You can do this by asking yourself the same questions we asked in the previous habit reversal technique.

Step One:

Induce hypnosis using a method of your choice.

Step Two:

Start to imagine that you have been out in the sunshine without sun cream during the day, and having got home there is an area of your body that has some heat emanating from it, and is coloured red and hot to the touch.

Become aware of that sensation in the area upon your skin, imagine it. Now imagine that someone touches it by mistake – notice how that sensation crawls through the surrounding area of your body, is signaled in your brain and the level of heighten sensitivity gives you goose-bumps and a slight pain, and you hold your body a certain way to compensate. Get a real-life sensation of what that is like in your mind, and when you notice yourself feeling that sensitivity, then imagine the word CRINGE in a bright neon colour flashing inside your mind.

Repeat this process a couple of times: following too much unprotected exposure to the sun, develop an acute and very real sensation of sensitivity, noticing the dryness, the tightness and the way you breathe just thinking about someone or something touching it. Then when you imagine something touching that sunburn, as soon as you notice the discomfort and sensitized feeling, flash the word CRINGE inside your mind in real bright colours.

When it flashes up, add an alarming hooter sound or an unpleasant alarm noise of some kind to it, and imagine the word cringe being spoken inside your head. When you think that you have truly installed the word cringe as a way of accessing that hyper sensitivity, then move on to the next step.

Step Three:

Now imagine being in the place where the habit used to typically happen. See the sights, hear the sounds, notice how you feel and behave. Take your time to create the scene and put yourself in it. Truly be in that scene, a target situation where the habit used to typically occur.

Start to notice the thoughts, feelings and behaviour happening that in the past led to the habit. Walk through the old process, and as soon as you notice the early signs of the habit starting, the word CRINGE flashes into your head. You feel the searing sensitivity on your skin, you hear the word loudly in your mind with the alarm and you stop with the habit and move totally differently.

Notice as soon as the habit starts, the word 'cringe' pops into your mind and you find yourself engulfed in that same sensitivity and slight discomfort. It consumes you and gets worse until you stop with the old habit. When you have run through that scenario in detail, then move on to the next step.

Step Four:

Repeat step three another 3-5 times, and each time make sure you get the association between the old habit and the word CRINGE, and that uncomfortable sensitivity all lodged in your mind. This is to ensure that it starts to happen in real-life scenarios too. When you have repeated that 3-5 times, then move on to the next step.

Step Five:

Imagine a future time now, a moment in your future – see yourself in that situation and notice the scenario and circumstances that used to cause the old habit to happen, but this time you are in control and there is no sign of the habit happening.

If the thoughts start or the old habit begins at all, you notice the word 'cringe' springs into your mind, along with its accompanying dominant feelings and sensations. You naturally stop the old behaviour, and as soon as you stop, the sensitive sensation dissipates. Run through this future scenario in detail, then move on to the final step.

Step Six:

Exit hypnosis by counting from one through to five.

You may find this type of process goes perfectly well in conjunction with other techniques that you are using to help overcome your unwanted habit.

The Craving Balloon

Not all habits necessarily have cravings. Lots do though. This next process is going to help you overcome cravings that used to lead to an unwanted habit occuring.

Christmas seems to start in the middle of October these days. The Christmas advertisements are on the television, the shop fronts are covered in sparkly adornments, and of course, we start reaching for those bigger trousers as our waist lines start to increase due to the scoffing that goes on at the festive time of year.

You should see the winter time mugs of hot chocolate that my wife makes when we go to the Beach Hut when the sun shines. All wrapped up watching the sea, the beach quiet and a stark contrast to the hustle and bustle of summer. She fills the mugs with hot chocolate, topped with whipped cream and brimming over with marshmallows.

The festive season…

Mince pies. Mulled wine. Turkey feasts with roast potatoes and those delicious pigs in blankets (sausages wrapped in bacon). There is chocolate of every denomination. Huge hams. Slabs of smoked salmon. It is the only time of year I eat dates and sugared almonds! There are snacks and nibbles that accompany every get together. There is the booze… We have boozy snowballs, which is cava with Advocaat, not to mention that we get a barrel of real ale in and so much wine and spirits, we could get an army inebriated.

It wears me out just thinking about it, and a problem is created when we eat to excess. The more we eat, the more our mind and body wants to eat. When we eat to excess (especially loads of simple carbs and refined sugars) and when we sleep less during party season and drink too much, general fatigue also contributes to us eating more. Then we start craving stuff. We crave and are only satiated when we are stuffed full and snoozing again. The cycle continues and takes all our might with our new year's resolutions to get us on the straight and narrow again.

The process that I am illustrating next originated as a means of dealing with cravings for cigarettes, and was used with hypnotherapy clients. The Red Balloon technique of Walch *(1976)* has been used extensively and championed in the work of Stanton *(1978)*. There are many versions of this type of process that you can find online and in books, but ideally tailor it for your own requirements and preferences. Although I am showing you how to use self-hypnosis with this process for dealing with food cravings, it is often used for emotional disorders that require to be let go of.

As I have repeatedly said with the techniques in this book, this process needs to be practiced formally a few times before it can be used in real-life scenarios. So run through this process in detail, step by step and then at the end I'll mention how to do this process without the formalised hypnosis session.

Step One:

Induce hypnosis using your method of choice.

Step Two:

Now start to imagine that you are walking along a pathway, a pathway of your life.

Notice what the path is made of and imagine hearing the sounds of your own feet walking along it. Become aware of where this path is – perhaps a place in nature, or in an urban landscape, or near the sea, or in the countryside, you choose. Notice the colours and details of the sights around you. Become aware of the textures and shades of the colours and all that you see. Notice how it makes you feel to be in this place and hear the sounds of the place, the volume of the various sounds, what is close up and what is distant.

Tell yourself that with each step you walk along the path, you go deeper inside your mind and take some time to use this to deepen the hypnosis you are experiencing. Once you have engaged your imagination as fully as possible and deepened for a while, then move on to the next step.

Step Three:

As you walk, notice that you are carrying a backpack of some kind. As you walk along the pathway, notice that it is heavy and getting heavier. Notice that it actually is weighing upon you. Imagine that the pack carries around with it all your cravings that you have accrued over recent times. Maybe it is those actual foods and drinks that are in this increasingly large pack on your back.

You notice that the pathway starts to move upwards slightly, and as you walk uphill and as more cravings and foods are piled into the bag, it is becoming harder and harder to move smoothly and enjoyably. Let yourself get to the top of this slope, feeling weighed down with those cravings and then move on to the next step.

Step Four:

At the top of the hill, you notice there is a large colourful hot air balloon tied to the ground, with a basket sitting underneath it. Now start to take one item at a time out of your backpack and place it into the basket. Notice what it is that comes out of the pack, become aware of what you were craving and notice that as you let go of them, you feel lighter and easier and more comfortable.

Let yourself start to be free of those cravings, place them all one at a time into the basket and notice that you feel lighter and more at ease with each and every item you place in there. Keep doing this, taking all the time necessary to completely empty the pack. Notice all the feelings attached to those foods, all the old desires and associations are leaving and being put into the basket. Watch it all sitting there in that basket.

Feel cleansed and free and in control of yourself. In fact spend some time to just feel a lighter sensation in your chest, in your stomach and your limbs. Now that you have shed these heavy burdensome cravings, truly experience a genuine sense of lightness and easiness in your shoulders. Once you have spent enough time noticing how much lighter you feel, then move on to the next step.

Step Five:

Now go over to the ties attaching the basket and hot air balloon to the ground and untie it. Watch all those foods, feelings, sensations, associations and cravings, all start to float away into nothingness. Watch it all drifting and floating into the distance. Smile as you wave goodbye to it all. Enjoy the sense of being in control that you get from this.

Watch it until it becomes a tiny speck very far away that eventually vanishes and is gone for good. Now start to take some good deep breaths and notice the lightness you experience – not just because you have let go of your cravings – but because you have also taken control of who and how you are, and that feels really good.

Step Six:

Once you have enjoyed the lightness for a while, and you are sure that the balloon is long gone and the cravings are no more, then open your eyes, wiggle your fingers and toes, take a couple of deeper breaths and go about your day.

Practice this process 4-6 times with real focus and concentration. Then, when you are out at a party or festive drinks, or if you are at home and it is not time for your proper meals, but you are presented with choices for more and more naughty stuff, then breathe deeply, close your eyes for a moment and imagine placing that craving or urge into the basket and letting it fly away.

Let it pass without resisting it or fighting the feeling; breathe deeply and then go and take some other action, engage in a conversation and congratulate yourself for taking control.

Chapter Thirteen:
Techniques for Specific Issues.

There is a good evidence base to support the use of hypnosis with specific ailments and issues. This chapter aims at giving you tools for specific issues, but again, the types of techniques can be applied to a wide variety of other issues too.

When I first start researching specific issues and ailments using hypnosis and hypnotherapy, it is always wonderful when firstly, the subject matter has some supporting evidence, and secondly, that supporting evidence is positive. One of the more impressive applications of hypnosis for a medical issue is when it is used to help deal with irritable bowel syndrome *(Whorwell et al., 1984; Palsson et al., 2002; Harvey et al., 1989; Talley et al., 1996).*

As the evidence suggests, with the repetition of these techniques you'll start to develop control and more of a notable response to them. This first process is designed to help soothe the symptoms of IBS, but also to heighten control of gut function. Speaking of which, anyone wishing to derive the most benefit from these types of processes (pertaining to IBS) will enhance the effectiveness of the processes with a good understanding of the physiology of the gut. I'd recommend that you google it, or look it up in an anatomy manual of some kind.

For example, get a good idea of whereabouts your colon, stomach, small intestine and large bowel is located. It'll demonstrate that the pain of IBS is not always deep in the pits of our lower abdomen, but can reach up to our ribs where our large bowel extends towards.

Sometimes, the pain, spasms and oversensitivity associated with IBS can seem out of our control, so repeated use of these processes are designed to give you a coping skill and a sense of control. Prior to starting, have a good think about your own ongoing symptoms with IBS (i.e. noting differences between diarrhoea and constipation) and with the symptoms in mind, then we can get set up and ready to start.

Hypnosis For Irritable Bowel Syndrome

Get yourself into a place where you'll be undisturbed for the period of time taken to run through the process. Ideally, be sat upright, with your feet flat on the floor and hands uncrossed, not touching each other. Then follow this step-by-step guide.

Step One:

Induce hypnosis using a method of your choosing.

A progressive relaxation process to enter hypnosis works well with this session, as IBS sufferers do benefit from the added physical relaxation.

Step Two:

Tune in to your gut. Firstly, just move your awareness to the general area of your gut.

How does it feel? Is there movement? Is there sound? Really tune in for a few moments and focus your attention and awareness on the area of your gut. As you focus in on it, let your breathing relax and notice how your gut responds to your gentle breathing.

Just focus in on the gut area while breathing, allowing each breath to keep you focused and aware of your gut region. Once you have begun to relax and feel that you are tuned in to your gut, then move on to the next step.

Step Three:

Start to imagine your gut as a flowing body of water. It can be the flow from a tap, a flowing river or a waterfall of some kind (choose whatever suits you best). Start to imagine that flow of water is warm and soothing. Spend a little while on this step to create the ideal flow of water, and imagine your gut as this flowing body of water.

Tell yourself that the flowing water is taking you deeper into hypnosis and deeper inside of your mind, then move on to step four.

Step Four:

Alter the speed of the water flow to suit your personal requirements. If you have been constipated, then make the water flow fast and strong, as much as is appropriate.

If you have had diarrhea, then let the flow of water slow. Be in control of the flow of the soothing water. Once you have set the correct and most useful speed for the flow of water, then spend some time observing it and enjoying it flowing at that pace.

Then, when you have tuned in and enjoyed being in control of the pace of the water, move on to the next step.

Step Five:

Engage deeply again with your breathing and with the entire area of the gut. Focus in on it, and now let the adjusted flow of water start to heal and soothe.

Let the water start to relax and warm through the entire area of the stomach, colon, intestine and bowels, spreading warmth and soothing senses throughout the abdomen. Perhaps imagine the water has a colour. Perhaps imagine the water has a sound. Notice how the feelings are experienced within your gut area as you imagine the warming, soothing, gentle sense of healing water flowing at the right pace, but relax with your breathing and the spreading throughout you.

Spend as much time on this step as you would like. Enjoy it, enjoy the control you have and when you have spent enough time enjoying the soothing, warming sense of the water, then move on to the next step.

Step Six:

Now accompany those great feelings with a positive and reinforcing cognition. Repeat a progressive cognition to yourself to enhance the warming effect. Use your internal dialogue and repeat to yourself something along the lines of: "I feel soothed" or "my stomach relaxes more and more" or "each breath I breathe soothes me and eases my stomach area."

Also suggest that the comfort, relief and sense of control is something that stays with you after this session has finished. Also tell yourself with some conviction that each time you use this technique it is working cumulatively better and more powerfully for you, and that you derive more benefit as you practice it. Really engage your cognitions, use your internal dialogue in a firm and convincing manner, then move on to the next step.

Step Seven:

You can spend some more time relaxing the area with the warm flowing water, and then when you are ready, bring yourself out of hypnosis by counting from one through to five.

There you have it, the first in our series of self-hypnosis skills and tools for helping deal with IBS – remember that repetition is King with these processes, and the more you practice this, the better the results are going to be.

Using a Warm Hand to Ease IBS

Following on from the previous process, here is another simple and easy process to help deal with IBS symptoms.

We are surely all aware that when we have experienced an upset tummy, that we often instinctively place our hand upon it, as a means of soothing – in much the same way that a parent may have done when we were smaller. Likewise, when I was in my early teens, I can remember being in bed with stomach cramps after sporting exertions and dehydration, and I found holding a hot-water bottle on my tummy helped it to relax, stop its spasms and eventually ease the pain.

This hypnosis session is similar to our previous one in terms of it helping to relax and ease the stomach area from the symptoms of irritable bowel syndrome; it also helps to establish a sense of self-efficacy in dealing with those symptoms and gives us a sense of personal control. Ideally when we start to rehearse these types of processes, they can be used not only as a preventative measure, but also can be used as a coping skill to abate and deal with symptoms if they occur in the future.

Get yourself into a comfortable, attentive, seated or lying position (if you are seated, ideally with your feet flat on the floor) with both your arms and legs uncrossed. Make sure that your dominant hand has your palm facing upwards, then we are ready to begin. Just follow these simple steps:

Step One:

Induce hypnosis using your preferred method.

Step Two:

Focus all your attention and all your awareness on your dominant hand that has its palm facing upwards. Imagine the area on the centre of the palm is starting to warm up. Just start with a small spot of warmth on the middle of the palm, and then imagine it spreading and widening, slowly and powerfully and surely.

There are a number of ways to use your imagination to help you with this.

Firstly, you might imagine a hot-water bottle being placed onto that hand as the heat spreads all over the hand.

Secondly, you might imagine the heat is a colour that you associate with heat and that colour spreads.

Thirdly, you may recall a time when you have been close to an open fire with the embers glowing, recall how you felt the heat. Imagine that your palm is held towards such glowing embers and you feel that intense heat spreading comfortably into the palm of your hand.

You might choose to use any other means of imagining your hand getting warmer and comfortably hotter. Tell yourself that your hand feels as if it is getting warmer, engage your imagination at the same time.

Let the sensation grow and as it does, let it take you deeper inside your mind. When you have a notable belief and sensation of warmth in your hand – which requires you to really engage your imagination, and believe and expect it to happen – then move on to the next step.

Step Three:

Ideally, just having to bend your arm at the elbow, move your warm hand and place it upon your stomach. In the centre of your stomach.

Using the least amount of effort, move your warm hand to the stomach area. As it arrives, start to imagine how warm it feels as it touches the stomach area. Start to spread warmth and a relaxing healing sensation into the stomach area. Imagine that it penetrates deeply into your stomach, your intestines, bowel and other areas, warming, relaxing, soothing.

Again, it is important to engage your imagination – whether it is the colour you spread into your tummy, or that you brought the hot-water bottle with your hand to the stomach, or that you brought the heat of the glowing embers to soothe and relax and warm deeply – do engage the imagination in whatever way is right for you.

Spend plenty of time on this step and continue to do so until you notice a warmth in your stomach that is really relaxing and soothing the stomach area.

Step Four:

Continue to allow the relaxation to grow and warm and soothe. As you do so, start to use your internal dialogue and cognitions to help amplify and enhance this process. Affirm to yourself to support the warming, healing, soothing sensations. For example, "my tummy is more and more relaxed" or "I enjoy these warm sensations as they soothe my tummy."

Make sure you say this to yourself in a way that you find to be convincing and believable, and in a way that enhances the warming soothing sensations that are spreading from your hand into your stomach and surrounding areas.

Once you have said this and repeated it over and over a few times to enhance the sensations, then move on to the next step.

Step Five:

Now you are going to mentally rehearse being in a situation of your life, maybe a situation that you used to avoid due to the worry of your IBS symptoms flaring up and causing you issues.

Imagine truly being in that situation and feeling these ongoing warming sensations from your hand, soothing, warming and easing the stomach area, keeping your stomach more and more comfortable and relaxed, in a stable state. Truly imagine being in that situation and taking control of how you feel, spreading this warmth. Start to associate the warmth and soothing sensation you have generated in this session, with the scenario you are imagining.

This requires some time and diligence to be thorough so that you can benefit the most from this part of the session. Tell yourself that you know you are becoming better and better at doing this process, and that anytime you require it, you can use the warm hand to soothe and ease your stomach area, and the old unwanted symptoms will lessen and lessen.

Be undeniably convincing. Affirm your belief in your ability to do this whenever you need it, and then move on to the next step.

Step Six:

Now finally, start to imagine that warming relaxation is emanating from the stomach area. It is starting to spread throughout your entire body. Engage in some progressive relaxation while you are letting that warming sensation spread from your warm stomach region throughout your body. To achieve this, choose any method that you prefer from our earlier chapter on using hypnotic relaxation.

Once you have relaxed your entire body, simply move on to the final step.

Step Seven:

Exit hypnosis by counting from one through to five.

Maintain the warmth in your tummy if pertinent, and keep on enhancing your belief in your own abilities to do this process in order to help you cope with and deal with situations in the future.

Reduce High Blood Pressure and Treat Hypertension

Those that read my weekly ezine "Adam Up", will know that back in 2011, my business partner Keith had a heart attack and we were incredibly worried. I wrote about it in the ezine. He worked hard on his physical activity and had regular visits to the hospital and became fitter than ever. We were delighted.

At that time I began researching the extent to which hypnosis could help reduce high blood pressure and a number of various other applications to help heart related issues. There are a number of impressive studies that show hypnosis as a great tool for treating hypertension and helping to lower blood pressure *(Friedman and Taub, 1977; Borckhardt, 2002; Sletvold et al., 1990).* With this in mind, the next technique is one using mental imagery and hypnosis to reduce high blood pressure.

Step One:

Induce hypnosis using whichever method you choose.

Step Two:

Start to engage your imagination and find yourself in a favourite place in nature. It can be somewhere you are creating right now in your mind, or somewhere you have been before, or any other favourite place outside.

Notice the sights, colours and shades of light that you can see all around you. Hear the sounds of life, notice the distance of sounds, even the sound of the breeze, if there is one. Feel how safe and comfortable it is in this place, feel the temperature, the air and smell the aromas of that fresh air, as it moves into your lungs through your nose. Engage all your senses and tune into this place.

As you relax here, start to imagine that your body is relaxing as you enjoy the peacefulness and serenity all around you. Notice your muscles softening, notice that you are becoming more still as you tune in to the surroundings. Tell yourself that you are drifting deeper into hypnosis, deeper into your mind as you continue to imagine being in this place as vividly as you can. Once you have noticed that you are still, relaxed and tuned into this place in nature, then move on to the next step.

Step Three:

Start to notice the plants in more detail around you. Start to notice the flowers and the shrubs – you decide to water them to help them enjoy being healthy in this place in nature.

Imagine somewhere nearby is a hosepipe in[?] your mind, that starts at a nearby lake, and serves as part of the irrigation system for this beautiful place in nature. You pick it up and with your thoughts of watering and spraying the plants around you, and the water begins to emerge from the hosepipe. It begins to come out of the hosepipe faster and stronger, and it becomes tough to handle and keep a hold of. In fact, it wriggles out of your grip and sprays harder and faster, and its bolts of fast water knock some of the shrubs over as it sprays. For a few moments, watch it firing water uncontrollably all over the area. As this happens, tell yourself you are going deeper inside of your mind and then move on to the next step.

Step Four:

You calmly, positively and easily take a comfortable hold of the hosepipe, and you instinctively start to breathe gently, deeply and purposefully. As you do so, the water stream starts to react and respond to your thoughts, your intention and your level of control. The water stream starts to respond to the rate of your breathing and your thoughts of calmness, and the flow of water becomes manageable, easy and gentle.

Watch as the stream of water flows gently and easily… And you go deeper inside your mind, relaxing more as you watch it. Take some time to do this step and then start to water all the plants and flowers around you, nurturing them, watering them. Get a sense of the landscape and benefit from this sense of comfort, easiness and the gentle flow of the water coming out of the hosepipe. Flowing freely and with just the right pressure that is steady and even, it has a truly healthy rhythm to it. The surroundings start to react and respond and the entire place starts to feel relaxed, calm and gentle again. The sounds, sights and feelings all tell you that everything is relaxed, calm and flowing with healthiness and vitality. When you have enjoyed this for a while, move on to the next step.

Step Five:

Now set the hosepipe at this healthy level of flow, and sit back and watch the tranquility[?] around you. As you do so, you breathe naturally and enjoy the fresh air. With each breath that you breathe you start to notice your own body beginning to synchronise with your surroundings. You can sense the flow of blood around your body adjusting itself to the correct and healthiest levels. Take some time and imagine that happening within you, as you enjoy breathing the clean, fresh, healthy air.

Notice the easy, gentle rhythm of life flowing through you. Imagine all the systems of your body joining in with the nature around you, setting itself to the rhythm that is optimal for you. As you enjoy the scenery, breath gently, letting the flow happen in a controllable and easy way before you. Enjoy this for as long as you like, getting your body in sync with nature, knowing its healthiest levels and then move on to the final step.

Step Six:

Tell yourself that this technique works better each time you practice it, and commit to practicing it regularly. As you imagine the comfortable, soothing flow of life within yourself, bring all that balance and easiness with you. As you wiggle your toes and fingers, take a couple of deeper, energizing breaths, and then open your eyes.

Do practice this process, the more you practice it, the more beneficial the results will be for lowering your blood pressure.

Using Self-Hypnosis to Lower High Blood Pressure

Further to the previous technique on this subject, this next process is aimed at lowering high blood pressure. There are a number of applications of hypnosis that I have used throughout the years to demonstrate the power of the mind over body, which have involved the control of blood flow. For example, when I have had people use hypnosis for pain relief, in particular when a glove anaesthesia process is employed, the arm that the client has imagined to be encased in ice (for subsequent anaesthesia purposes) is noticeably more pale; as the blood has drained away, it feels cooler to touch and is a very visual and obvious means of seeing the body respond to the mind, imagination and hypnotic suggestion.

Likewise, blood perfusion is often done with hypnosis; that is, the process of mobilising blood into other parts of the body. Research exploring this has even included encouraging results working with haemophiliac patients by using hypnosis to control bleeding *(LaBaw, 1975 and 1992; Fung and Lazar, 1983; LeBaron and Zeltzer, 1984; Swirsky-Sacchetti and Margolis, 1986).*

When I have demonstrated analgesia and/or anaesthesia using hypnosis, and I have put a pin through someone's arm, suggestions can be given that when the pin is taken out, the slight bleeding only happens in one of the holes made on the pin's exit – and it happens. It is amazing to see. Having seen so much of this, it seems natural to me that hypnosis can and should be used for great effect in the process of lowering and reducing high blood pressure.

Step One:

Induce hypnosis using a method of your choosing.

Step Two:

Imagine sitting in a chair that has been designed and created especially for you. Notice the way it molds and melds itself to the contours of your body, how it supports you in all the right areas and how your body settles deeply into the chair in other places. Start to imagine that the chair is holding and supporting you, rather than you resting in and on it. As unusual as that may initially sound, I want you to use your imagination to make a somatic difference to the way you perceive yourself resting in the chair.

Let the material of the chair be your own favoured choice, let it be the colour and size that you wish. Spend all the time necessary to enjoy being sat in this chair that is designed and created by your mind, that is simply perfect for you and your body. Tell yourself that each moment spent sat and supported in this chair, you go deeper into hypnosis and drift deeper inside your mind, while remaining focused of mind your body continues to relax further. When you have truly engaged in this and feel notably more relaxed, move on to the next step.

Step Three:

Imagine that you are now sat in your chair in a spacious, white room. All around you is white, unblemished, perfect white. Pure white. You can only just make out the places where the walls meet the floor and ceiling. Be filled with a sense of purity and receptivity, as you truly engage in this white room, this white space. Continue to tell yourself that you are drifting deeper into your mind, that you are physically relaxing deeper, and that you remain focused. When you are engaged and tuned into this white space, with the colour of white dominating your thoughts and senses, then move on to the next step.

Step Four:

Let your mind recall a time when you were fit, healthy and well, and your blood pressure was optimum and healthy. A time when you felt good to be alive and with a sense of physical freedom and vigour.

As you do so, the walls start to be filled with details of being in that place again… Notice colours, shades of light and images begin to fill the walls. As you remember more of the details of this time in your life when you were filled with vitality and physical well-being, notice the sounds of the place start to resonate around the room, and enjoy the feelings that are starting to occur within you as you truly imagine being in this place.

As the walls fill with the detail of being in this place, your mind starts to notice and recall how your blood pressure was in these circumstances. Your body starts to adjust and alter to match that sensation and level of well-being. Notice the beat of your heart adjusting, the flow adjusting itself to its optimum state, the level of pressure just right for your physical well-being. Notice the sensation of your body functioning correctly and beautifully in this way.

Engage with your surroundings, continue to notice the sounds, sights and most importantly, enjoy the feelings of this environment. Your mind has a blueprint of how you functioned at this time; so allow that blue print to be brought to the forefront of your mind now. Let your mind imprint that blueprint of healthy information, healthy blood flow and comfortable blood pressure upon your mind and body again, here in this moment. Enjoy the comfort, enjoy the steady flow and rhythm of your blood, tune in and feel it and love the sensation. When you feel truly engaged in the surroundings, and can notice the adjustments being made within you, then move on to the next step.

Step Five:

Now imagine and think of your blood flowing healthily, safely and optimally through your entire system. Notice the healthy flowing sensation running through your body, and you become part of that flow. Move your awareness further inside of yourself, focus on you and nothing else for a while. Engage exclusively in the enjoyable process of your blood flowing healthily through your body, pumped comfortably and easily by your heart. Imagine the system of canals being soft, gentle and comfortable, as the blood flows harmoniously through you. Maybe you can imagine the sound of the healthy blood flow as you engage with it; perhaps you can even feel its wonderful harmony as it moves knowingly and healthily through every channel within you.

Notice a warmth and easiness of sensation flowing through you. Imagine your blood being warm, gentle, flowing smoothly and easily. Spend some time with this step, truly engaging in the free-flowing sensation of your blood moving healthily around you, relaxing more, drifting deeper into your mind and remaining absolutely focused. When you have spent enough time on this step and have enjoyed it for long enough, move on to the next step.

Step Six:

Trust and confirm with yourself that as a result of this session, your body and mind continue to function in this healthy, optimum way. You can then bring this session to an end by counting yourself up and out from one through to five.

Practice this process over and over. Let your body relearn how to respond calmly to control your blood pressure, enjoying the sensations that stay with you.

Let Go of Anger With a Clenched Fist?

Often when a closed fist is mentioned, people might think about it being a symbol of anger, a symbol of might or strength, or maybe as a symbol of violence. Others might perceive a closed fist as a sign of aggression, or celebration, or as a means to inspire someone. For some it represents power or a sense of freedom, and it is a sense of freedom that I want to promote in this next technique, which uses a fist combined with hypnosis, for great therapeutic effect to help let go of anger.

This kind of process does not have to be limited to people that may think they have an anger problem. Rather, it may well be used by anyone hoping to overcome an angry episode. Likewise, it is a great tool for overcoming stress, anxiety or any other unwanted emotional issue. Many people often need to be shown how to let go of a negative impulse (in this case we are focusing on anger) that they experience. Especially if that negative experience has some accompanying physical tension. With this closed-fist technique, you are encouraged to make a fist in order to contain and control unwanted sensations of anger.

Step One:

Get yourself into a comfortable position, one whereby you are going to be undisturbed for the duration of this exercise. Make sure your feet are flat on the floor and place your dominant hand in your lap with your palm facing upwards. Then in that position, hypnotise yourself using the method of your choice and move on to the next step.

Step Two:

Tune into how you are feeling right now, move your awareness to scan through your entire body and identify any areas where anger is felt. Get in touch with the sensation of anger, knowing that you are soon going to let it go and diffuse it, without harming anyone, including yourself. Really look forward to letting go of it totally and safely for now.

Be aware first of all of your feet. Is there any sign of anger there? If so, move it up, through your body and into the hand that you have placed palm up in your lap. Bring all the angry feelings there and put them in the palm of that hand.

Continue to scan through the entire lower part of body (everything from waist down), methodically and systematically, moving all the feelings of anger upwards into that palm. Take all the time you need to do this surely and thoroughly. When you have all of those feelings resting in the palm of that hand, then move on to the next step.

Step Three:

Just as you did with the lower body, now do the same with the upper body. Is there any anger at the top of your head? If so, start moving it down toward the palm in your lap. Move and scan through the face, shoulders, chest, stomach, back, and everywhere else in between and around the upper body, methodically and systematically finding and locating any anger and mobilising it toward the palm. Let it all gather up and settle in the palm of that hand.

Tell yourself that there is no need to keep the anger in any other place, and that you are forming a sort of temporary coral that you are herding the anger into and onto - the palm of your hand. Start to notice the absence of it from the places you are removing it from, you can let those places relax if you want. When you are sure that all the anger is on the palm, having spent the time doing that thoroughly, then you move on to the next step.

Step Four:

Imagine that your hand is closing around the anger. Start to then actually close your hand to make a fist. As it does so, imagine your hand is machine-like in the way it is compacting the anger. Imagine the anger getting smaller as the fist closes tighter and stronger.

Make a tight fist, close your hand, make a fist of strength that is capable of containing the anger. Tell yourself that you are stronger and better than the anger, and repeat that message to yourself as you sense the anger diffusing and dispelling. Start to notice how much effort it takes to hold an increasingly tighter fist, notice the energy you use to compact and contain all that anger in your hand. When you start to notice a slight strain, and your fist is so tight that it has all your focus and attention driven into it, move on to the next step.

Step Five:

As you notice the effort that it takes to maintain the closed tight fist, start to think about how much effort it takes to be angry. It takes a lot of effort to experience anger. You want to be healthy and well and happy, and tell yourself that right now. Start to tell yourself that you are going to let the anger go, for your own well-being. Imagine the anger is leaving and taking all the tension and unwanted feelings away with it, leaving your mind and body free and more clear.

When you are ready to relax your body more and more and let go of the anger totally, then slowly open your fist, relax the muscles in your hand. Open the fist and imagine the anger leaving, dissipating, diffusing and going.

Let it disappear into the distance, let it evaporate and become harmless nothingness.

As you do that, as you let go, breathe deeply and start to relax your body. Any breathing technique or progressive muscle relaxation process you know, spend some time doing that to get your body relaxed and enjoy being free of the anger. When you are sure it is all gone and you feel deeply relaxed, then move on to the next step.

Step Six:

Reflect intelligently upon the anger while you are now deeply relaxed. Think about how you will choose to be in the future and how you strive to continue to make healthy choices for your body and mind – reflect upon how one affects and influences the other so greatly.

If you feel it will do you some good, make a decision to go and explain your thoughts and feelings to someone that will hear and not judge you. Continue to let your hand and body relax, continue to breathe deeply while you reflect intelligently, and when you have done so to your satisfaction, then move on to the final step.

Step Seven:

Count yourself up and out of hypnosis from one through to five.

Using 'The Healing Force'

As we near the end of the book, I wanted to offer up a generic healing protocol for you to use with a wide range of issues and ailments. It can be adapted and used in a variety of differing formats.

This process encourages the use of 'the healing force.' I know, I know…. It sounds a bit 'wooo'[not sure what this signifies?], which I hope that you know is quite unlike me. However, the process has some sound principles and is wonderful in its simplicity, which means it is easy to apply, even if you are not totally motivated to engage in psychological processes while injured or poorly.

The use of the term 'healing force' does have a bit of ambiguity within it, and it is also a little bit tongue in cheek. I mean, how many times do I get to incorporate a Star Wars-type of phrase into my work? When I say ambiguity, it is actually something that you get to interpret in a way that suits you best, rather than being spoon-fed by my own preferences.

The process is based on a process that Donald Liggett *(2000)* trialed with a group of 10 athletes who were injured. Using this type of technique when hypnotized, he compared their recovery to 20 other athletes, and although the study was not able to be published, it is encouraging none the less. The recovery rate of the hypnotised group was quicker than the control group, who tended to recover at the same rate as the estimated timeframe given by the professionals they were dealing with.

Prior to starting with the session, think of a positive, healing cognition (an affirmation or phrase) that you can use later in the upcoming session. A good example might be *"I am healing faster"* or *"I feel more comfort"* – make it present tense (i.e. it is happening now) and use the kind of language and phrase that suits you best.

Ensure that you are in a comfortable position, ideally seated, but if you have an injury, just get in whatever position you can to experience the most comfort. You'll want to ensure your arms and legs are uncrossed, and that you are going to be undisturbed for the duration of this exercise. Then follow the steps.

Step One:

Induce hypnosis using your preferred method.

Step Two:

Take a few deep breaths, and then allow your breathing to gently continue going deeper. Imagine that you go deeper into hypnosis with each deeper breath. Tell yourself this is happening. That is, use your cognitions to tell yourself with belief that you are going deeper into hypnosis. Notice the sensation that you get as you breathe deeper. For some it is like an energised feeling.

Become aware of an uplifting, energised sensation as you breathe deeply and gently; enjoy the sensation, and once you have noticed it for a couple of breaths, move on to the next step.

Step Three:

As you inhale, imagine that you are breathing in an energised, healing force. Imagine a spark of healthy, well-being somewhere inside you. Notice a small sign of the good feeling, like it is a spark of light of some kind. Then start to imagine that each breath starts to make that feeling bigger.

With each breath inwards, imagine that you are building up a ball of concentrated energised healing force – whatever that means to you, however you interpret it, imagine that in your own way. Let the healing force get bigger and more concentrated and more powerful. Notice the qualities of it – the colour, the movement, the sound of it, and how it feels to have this powerful, concentrated ball of healing and well-being in that place within you.

I imagine it being like a shimmering, golden globe, which was inspired by a particular sci-fi film I love. Find your own inspirational source, and when the ball is at a good size, then move on to the next step.

Step Four:

Now send this mobilised, concentrated ball of healing force to the area of the injury. Take some time to imagine it arriving there and dominating that area with its colour and sound (ideally they are healing sounds and colours).

Then start to imagine the ball melting into the area in and around the injury. Imagine that the area becomes free of pain and discomfort. You might notice a slight sensation of some kind as it melts into the area, especially if you expect it. Some people imagine that curative fluids are being transported to the area of the injury, and that they start to enhance and speed up the natural healing process. Some people imagine it is like an ointment or cream that has been applied and is soaking into the area, having a fabulous effect. Use your imagination and do what is best for you. Once you have moved the ball to the area, and it is melting in and being absorbed by the injured area, move on to the next step.

Step Five:

While the healing force continues to get to work, start to repeat your progressive cognition to yourself: the one you chose prior to starting this process. Say it in a way that is convincing so that you believe. Say it like you absolutely mean it, and repeat it over and over with a gentle reassured sense. All the time imagine the effects of the healing force getting more profound and beneficial. Then move on to the final step.

Step Six:

Take a couple more deep breaths, then exit hypnosis by counting up from one through to five.

Chapter Fourteen:
Being a Self-Hypnotist

As we arrive at the final chapter of this book, I thought we could metaphorically wave some smelling salts under your nose and enliven the senses.

Hypnosis often gets associated with being relaxed, zonked out or heavy-limbed, as if the Svengali himself has put us under his spell. It does not have to be that way, as I hope you have realised by now. It strikes me that the following technique may have been a good one to share at the beginning of this book – to help keep you focused and concentrating with a sharpness of mind– but having it towards the end seems just as appropriate, as all the reading and self-hypnosis sessions will have kept you alert and sharp.

Back in 2010, I watched a brilliant TV series (brilliant in my opinion), based on a true story about the US marines that were sent into Iraq to spearhead the invasion aimed at toppling the regime. The series was called *Generation Kill.* Sgt. Brad Colbert (played by Alexander Skarsgård) was known as the Iceman, and he also coined a phrase that became the tag line for the entire series. Whenever they were going out on scouting missions, or going into battle, or on a recon mission into a town that they knew contained opposition fighters, he would say to his team, "stay frosty."

This term was about remaining cool and calm, but most importantly to keep alert and stay on your toes, so to speak.

This next self-hypnosis technique is all about how to 'stay frosty' and with it by using self-hypnosis to keep alert and on our toes. In my second year of University, I lived and studied in Finland for 6 months. My mother is Norwegian and so I have a lot of love for Scandinavia in general. I attended the University of Tampere and lived in the city that was twinned with Manchester University that I attended. The city port looks very similar to parts of Manchester too. Part of Finnish life is the sauna. Every home and building has its own sauna, and the health benefits are considered important to all local people. Even my student accommodation had its own sauna facilities.

At one of the international students association's gatherings, we were taken to a sauna out in the forest on the edge of the city, which could only be reached by walking (an hour walk) to a cabin by a frozen lake. We enjoyed the sauna there, and they had a real-life ice cutter that cut into the frozen lake (like you see on cartoons) to remove the ice and reveal wooden steps. We then would step out of the sauna, jump into the frozen lake and climb out again.

The initial sensation of entering the extremely cold water in a forest, where the temperature was minus 20 degrees in the middle of January (it was actually deemed a mild evening) was literally breath taking. I could not breathe. My breath vanished, it scarpered, my body shook and I scampered to the steps and climbed out. The funny thing was, even though it was so cold, our core temperature was hot from the sauna, so we then stood outside in a forest, in the glow of the cabin, completely naked, drinking beer and chatting as if it was totally normal. This self-hypnosis process is going to combine some of these ideas and has inspired me to develop a process using hypnosis for alertness that I have seen suggested in a number of other places.

Keeping Frosty And Alert Using Hypnosis

Step One:

Induce hypnosis using whichever method you choose.

Step Two:

Imagine being in a shower room. It can be a dream shower room, or one you have actually been to before. Engage your imagination, take all the time necessary to be in this place. Notice the colours, shades of light and details of the place. Hear the sounds and notice how sounds travel in this space when you make them. Feel comfortable here and imagine reaching deeper inside your mind, as you create this perfect shower room for you. When you have truly engaged with this environment, then move on to the next step.

Step Three:

Now step underneath the shower itself. Stand underneath it and start to anticipate the water pouring down, start to anticipate how it is going to feel and how you are going to react to the cold water reaching you and showering your skin.

As you are imagining and anticipating, at the moment you least expect it, the icy cold water fires out and down upon you. It is not a gentle shower, but a hard and fast shower bolting water down upon you, like standing underneath a mountainside waterfall. Notice how your skin reacts and breath reacts as it pours down upon you.

Notice the effect it has on your senses. As and when you feel enlivened, imagine stepping forward, out of the water as it falls. Step forward and shake your body to get some of the water off and move on to the next step.

Step Four:

As you step forward and out of the water, as you shake your body, the floor falls away from you suddenly and safely, and you plunge straight into an ice pool. As you drop into the water, notice how it takes your breath away, notice the initial 'gasp' and the effect it has upon your entire body, as you are temporarily completely immersed in icy cold water.

As your head comes up and out of the water, you catch your breath. Find the steps easily as you reach out in front of you and climb out. Notice your breathing sending oxygen throughout your body, invigorating you and bringing your senses to life. As you climb out, feeling more invigorated and comfortable with each step, move on to the next step.

Step Five:

Imagine the feelings flowing through your body now, notice your mind being alert, your senses tuned into the world around you. Then take a couple of more energising, alertness enhancing breaths, open your eyes and bring this session to an end by counting from one through to five.

Stretch your limbs out, take a couple of more deeper breaths and go about your day, filled with a level of focus and alertness that is going to serve you wonderfully well.

Stay frosty!

Being a Self-Hypnotist

Being a self-hypnotist has given me a sense of belief in my own capability in a wide of areas of my life. The skill is one that I use when I have a cold, when I am running (and planning on running), when I am studying, worrying about my children, travelling, teaching and many other facets of my life. It is inherent in so much of what I do. Not just in a structured fashion as described throughout this book, but also in a manner that ensures the internal environment of my mind is equipped. It is not perfect and I cannot profess to being mentally invincible, but certainly I feel I have a degree of control and assuredness that gives me a quality of life that I am happy with.

The aim of this book has been to show you how to use self-hypnosis in an evidence-based way as much as possible. However, much of the evidence you are presented with, the things that contribute to you being a self-hypnotist are unique to you: your imagination, your cognitions, your expectancies, attitudes and so on. Therefore, what being a self-hypnotist means to you is something you can create, craft and enjoy in your own way.

This book has offered a conceptualisation of hypnosis as a mindset, a cognitive strategy that anyone can learn, and then develop for improvement. In this book I have shown you how to draw upon a range of comprehensive strategies to deliver suggestions to yourself in (and out of) self-hypnosis sessions, and to make those suggestions as effective as possible. We then looked at how to use self-hypnosis for relaxation, for stress and anxiety relief, for enhancing sleep, controlling pain, elevating mood, overcoming habits and much more.

There are lots of other effective applications of self-hypnosis that I have used to

- distort my perception of time when flying on planes,

- increase concentration when studying,

- advance my ability to recover from training for marathons

- diminish the symptoms of the common cold.

There have also been some other seemingly incredible applications (not mentioning the things that many of my students profess to have done) but the evidence base is lacking or non-existent, and therefore there is no point writing a book about evidence based self-hypnosis and then including material supported purely by my own opinion or anecdotal evidence.

However, many, many more techniques can be found on my blog, which can be accessed for free, for you to use in conjunction with the basic structures you have been shown in this book: **www.adam-eason.com/blog**

Please do connect with me:

Facebook: **http://twitter.com/adameason**

Twitter: **www.facebook.com/hypnotistadam**

My own hub, a community which is free to join where I offer a wide range of ongoing resources, techniques, advice and support for self-hypnotists, and where you can learn from other self-hypnotists too:
www.adamshypnosishub.com

Many of the processes in this book are available to buy as an audio download from my website, whereby I guide you through the process instead of you having to keep doing it for yourself:
www.hypnosisfordownload.com

Final Thanks

A word of thanks from me to all the authors, researchers, scholars, clinicians, academics, explorers and professionals for contributing such a fabulous body of evidence that I have been able to draw upon throughout this book. You are the foundations upon which this field is building – I doff my cap and offer eternal thanks and appreciation to you all. I hope this field continues to develop and there is more research and study for us all to read, enjoy and benefit from. It is indeed an exciting time to be a hypnosis professional as I am.

My apologies for so much repetition of the point that you need to repeatedly practice the techniques in this book.

Most importantly though, I hope you have enjoyed this book and

that you feel well prepared to use these skills to improve the quality of your life in some way.

In my opinion, there are not enough people in the world who have these skills. Self-hypnotists have the opportunity to make real beneficial changes that make each day an exciting prospect; the self-hypnosis adventure and exploration starts here.

I wish you every success.

Thank you for reading.

Also By Adam Eason

Available from Amazon as Paperback or Kindle E-Book

Audio Versions By Adam Eason

The audio versions available from Adam's Online Store bring to life the scripts presented in his books.

www.hypnosisfordownload.com

References

Anderson, J. A. Basker, M. A., & Dalton, R. (1975)

Migraine and Hypnotherapy',

International Journal of clinical and Experimental Hypnosis, 23: 48-58.

Andreychuk, T. and Skriver, C. (1975)

'Hypnosis and Biofeedback in the Treatment of Migraine Headache',

International Journal of Clinical and Experimental Hypnosis, 23: 172-183.

Alladin, A. (2008)

Handbook of Cognitive Hypnotherapy for Depression: An Evidence-Based Approach.

Wiley-Blackwell.

Alladin, A. and Alibhai, A. (2007)

'Cognitive Hypnotherapy for Depression',

International Journal of Clinical and Experimental Hypnosis, 55: 147-166.

August, R. V. (1975)

'Hypnotic Induction of Hyperthermia: An Additional Approach to Postoperative Control of Cancer Recurrence',

American Journal of Clinical Hypnosis, 18: 52-55.

Azrin, N. H. and Nunn, R. G. (1977)

Habit Control In a Day.

New York: Simon and Schuster.

Bandura, A. (1977)

'Self-efficacy: Toward a Unifying Theory of Behavioral Change',

Psychological Review, 84(2): 191-215.

Banyai, E. I. and Hilgard, E. R. (1976)
'A Comparison of Active-alert Hypnotic Induction with Traditional Relaxation Induction',
Journal of Abnormal Psychology, 85(2): 218-224.

Barabsz, A. F. and McGeorge, C. M. (1978)
'Biofeedback, Mediated Biofeedback and Hypnosis in peripheral Vasodilation Training',
American Journal of Clinical Hypnosis, 21: 28-37.

Barber, T. X. (1969)
Hypnosis: A Scientific Approach.
South Orange, NJ: Power Publishers.

Barber, T. X. (1985)
'Hypnosuggestive Procedures as Catalysts for Psychotherapies'. In S. J. Lynn and J. P. Garske (Eds.), Contemporary Psychotherapies: Models and Methods, pp. 333-376.
Columbus, OH: Charles E. Merrill.

Barber, T., Spanos, N. and Chaves, J (1974)
Hypnotism, Imagination and Human Potentialities.
New York: Pergamon.

Barkley, R. A., Hastings, J. E. and Jackson, T. L. (1977)
'The Effects of Rapid Smoking and Hypnosis in the Treatment of Smoking Behaviour',
International Journal of Clinical and Experimental Hypnosis, 25: 7-17.

Baudouin, C. (1927)
Suggestion & Autosuggestion.
Kessinger Publishing.

Beck, A. (1967)

Depression: Causes and Treatment.

Philadelphia: University of Pennsylvania Press.

Beck, A. (1976)

Cognitive Therapy and the Emotional Disorders.

New York: New American Library.

Beck, A., Rush, A., Shaw, B. and Emery, G. (1979)

Cognitive Therapy of Depression.

New York: Guildford Press.

Beck, J. S. (2011).

Cognitive Behavior Therapy,

Second Edition: Basics and Beyond.

Guildford Press.

Benson, H. and Hoffman J.W. (1981)

'The Relaxation Response and Hypnosis',

International Journal of Clinical and Experimental Hypnosis, 29: 259-270.

Benson, H., Frankel, F. H., Apfel, R., Daniels, M. D., Schniewind, H. E., Nemiah, J. C., Sifneos, P. E., Crassweller, K. D., Greenwood, M. M., Kotch, J. B., Arns, P. A. and Rosner, B. (1978)

'Treatment of Anxiety: A Comparison of the Usefulness of Self-Hypnosis and a Meditational Relaxation Technique - an Overview',

Journal of Psychotherapy and Psychosomatic, 30: 229-242.

Benson, H. (1975)

The Relaxation Response.

New York: William Morrow.

Borckhardt, J. J. and Nash, M. R. (2002)

'A Case Study Examining the Efficacy of a Multi-modal Psychotherapeutic Intervention for Hypertension',

International Journal of Clinical and Experimental Hypnosis, 50: 114-148.

Boutin, G. E. and Tosi, D. J. (1983)

'Modifications of Irrational Ideas and Test Anxiety Through Rational Stage Directed Hypnotherapy (RSDH)',.

Journal of Clinical Psychology, 39: 382-391.

Brom, D., Kleber, R. J. & Defares, P. B. (1989)

'Brief Psychotherapy For Post-traumatic Stress Disorders',

Journal of Consulting and Clinical Psychology, 57: 607-612.

Burns, D. (1980)

Feeling Good: The New Mood Therapy.

New York: Avon Books.

Casiglia, E., Mazza, A., Ginocchio, G., Onesto, C., Pessina, A. C. and Rossi, A. (1997)

'Hemodynamics Following Real and Hypnosis-simulated Phlebotomoy',

American Journal of Clinical Hypnosis, 40(I): 368-375.

Chambless, D. L. and Hollon, S. D. (1998)

'Defining Empirically Supported Therapies',

Journal of Consulting and Clinical Psychology, 66: 7-18.

Chapman, L. F., Goodell, H. and Wolff, H. G. (1959)

'Augmentation of The Inflammatory Reaction by Activity of The central Nervous System',

Archives of Neurology, I: 557-572.

Chiasson, S. W. (1973)

A Syllabus on Hypnosis.

American Society of Clinical Hypnosis, Education, and Research Foundation.

Clark, D. A. (ed.) (2005)

Intrusive Thoughts in Clinical Disorders: Theory, Research, and Treatment,

New York: Guildford Press.

Clarke, R. E. and Forgione, A. G. (1974)

'Gingival and digital vasomotor response to thermal Imagery in Hypnosis',

Journal of Dental Research, 53: 792-796.

Coué, E. (1922)

Self-mastery Through Conscious Autosuggestion.

New York: American Library.

Coué, E. (1923)

How to Practice Suggestion & Autosuggestion.

Kessinger Publishing.

Coué, E. (1923)

My Method.

Kessinger Publishing.

Dikel, W. and Olness, K. (1980)

'Self-hypnosis, Biofeedback, and Voluntary Peripheral Temperature Control in Children',

Pediatrics, 66: 335-340.

Eason, A. D. (2012)

Hypnosis for Running: Training Your Mind to Maximise Your Running Performance.

Poole: Awake Media.

Edelson, J. and Fitzpatrick, J. L. (1989)

'A Comparison of Cognitive-behavioral and Hypnotic Treatments of Chronic Pain',

Journal of Clinical Psychology, 45(2): 316-323.

Edinger, J. (2001)

'Cognitive Behavioral Therapy for Treatment of Chronic Primary Insomnia: A Randomized Controlled Trial',

Journal of the American Medical Association, 285: 1856-1864.

Edmonston, W. E. (1981)

Hypnosis and Relaxation: Modern Verification of an Old Equation.

John Wiley and sons.

Ellis, A. (1987)

'The Evolution of Rational Emotive Therapy (RET) and Cognitive Behavior Therapy (CBT)'.

In J. Zeig (ed.) The Evolution of Psychotherapy, pp. 107-125.

New York: Brunner/Mazel.

Ellis, A. (1994)

Reason and Emotion in Psychotherapy, rev.edn.

New York: Birch Lane Press.

Ellis, A. (1997)

'The Evolution of Albert Ellis and Rational Emotive Behavior Therapy'.

In J. Zeig (ed.) The Evolution of Psychotherapy, pp. 69-78.

New York: Brunner/Mazel.

Elman, D. (1984)

Hypnotherapy

Glendale, CA: Westwood Publishing.

Erickson, M. H. (1948)

'Hypnotic Psychotherapy'.
In The Medical Clinics of North America (pp. 571-583).

New York: W. B. Saunders.

Erickson, M. H. and Rossi, E. L. (1979)

Hypnotherapy: An Exploratory Casebook.

New York: Irvington.

Erickson, M. H. (1980)

'Explorations in Hypnosis Research'.
In M. H. Erickson and E. L. Rossi (Ed.), The Collected Papers of
Milton H. Erickson (Vol II),

New York: Irvington.

Espie, C., Lindsay, W. R., Brooks, D. N. et al. (1989)

'A Controlled Comparative Investigation of Psychological
Treatments for Chronic Sleep-onset Insomnia',

Behaviour Research and Therapy, 27: 79-88.

Eysenck, H. (1957)

Sense and Nonsense in Psychology.

London: Pelican.

Faymonville, M. E., Laureys, S., Degueldre, C., DelFiore, G., Luxen, A. and
Franck, G. (2000).

'Neural mechanisms of Antinociceptive Effects of Hypnosis',

Anesthesiology, 92(5): 1257-1267.

Faymonville, M. E., Roediger, L., DelFiore, G., Delgueldre, C., Phillips, C.and Lamy, M. (2003)

'Increased Cerebral Functional Connectivity Underlying the Antinociceptive Effects of Hypnosis',

Brain Research: Cognitive Brain Research, 17(2): 255-262.

Fingelkurts, A. A., Kallio, S. and Revonsuo, A. (2007)

'Cortex Functional Connectivity as a Neurophysiological Correlate of Hypnosis: An EEG Case Study',

Neuropsychologia 45(7): 1452.

Foreyt, J. P. and Goodrick, G. D. (1993)

'Evidence for Auccess in Behaviour Modification in Weight Loss and Control',

Annals of Internal Medicine, 119: 698-701.

Franklin, J. (1981)

'The Measurement of Sleep-onset Insomnia',

Behaviour Research and Therapy, 19: 547-549.

Freeman, R. M., Macauley, A. J., Eve, L., Chamberlain, G. V. and Bhat, A. V. (1986)

'Randomised Trial of Self-hypnosis for Analgesia in Labour'.

British Medical Journal, 292: 657-658.

Friedman, H. and Taub, H. A. (1977)

'The Use of Hypnosis and Biofeedback Procedures for Essential Hypertension',

International Journal of Clinical and Experimental Hypnosis, 25: 335-347

Friedman, H. and Taub, H. A. (1984).

'Brief Psychological Training Procedures in Migraine Treatment',

American Journal of Clinical Hypnosis, 26(3), 187-200.

Fromm, E. and Kahn, S. (1990)

Self-hypnosis: The Chicago Paradigm.

New York: Guildford Press.

Fromm, E. (1981)

'Ego-psychological Parameters of Hypnosis and Their Clinical Applications'.

In H. Wain (Ed), Theoretical and Clinical Aspects of Hypnosis,

Miami, FL: Symposia Specialists.

Fromm, E., Brown, D. P., Hurt, S. W., Oberlander, J. Z., Boxer, A. M. and Pfeifer, G. (1981)

'The Phenomena and Characteristics of Self-hypnosis',

International Journal of Clinical and Experimental Hypnosis, 29: 189-246.

Gardner, G. (1981)

'Teaching Self-hypnosis to Children',

International Journal of Clinical and Experimental Hypnosis, 29: 300-312.

Gay, M., Philipport, P. and Luminet, O. (2002)

'Differential Effectiveness of Psychological Interventions for Reducing Osteoarthritis Pain: A Comparison of Erikson Hypnosis and Jacobson Relaxation'

European Journal of Pain, 6: 1-16.

Gilliland, B. E. and James, R. K. (1983)

'Hypnotherapy and Cognition: A Combinatorial Approach', Medical Hypnoanalysis:

Journal of the Society of Medical Hypnonalysts, 4: 101-113.

Golden, W. L., Dowd, E. T. and Friedberg, F. (1987)

Hypnotherapy: A Modern Approach.

New York: Pergamon Press.

Gorassini, D. R. and Spanos, N. P. (1986) '

A Social-cognitive Skills Approach to the Successful Modification of Hypnotic Susceptibility',

Journal of Personality and Social Psychology, 50: 1004-1012.

Green, J. P., Barabasz, A., Barrett, D. and Montgomery, G. H. (2005)

Forging Ahead: The 2003 APA Division 30 Definition of Hypnosis',

International Journal of Clinical and Experimental Hypnosis, 53: 259-264.

Green, J. P. and Lynn, S. J. (2000)

'Hypnosis and Suggestion-based Approaches to Smoking Cessation: An Examination of the Evidence',

International Journal of Clinical and Experimental Hypnosis, 48: 195-224.

Haanen, H. C., Hoenderdos, H. T., van Romunde, L. K., Hop, W. C., Mallee, C. and Terwiel, J. P. (1991)

'Controlled Trial of Hypnotherapy in the Treatment of Refractory Fibromyalgia',.

Journal of Rheumatology, 18(I): 72-75.

Hardy, J. D., Wolff, H. G. and Goodell, H. (1952)

Pain Sensations and Reactions.

New York: Williams and Wilkins.

Harmon, T. M., Hynan, M. T. and Tyre, T. E. (1990)
'Improved Obstectric Outcomes Using Hypnotic Analgesia and Skill Mastery With Childbirth Education',
Journal of Consulting and Clinical Psychology, 58: 525-530.

Harvey, R. F., Hinton, R. A., Gunary, R. M. and Barry, R. E. (1989)
'Individual and Group Hypnotherapy in Treatment of Refractory Irritable Bowel Syndrome',
Lancet, 1: 424-425.

Heap, M. and Aravind, K. (2002)
Hartland's Medical & Dental Hypnosis (Fourth ed.).
Churchill Livingstone.

Healy, D. (1998)
The Antidepressant Era. Cambridge, MA:
Harvard University Press.

Herzberg, A. (1945)
Active Psychotherapy.
New York: Grune & Stratton.

Hilgard, E. R. (1965)
Hypnotic Susceptibility.
Harcourt, Brace & Jovanovich.

Hofbauer, R. K., Rainville, P., Duncan, G. H. and Bushnell, M. C. (2001).
Cortical 'Respresentation of The Sensory Dimension of Pain',
Journal of Neurophysiology, 86(I): 402-411.

Holroyd, J. D. (1980)
'Hypnosis Treatment for Smoking: An Evaluation Review',
International Journal of Clinical and Experimental Hypnosis, 4: 241-357.

Horne, J. (1992)

'Insomnia',

The Psychologist, 5: 216-218.

Hunt, W. and Bespalec, D. (1974) '

An Evaluation of Current Methods of Modifying Smoking Behaviors',

Journal of Clinical Psychology, 30: 431-438.

Hull, C. (1933)

Hypnosis and Suggestibility.

Carmarthen: Crown House Publishing.

Jacobs, G. D. (1993)

'Multifactoral Behavior Treatment of Chronic Sleep-onset Insomnia Using Stimulus Control and The Relaxation Response. A Preliminary study',

Behavior Modification, 17: 498-509.

James, W. (1884)

'What is an Emotion?',

Mind, 9, 188-205.

Jensen, M., Barber, J., Romano, J. M., Hanley, M. A., Raichle, K. and Molton, I. R. (2009)

'Effects of Self-hypnosis Training and EMG Biofeedback Relaxation Training on Chronic Pain Persons with Spinal Cord Injury',

International Journal of Clinical and Experimental Hypnosis, 57: 239-268.

Jensen, M., Barber, J., Romano, J. M., Hanley, M. A., Raichle, K. and Osborne, T. L. (2009). '

A Comparison of Self-hypnosis Versus Progressive Muscle Relaxation in Patients With Multiple Sclerosis and Chronic Pain',

International Journal of Clinical and Experimental Hypnosis, 57: 198-221.

Jensen, M., Ehde, D. M., Gerts, K., Stoelbe, B. L., Dillworth, T. M. and Hirsch, A. T. (2011)

'Effects of Self-hypnosis Training and Cognitive Restructuring on Daily Pain Intensity and Catatrophizing in Individuals With Multiple Sclerosis and Chronic Pain',

International Journal of Clinical and Experimental Hypnosis, 59: 45-63.

Johnson, L. S. (1981)

'Current Research in Self-hypnotic Phenomenology: The Chicago Paradigm',

International Journal of Clinical and Experimental Hypnosis, 29 (3), 247-258.

Johnson, L. S., Dawson, S. L., Clark, J. L. and Sirkorsky, C. (1983)

Self-hypnosis Versus Hetero-hypnosis: Order Effects and Sex Differences in Behavioral and Experiential Impact',

International Journal of Clinical and Experimental Hypnosis, 31: 139-154.

Johnson, L.S. (1979)

'Self-hypnosis: Behavioral and Phenomenological Comparisons With Heterohypnosis',

International Journal of Clinical and Experimental Hypnosis, 27: 240-264.

Johnston, E. and Donoghue, J. (1971).

'Hypnosis and Smoking: A Review of The Literature',

American Journal of Clinical hypnosis, 13: 265-272.

Jones, M. C. (1924a)

'A Laboratory Study of Fear: The Case of Peter',

The Pedagogical Seminary, 31: 308-315.

Jones, M. C. (1924b)

The Elimination of Children's Fears',

Journal of Experimental Psychology, 7: 382-390.

Kahn, S. P., Fromm, E., Lombard, L. S. and Sossi, M. (1989)

'The Relation of Self-Reports of Hypnotic Depth in Self-hypnosis to Hypnotizability and Imagery Production',

International Journal of Clinical and Experimental Hypnosis, 37: 290-304.

Katz, E. R., Kellerman, J. and Ellenberg, L. (1987)

'Hypnosis in The Reduction of Acute Pain and Distress in Children with Cancer',

Journal of Pediatric Psychology, 12: 379-393.

Kirsch, I. (1985)

'Response Expectancy as a Determinant of Experience and Behavior',

American Psychologist, 40 (11): 1189–1202.

Kirsch, I. (2009)

The Emperor's New Drugs: Exploding the Antidepressant Myth.

London: Bodley Head.

Kirsch, I., Montgomery, G. and Sapirstein, G. (1995)

'Hypnosis as an Adjunct to Cognitive-behavioral Psychotherapy: A Meta-analysis',

Journal of Consulting and Clinical Psychology, 63: 214-220.

Kirsch, I., Silva, C. E., Carone, J. E., Johnston, J. D. and Simon, B. (1989)
'The Surreptitious Observation Design: An Experimental Paradigm for Distinguishing Artefact From Essence in Hypnosis',
Journal of Abnormal Psychology, 98(2): 132-136.

Kirschenbaum, D. S. (1994)
Weight Loss Through Persistence: Making Science Work For You.
Oakland, CA: New Harbinger.

Klapow, J. C., Patterson, D. R., and Edwards, W. T. (1996)
'Hypnosis as an Adjunct to Medical Care in the Management of Burger's Disease: A Case Report,'
American Journal of Clinical Hypnosis, 38(4), 271-276.

Krasner, A. M. (1990)
The Wizard Within.
American Board of Hypnotherapy Press.

Kroger, W. S. (1977)
Clinical and Experimental Hypnosis (2nd ed.).
Philadelphia: J. B. Lippincott.

Lazarus, A. (1984)
In the Mind's Eye: The Power of Imagery for Personal Enrichment (2nd edition).
Guildford Press.

Liggett, D. (2000)
Sport Hypnosis.
London: Human Kinetics.

Logue, E. E., Jarjoura, D. G., Sutton, K. S., Smucker, W. D., Baughman, K. R. and Capers, C. F. (2004)
'Longitudinal Relationship Between Elapsed Time in The Action Stages of Change and Weight Loss,'
Obesity Research, 12: 1499-1508.

Lynn, S. J., and Kirsch, I. (2006)
Essentials of Clinical Hypnosis: An Evidence-Based Approach.
Washington: APA.

Lynn, S. J., Kirsch, I. and Hallquist, M. N. (2008)
'Social Cognitive Theories of Hypnosis'.
In M. R. Nash and A. J. Barnier (Eds.). The Oxford Handbook of Hypnosis: Theory, Research and Practice, pp. 111-139.
Oxford: Oxford University Press.

Lynn, S. J., Martin, D. J. and Frauman, D. C. (1996)
'Does Hypnosis Pose Special Risks For Negative Effects?',
International Journal of Clinical and Experimental Hypnosis, 44:1, 7-19.

Lynn, S. J. and Nash, M. R. (1994)
'Truth in Memory: Ramifications For Psychotherapy and Hypnotherapy',
American Journal of Clinical Hypnosis, 36:3, 194-208.

Lynn, S. J., Neufeld, J. and Maré, C. (1993)
'Direct Versus Indirect Suggestions: A Conceptual and Methodological Review',
International Journal of Clinical and Experimental Hypnosis, 41: 124-152.

Lynn, S. J. and Rhue, J.W. (1991)
Theories of Hypnosis: Current Models and Perspectives.
Guildford Press.

MacHovec, F. J. and Man, S. C. (1978)

'Acupuncture and Hypnosis Compared: Fifty-eight Cases',

American Journal of Clinical Hypnosis, 88: 129-130.

Mallot, J. M. (1984) '

Active-alert Hypnosis: Replication and Extension of Previous Research',

Journal of Abnormal Psychology, 93(2): 246-249.

Marcus Aurelius (2006)

Meditations: Living, Dying and the Good Life.

London: Penguin Classics.

Martin, A. A., Schauble, P. G., Rai, S. H. and Curry, R. W. (2001).

'The Effects of Hypnosis on The Labour Processes and Birth Outcomes of Pregnant Adolescents',

Journal of Family Practice, 50: 441-443.

McConkey, K. M. (1986)

'Opinions About Hypnosis and Self-hypnosis Before and After Hypnotic Testing',

International Journal of Clinical and Experimental Hypnosis, 34: 311-319.

Mehl-Madrona, L. E. (2004)

'Hypnopsis to Facilitate Uncomplicated Birth',

American Journal of Clinical Hypnosis, 46: 229-312.

Meyers, A. W. and Shleser, R. A. (1980) '

A Cognitive-behavioral Intervention For Improving Basketball Performance',

Journal of Sports Psychology, 3: 69-73.

Montgomery, G., DuHamel, K. and Redd, W. (2000)
'A Meta-analysis of Hypnotically Induced Analgesia: How Effective is Hypnosis?',
International Journal of Clinical and Experimental Hypnosis, 48: 134-149.

National Institutes of Health (2005)
NIH State-of-the-Science Conference Statement on Manifestations and Management of Chronic Insomnia in Adults.,
Washington, DC: National Institutes of Health.

Nash, M. R. (1987)
'What, if Anything, is Regressed About Hypnotic Age Regression? A Review of Empirical Literature',
Psychological Bulletin, 102: 42-52.

Nash, M. R. and Barnier, A. J. (2008)
The Oxford Handbook of Hypnosis: Theory, Research and Practice.
Oxford University Press.

Olness, K. (1981)
'Imagery (self-hypnosis) as Adjunct Therapy in Childhood Cancer: Clinical Experience With 25 Patients',
American Journal of Pediatric Hermatology/Oncology, 3: 313-321.

Orne, M. T. and McConkey, K. M. (1981)
'Toward Convergent Inquiry Into Self-Hypnosis',
International Journal of Clinical and Experimental Hypnosis, 29: 313-323.

Orne, M. T. and McConkey, K. M. (1981)
'Hypnosis and Self-hypnosis'. In L. Kristal (ed.), The ABC of Psychology, pp. 115-118.
London: Multimedia Publications.

Otani, A. (1990)

'Structural Characteristics and Thematic Patterns of Interspersal Techniques of Milton H Erickson: A Quantitative Analysis of The Case of Joe'. In Lankton, S. R (ed.) Ericksonian Monographs, Number 7: The Broader Implications of Ericksonian Therapy, p. 40

New York: Brunner/Mazel.

Palsson, O. S., Turner, M. J., Johnson, D. A., Burnett, C. K. and Whitehead, W. E. (2002)

'Hypnosis Treatment For Severe Irritable Bowel Syndrome',

Digestive Diseases and Sciences, 47: 2605-2614.

Parkes, J. D. (1985)

Sleep and its disorders.

London: Saunders.

Pederson, L. L., Scrimgeour, W. G. and Lefcoe, N. M. (1975)

'Comparison of Hypnosis Plus Counselling, Counselling Alone, and Hypnosis Alone in a Community Service Smoking Withdrawal Program',

Journal of Consulting and Clinical Psychology, 43: 920.

Perls, F. S., Hefferline, R. and Goodman, P. (1951)

Gestalt Therapy: Excitement and Growth in the Human Personality.

Gestalt Journal Press.

Platonov, K. I. (1959).

The Word as a Physiological and Therapeutic Factor: The Theory and Practice of Psychotherapy According to I. P. Pavlov.

Moscow: Foreign Languages Publishing House.

Rainville, P. (2002)

'Brain Mechanisms of Pain Affect and Pain Modulation',

Current Opinion in Neurobiology 12(2): 195-204.

Robertson, D. (2008)

'The Discovery of Hypnosis: The Complete Writings of James Braid'.

In National Council For Hypnotherapy, [page range?]. [place: publisher?].

Rock, N. L., Shipley, T. E. and Campbell, C. (1969)

'Hypnosis With Untrained Volunteer Patients in Labor',

International Journal of Clinical and Experimental Hypnosis, 18: 25-36.

Ruch J.C. (1975)

'Self-hypnosis: The Result of Heterohypnosisor Vice-versa?',

International Journal of Clinical and Experimental Hypnosis, 23: 282-304.

Sanders, S. (1991)

Clinical Self-Hypnosis: The Power of Words and Images.

New York: The Guildford Press.

Sarbin, T. R. (1950)

'Contributions to Role-taking Theory: In Hypnotic Behavior',

Psychological Review, 57: 255-270.

Sarbin, T. R. (1954)

'Role Theory'. In G. Lindzey (ed.), Handbook of Social Psychology, Vol. 1, pp. 223-258.

Cambridge, MA: Addison-Wesley.

Sarbin, T. R. and Andersen, M. L. (1967)

'Role-theoretical Analysis of Hypnotic Behavior.
In J. E. Gordon (ed.) Handbook of Clinical and Experimental
Hypnosis, pp. 319-344.

New York: Macmillan.

Schill, T., Monroe, S., Evans, R. and Ramanaiah, N. (1978)

'The Effects of Self-Verbalizations on Performance: A Test of
The Rational-emotive Position',

Psychotherapy: Theory, Research, and Practice, 15: 2-7.

Schoenberger, N. E., Kirsch, I., Gearan, P., Mongomery, G. and Pastyrnak, S. L.
(1997)

'Hypnotic Enhancement of a Cognitive Behavioural Treatment
For Public Speaking Anxiety',

Behaviour Therapy, 28: 127-140.

Schoenberger, N. (2000)

'Research on Hypnosis as an Adjunct to Cognitive-Behavioral
Psychotherapy',

International Journal of Clinical and Experimental Hypnosis, 48: 154-169.

Seligman, M. (1990)

Learned Optimism.

New York: Alfred A. Knopf.

Sellick, S. M. and Zaza, C. (1998)

'Critical Review of 5 Non-pharmacologic Strategies For
Managing Cancer Pain',

Cancer Prevention and Control, 2: 7-14.

Sheehan, P. W. (1991)

'Hypnosis, Context, and Commitment'.

In S. J. Lynn and J. W. Rhue (ed.) Theories of Hypnosis: Current Models and Perspectives, pp. 520-541.

New York: Guildford Press.

Sheehan, P. W. and McConkey, K. M. (1979)

'Australian Norms For The Harvard Group Scale of Hypnotic Susceptibility, Form A',

International Journal of Clinical and Experimental Hypnosis, 27: 294-304.

Sheehan, P. W. and McConkey, K. M. (1982)

Hypnosis and Experience: The Exploration of Phenomena and Process.

Hillsdale, NJ: Erlbaum.

Shor, R. E. and Easton, R. D. (1973)

'A Preliminary Report on Research Comparing Self - and Hetero-hypnosis',

American Journal of Clinical Hypnosis, 16: 37-44.

Sletvold, H., Jensen, G. M. and Gotestam, K. G. (1986)

'The Effect of Specific Hypnotic Suggestions on Blood Pressure in Normotensive Subjects',

Pavlovian Journal of Biological Science, 25: 20-24.

Smith, C. A., Collins, C. T., Cyna, A. M. and Crowther, C. A. (2006)

'Complementary and Alternative Therapies For Pain Management in Labour,'

Cochrane Database of Systematic Reviews, 4: CD003521.

Soskis, D. (1986)

Teaching Self-Hypnosis.

London: Norton & Co.

Spanos, N. P. (1991)

'A Sociocognitive Approach to Hypnosis'.

In S. J. Lynn and J. W. Rhue (Eds.), Theories of Hypnosis: Current Models and Perspectives, pp. 324-361.

New York: Guildford Press.

Spanos, N. P. and Barber, T. X. (1974)

'Toward a Convergence in Hypnosis Research',

American Psychologist, 29: 500-511.

Spanos, N. P. and Chaves, J. F. (1989)

Hypnosis: The Cognitive-behavioral Perspective.

Buffalo, NY: Prometheus Books.

Spiegel, D. (1996)

'Dissociative Disorders'.

In R. E. Hales and S. C. Yudofsky (ed.) Synopsis of Psychiatry, pp. 583-604.

Washington, DC: American Psychiatric Press.

Spiegel, D. and Bloom, J. R. (1983)

'Group Therapy and Hypnosis Reduce Metastatic Breast Carcinoma Pain',

Psychosomatic Medicine, 45: 333-339.

Spiegel, H. and Spiegel, D. (1978)

Trance and Treatment: Clinical Uses of Hypnosis.

New York: Basic Books.

Stanton, H. E. (1992)

'Using Hypnotic Success Imagery to Reduce Test Anxiety',

Australian Journal of Clinical and Experimental Hypnosis, 20: 31-37.

Stepanski, E., Zoric, F., Roehrs, T. et al. (1988)
'Daytime Alertness in Patients With Chronic Insomnia Compared With Asymptomatic Control Patients',
Sleep, 11: 54-60.

Sternbach, R. A. and Tursky, B. (1965).
'Ethnic Differences Among Housewives in Psychophysical and Skin Potential Responses to Electric Shock',
Psychophysiology, 1: 241.

Stewart, J. H. (2005)
'Hypnosis in Contemporary Medicine',
Mayo Clinic Procedings, 80: 511-524.

Straus, R. (1982)
Strategic Self-Hypnosis: How to Overcome Stress, Improve Performance, and Live to Your Fullest Potential.
Lincoln, NE: iUniverse.

Syralja, K. L., Cummings, C. and Donaldson, G. W. (1992)
'Hypnosis or Cognitive Behavioral Training For The Reduction of Pain and Nausea During Cancer Treatment: A Controlled Clinical Trial',
Pain, 48: 137-146.

Syralja, K. L., Donaldson, G. W., Davis, M. W., Kippes, M. E. and Carr, J. E. (1995)
'Relaxation and Imagery and Cognitive-behavioral Training Reduce Pain During Cancer Treatment: A Controlled Clinical Trial',
Pain, 63: 189-198.

Talley, N., Owen, B. K., Boyce, P. and Paterson, K. (1996)
'Psychological Treatments For Irritable Bowel Syndrome: A Critique of Controlled Treatment Trials',
American Journal of Gastroenterology, 91: 277-286.

Taylor, C. B. (1982)
'Adult Medical Disorders'.
In A. S. Bellack, M. Hersen and A. E. Kazdin (ed.) International Handbook of Behaviour Modification and Therapy, pp. 467-500.
New York: Plenum Press.

Teitelbaum, M. (1969)
Hypnosis Induction Technics.
Springfield, IL: Charles C Thomas.

Toomey, T. C. and Sanders, S. (1983)
'Group Hypnotherapy as an Active Self-Control Strategy in Chronic Pain',
American Journal of Clinical Hypnosis, 26 (1): 20-25.

Turner, R. M. and Ascher, L. M. (1979)
'Controlled Comparison of Progressive Relaxation, Stimulus Control and Paradoxical Intention Therapies For Insomnia',
Journal of Consulting and Clinical Psychology, 47: 500-508.

Van Dyck, R. and Spinhoven, P. (1997)
'Does Preference For Type of Treatment Matter? A Study of Exposure in Vivo With or Without Hypnosis in The Treatment of Panic Disorder With Agoraphobia',
Behavior Modification, 21: 172-186.

Viswesvaran, C. and Schmidt, F. (1992)
'A Meta-analytic Comparison of the Effectiveness of Smoking Cessation Methods',
Journal of Applied Psychology, 77: 554-561.

Von Dedenroth, T. (1964)

'The Use of Hypnosis With "Tobaccomanics",

American Journal of Clinical Hypnosis, 6: 326.

Wadden, T. A. and VanItallie, T. B. (ed.) (1992)

Treatment of The Seriously Obese Patient.

New York: Guildford Press.

Wall, V. J. and Womack, W. (1989)

'Hypnotic Versus Active Cognitive Strategies For Alleviation of Procedural Distress in Pediatric Oncology Patients',

American Journal of Clinical Hypnosis, 13: 181-191.

Wallace, B. and Kokoszaka, A. (1992)

'Experience of Peripheral Temperature Change During Hypnotic Analgesia',

International Journal of Clinical and Experimental Hypnosis, 40: 180-193.

Wenzlaff, R. M. and Wegner, D. M. (2000)

'Thought Suppression',

Annual Review of Psychology, 51: 59-91.

Whorwell, P.J., Prior, A. and Farragher, E.B. (1984)

'Controlled Trial of Hypnotherapy in The Treatment of Severe Refractory Irritable Bowel Syndrome',

Lancet, 2:1232-1234 (I actually referred to this study via a review of the study conducted and published in the International Journal of Clinical and Experimental Hypnosis).

Wik, G., Fischer, H., Bragee, B., Finer, B. and Fredrikson, M. (1999)

'Functional Anatomy of Hypnotic Analgesia: A PET Study of Patients With Fibromyalgia',

European Journal of Pain, 3(I): 7-12.

Winocur, E., Gavish, A., Emodi-Perlman, A., Halachmi, M. and Eli, I. (2002)
'Hypnorelaxation as Treatment For Myofascial Pain Disorder: A Comparative Study',
Oral surgery Oral Medicine Oral Pathology, 93: 429-434.

Wolberg, L. R. (1948a)
Medical Hypnosis (Vol. 1).
New York: Grune & Stratton.

Wolberg, L. R. (1948b)
Medical Hypnosis (Vol. 2).
New York: Grune & Stratton.

Wolpe, J. (1954)
'Reciprocal Inhibition as The Main Basis of Psychotherapeutic Effects',
Archives of Neurology & Psychiatry, 72: 205-226.

Wolpe, J. (1958)
Psychotherapy by Reciprocal Inhibition.
CA: Stanford University Press.

Wolpe, J. (1990)
The Practice of Behavior Therapy Techniques: A Guide to the Treatment of Neuroses.
Long Island City, NY: Pergamon.

World Health Organization (2002)
The World Health Report 2002: Reducing Risks, Promoting Healthy Life.
Geneva: World Health Organization.

Yapko, M. (1992)

Hypnosis and the Treatment of Depressions: Strategies for Change.

New York: Brunner/Mazel.

Yapko, M. (1995)

Essentials of Hypnosis.

New York: Brunner/Mazel.

Yapko, M (1997)

Breaking the Patterns of Depression.

New York: Random House/Doubleday.

Yapko, M (2001)

Treating Depression With Hypnosis: Integrating Cognitive-Behavioral and Strategic Approaches.

New York: Brunner/Routledge.

Yapko, M. (2003)

Trancework.

New York: Brunner/Routledge.

Yapko, M. (ed.) (2006)

Hypnosis and Treating Depression: Applications in Clinical Practice.

New York: Routledge.

Zeltzer, L. and LeBaron, S. (1982)

'Hypnosis and No-hypnotic Techniques For Reduction of Pain and Anxiety During Painful Procedures in Children and Adolescents With Cancer',

Journal of Pediatrics, 101: 1032-1035.